JUDGING CREDENTIALS

JUDGING CREDENTIALS
NONLAWYER JUDGES
AND THE POLITICS
OF PROFESSIONALISM

DORIS MARIE PROVINE

94-65

University of Chicago Press
Chicago and London

DORIS MARIE PROVINE is associate professor of political science at Syracuse University. She is the author of *Case Selection in the U.S. Supreme Court,* also published by the University of Chicago Press, and one of the coauthors of *Law: Its Nature, Functions, and Limits* (3d ed.). From 1978 to 1982 she served as Town Justice in Virgil, New York.

The University of Chicago Press, Chicago 60637
The University of Chicago Press, Ltd., London
© 1986 by The University of Chicago
All rights reserved. Published 1986
Printed in the United States of America

95 94 93 92 91 90 89 88 87 86   5 4 3 2 1

Library of Congress Cataloging-in-Publication Data

Provine, Doris Marie.
  Judging credentials.

  Includes bibliographical references and index.
  1. Lay judges—United States. 2. Judicial process—
United States. I. Title.
KF8788.P76   1986   347.73′14   85-16516
ISBN 0-226-68470-9   347.30714
ISBN 0-226-68471-7 (pbk.)

For my favorite nonlawyer,
William B. Provine

CONTENTS

ACKNOWLEDGMENTS

I have had lots of help in producing this book. I owe perhaps my greatest debt to the many judges across New York State who answered my survey, and to the smaller number I studied intensively. All of my interviewees were most generous with their time and thoughtful in their responses to my many questions.

The financial wherewithal to carry out this study came from the Law and Social Sciences Program of the National Science Foundation (grant number SES-8012589) and from Syracuse University. Together these two institutions contributed over $100,000 toward the completion of this research. Dr. Felice Levine, who directs the law and social sciences program for the National Science Foundation, also contributed much of her own time to this project, offering many useful suggestions regarding its design.

I received other types of assistance in the course of analyzing my data and digging through the relevant literature on nonlawyer judges. Bruce Riddle at Syracuse University was enormously helpful in planning and executing the necessary computer runs. Susan Green at Cornell Law School patiently worked through much of the necessary typing and retyping.

Two other Cornellians, Dan Decker in Natural Resources and Phil Taietz in Rural Sociology provided important information at this stage in my work. Eugene Goss, the Kentucky lawyer who took *North v. Russell* to the Supreme Court, and Barbara Fromm, a research consultant in Syracuse, New York, also provided valuable assistance with some parts of the analysis.

Once I had completed a draft of the manuscript, I prevailed on friends to read it, and many did. My debts at Cornell University are particularly weighty. Professors Fred Aman, Carol Greenhouse, Russell Osgood, and Fred Somkin read some or all of the manuscript. Two of my colleagues at Syracuse University, Linda Fowler and Jeff Stonecash, read the whole manuscript and provided many valuable ideas. Steve Wasby (State University of New York at Albany) and James Jacobs (New York University Law School) also offered comments and encouragement. I received particularly detailed and thoughtful ideas and criticisms from Lawrence Baum of Ohio State University, who performed the same wonderful service for my last book. Other helpful readings came from outside the academic world: Judge Helen Burnham, Herbert Kline, Esq., and my parents, Charles and Edith Long.

I owe my husband Will and my two sons, Charles and Stuart, a different kind of special thanks. They provided tolerance and support throughout this book's long gestation. I am very grateful to them.

INTRODUCTION

Popular images of courts at work feature a judge with the wisdom and authority of a parent and the bearing of one steeped in the austere dignity of law. The judge, it almost goes without saying, is a lawyer. We take for granted the importance of legal education to judicial performance. The job seems to require a lawyer's expertise.

The image of the judge as lawyer is accurate as far as major state and federal judgeships are concerned. Lawyers enjoy a virtual monopoly on judicial office at this level, but not at the bottom of the judicial hierarchy, in the local courts that decide traffic cases and the other minor matters that bring ordinary citizens to court. Approximately 13,000 lay persons hold judgeships in courts of limited jurisdiction, typically in the towns and villages outside major metropolitan areas. The power of lay judges varies from state to state, but it often includes the authority to resolve traffic matters, small civil claims, and minor criminal cases. Only in Vermont do lay persons adjudicate serious criminal charges, including murder, and they do so there only on panels with a lawyer judge presiding.

The practical significance of nonlawyer judges lies in their numbers and the number of cases they handle.

Forty-three states currently authorize them, and in many of these states they outnumber lawyer judges in comparable courts, though their caseloads tend to be much smaller. In New York, for example, there are more nonlawyer judges (about 1,600) than the total of lawyer judges in all courts at every level. Lay judges in New York resolve nearly three million cases a year and collect about $45 million in fines and penalties. Nonlawyer judges are thus an important element in the state court system, whether the standard is caseload, revenues collected, or citizen contact.

This book considers the role nonlawyer judges play in the American judicial system and the controversy their participation provokes. Such judges are interesting, not just because they perform an important legal role without professional credentials but because they are associated with a distinctive style of adjudication. Modern nonlawyer judges are the descendants of the venerable justice of the peace. Traditionally, the justice of the peace was a part-time, elective office open to persons without formal training in the law. Always a local resident and often a leader in the community, the justice of the peace served for a short term and without pay, except for fees collected from litigants. The office began to disappear from the cities early in this century but remained important in the countryside much longer. Outside the cities, the power of the justices to resolve disputes came primarily from the regard in which they were held by their communities, not from their share of state authority. Procedures were ordinarily informal and familiar, like the communities that supported these courts.

Time has not dramatically altered this picture. Nonlawyer judges still bring to mind the amateur's independence from central and professional controls, informality in proceedings, and local democracy in the disposition of law. This Jeffersonian concept of adjudication rooted in local authority runs counter to presuppositions about judging which the legal profession seeks to foster. The profession's concept of fair adjudication requires a judge independent of local influence, trained in the requirements of state and federal law, and ready to apply these procedural and substantive standards in a dignified courtroom. Out-of-court ties between the judge and parties to litigation are minimized or absent so that the rule of law and the right to dispassionate adjudication can be protected. The trial judge is accountable to the legal profession, appellate bodies, and, indirectly, to the public, but not to the local community.

Both models of adjudication and accountability have been important in the development of the machinery of adjudication in America, though the professional view seems more appropriate to modern conditions. Urbanization, specialization, the growth of government and legislation, and more widespread reliance on professional judgment in a variety of endeavors all favor legal experts as adjudicators and centralization in the administration of law. Yet, at the same time, Americans have been unwilling to embrace without qualification the professional perspective on adjudication. The jury system, local election of judges, our tolerance for plea bargaining, the movement in the last decade toward mediation as an alternative to adjudication—all of these institutions bespeak sensitivity to values that compete with professionalism.

Our enthusiasm for extraprofessional values and roles in the judicial process, however, has limits. Most lay participation in adjudication takes place under professional supervision, or within restraints established by the profession; these boundaries help make the nonprofessional's role more palatable to lawyers. Lay judges, on the other hand, operate independent of professional authority, and they even have the power to discipline lawyers who appear before them. It should be no surprise that this form of lay participation has provoked the loudest complaints from lawyers and the bar's most sustained efforts at reform. Some of these efforts have been successful—most have not.

In assailing state laws that make judgeships available to lay persons, lawyers take the position that they alone are experts on matters relevant to adjudication. They want the law to reflect their professional perspective. Medical doctors and other professional groups have fought analogous battles to establish the prerogatives of expertise. "Every profession," Everett Hughes has observed, "considers itself the proper body to set the terms in which some aspect of society, life, or nature is to be thought of, and to define the general lines, or even the details, of public policy concerning it."[1]

The arguments the legal profession has used against lay judges have been revealing, if not always effective. Lawyers and their allies have relied on self-serving assumptions regarding the demands of adjudication in limited-jurisdiction courts and the beneficial impact of legal education and practice. The bar has, in effect, deduced the inferiority of nonlawyer judges from its own premises about adjudication and legal education. Lawyers interested in reform have pressed these arguments for nearly a century in the courts, state legislatures, and, most successfully, before the lawyers who make up state and federal court-reform commissions.

The actual inferiority or incompetence of nonlawyer judges has never been demonstrated and, in my opinion, will not be demonstrated. Nonlawyer judges, my evidence and other research suggests, are virtually indistinguishable from lawyer judges in how they conceive and perform the key elements of their jobs. Distinctions between individual judges are real enough, but legal education or its absence does not determine judicial attitudes or behavior in ways that are significant to the litigants who come before judges at this level.

From a consumer's perspective, the absence of empirical evidence of lay inferiority in adjudication might seem striking, for the burden of proof seems naturally to fall on those who would eliminate the nonprofessional element. Nonlawyer judges cost taxpayers less and are more convenient to litigants than the lawyer judges who would replace them. These are the practical considerations that preserve lay judges in a legal system grown accustomed to the idea that only lawyers should be judges.

Conflict over the credentials appropriate to the lower judiciary is not confined to the United States. Adjudication by nonlawyers is a significant feature in many court systems. Forms of lay participation vary somewhat across systems, but the fundamental rationale for lay participation is similar everywhere: it brings judicial power closer to the citizenry and thereby legitimizes the exercise of state power through courts. Lawyers elsewhere complain of inefficiency and ignorance of law and procedure among lay judges, yet these critics, like their counterparts in America, provide little reliable evidence of lay inferiority.

For more dispassionate observers, the survival of lay judges raises a number of questions that invite investigation. What do judges actually do at this level, and what educational prerequisites, if any, are appropriate? Doesn't organizational rationality demand full-time, career judges? How have professional groups and reform-minded individuals fought for the elimination of "unqualified" judges, and what obstacles have they faced? To what extent have these arguments for reform, so condescending toward nonprofessionals, aroused the lay public?

The first three chapters of this book describe the efforts of the American legal profession to eliminate lay persons from every level in the judiciary. Professional opposition to nonlawyer judges paid off quickly and handsomely at first, with lawyers assuming the most important judgeships when the courts reopened after the American Revolution. The first chapter considers how lawyers were able to persuade legislators that legal education should be a prerequisite for judicial office in a period when nonlawyers held most judgeships.

The second and third chapters examine the bar's less-focused and less-successful twentieth-century campaign to eliminate nonlawyer judges from courts of limited jurisdiction, their last toehold in the judicial system. This reform effort has involved patient legislative lobbying as well as litigation; arguments in both arenas reveal the mindset and politics of a mature legal profession. The limited success these advocates have enjoyed indicates how difficult it is to mobilize lawyers for coordinated political activity and how hard it is to reorganize the lower courts.

Chapter 4 compares decision making by lay and lawyer judges in New York, a state that relies more heavily on nonlawyer judges than most. The arguments reformers have used against nonlawyer judges provided the basis for comparison. Data came from a mail survey, courtroom observation, and interviews with judges and other court personnel. The questionnaire went to 2,222 New York judges, while observation and interviews focused on twenty-six lay and lawyer judges upstate. Though exhaustive, this study did not uncover any significant distinctions between lay and lawyer judges in their understanding of due-process guarantees or in their approach to the exercise of discretion. Both findings are in keeping with the relevant published evidence, which is also presented in this chapter.

Chapter 5 considers the institutional parameters within which nonlawyer judges work. Characteristics peculiar to the level in the court system in which nonlawyer judges predominate, this chapter argues, define our image of lay adjudication. Detailed analysis is again limited to New York in order to make clear how local politics, finances, and habit support a system of nonlawyer judges but, at the same time, rob it of legitimacy.

The final chapter considers lay participation in adjudication in a broader context. It focuses on the conflict between professional values and adjudication by nonprofessionals and considers the role of the laity in this conflict. Americans, this chapter suggests, are too committed to the significance of credentials and to the legal profession's vision of the judicial process to respond very favorably to nonlawyer judges, no matter how they perform. The public reveals in its lack of enthusiasm for lay legal authority its own alienation from law. American political sensibilities thus contain a curious contradiction: while we venerate rule by democratically established law as the foundation of our political traditions, we are uncomfortable with democracy in adjudication. Americans are not exceptional, however, in turning to experts to safeguard legal rights, as Chapter 6 points out in a brief survey of lay adjudication outside the United States. Nearly everywhere lay participation in adjudication is on the decline, despite ever-increasing pressure from the public for more access to dispute-resolution institutions. Law and the protection of legal rights become matters for experts in a complex society. Legal authority in a non-professional is suspect, even among nonlawyers.

1 LAWYERS AND THE JUDICIARY IN EARLY AMERICA

Settlement-era America had few lawyers and virtually no lawyer judges. Men began to take up the practice of law with some regularity only in the early 1700s, when the colonies had grown more populous and prosperous. As the century progressed, law practice proved highly profitable in the centers of business and colonial affairs. These lawyers argued their cases before judges who had never studied or practiced law themselves. This was true for a short time even in many of the highest courts of the newly established states. The situation soon began to change, however, with lawyer judges becoming more numerous from the late 1700s on. This change occurred first in the areas where commerce had grown most and the profession was best established.

The trend toward lawyer judges continued in the early 1800s as the economy developed and the profession grew larger. By mid-century, law-trained judges had become predominant nearly everywhere. Lay judges survived only in the frontier areas where lawyers were unavailable and as justices of the peace. The legal profession never lost this grip on judicial office established in the decades following the transition to nationhood.

How did early American lawyers persuade their fellow

citizens that legal training should be a prerequisite for higher judicial office? This achievement is all the more remarkable if one considers the self-confidence ordinary citizens in that period displayed about handling their own legal affairs, and the uneven quality of legal apprenticeships, the standard method of legal education then. Economic growth and differentiation helped the profession grow and prosper, and helped put lawyers in a position to dominate the judiciary, but the association between professional and economic growth appears to have been complex, mediated by organizational and ideological changes that came with the American Revolution.

This chapter examines the emergence of an all-lawyer higher-court bench in the new republic. This development laid the groundwork for the twentieth-century campaign to make all judges at every level lawyers. Related themes in contemporary court reform also have their roots in early America. Rural-urban differences in attitudes toward courts and court reform were evident before 1800, as was the relative shortage of lawyers in rural areas. The tendency to associate lawyers with sensitivity to procedural rights and strict application of rules, and to contrast these traits with the nonlawyer's presumed common sense and attention to substantive justice was also evident early. Americans with wealth and status to protect came to prefer the professional's approach to justice, with its promise of procedural regularity and predictable decisions, much as they do today. Developments in eighteenth-century America thus illuminate modern conflict over judicial credentials and help us unravel the complex relationship between economic, legal, and institutional change.

Judicial Process in Colonial America

The seventeenth century in New England was, according to one historian of the colonial period, "the miraculous era of law without lawyers."[1] Neither practitioners nor law-trained judges seemed necessary elements in the settlement-era political structure. The lay leadership, whether secular or religious, formulated law as necessary, and the same leadership at first adjudicated cases as they arose.[2] Even as recognizable court structures developed, colonial legislatures willingly entertained the private bills of unsuccessful petitioners. The idea of a technically skilled, independent judiciary, protected by the doctrine of separation of powers, had not yet taken hold.[3] The role of the judge was further circumscribed by the power of juries and the failure to distinguish between matters of law and matters of fact in trials or appeals.[4]

While legislatures and juries in this period decided some issues that would be reserved now for judges, it should be noted that court systems were much like our own in other respects. The courts considered many claims involving indebtedness and personal misbehavior, the kinds of cases courts often hear today. Surviving records also indicate that judges recognized the authority of civil legislation and precedent and had incorporated procedures traditionally deemed fundamental to fair adjudication.[5] The docket books of Springfield, Massachusetts, courts in the late seventeenth century, for example, indicate that, even in a rural area with no lawyers, judges were sensitive to procedural regularities. Joseph H. Smith, who edited these records, found that

> the standards of judicial administration ... compare favorably with that found in courts on the lower jurisdictional levels of the Bay. The few appeals taken and contempts of court recorded indicate that these standards were generally acceptable to offenders and litigants coming before the successive courts. ... The *Record* shows no significant mutations or deviations, substantively or procedurally, attributable to so-called "frontier" influences.[6]

The available evidence suggests that lay judges of the period were not usually ignorant of law—in fact, they tended to have considerably more legal knowledge than the laity has today. They were sometimes, however, unwilling to sacrifice the proper outcome to technicalities:

While . . . the judges adhered as closely as possible to the long established procedure borrowed from the English courts, they were nevertheless likely to become quite impatient with any attempts on the part of counsel to use such procedural methods as a means to an end.[7]

At this time England governed the colonies with a light hand and was not very much involved in colonial legal arrangements. The colonies were too distant and too insignificant to warrant close, sustained supervision over adjudication. Nor was consistency with English law a major concern in the colonies; some colonial authorities even refused to permit appeals to England.[8] Legal procedures were the remembered formalities of English justices of the peace, Old Bailey, and the county courts. Law books were rare, and manuals like Dalton's *Justice of the Peace* were virtually the sole source of definitive legal enlightenment.[9] The few early settlers that had any legal background at all tended to have been justices of the peace in England.

Lawyers in Colonial America

Law-trained settlers were rare in this period largely because the agrarian economy could not readily support a lawyer class. According to colonist William Byrd:

> It was a Place free from those three great Scourges of Mankind, Priests, Lawyers, and Physicians. . . . The People were yet too poor to maintain these Learned Gentlemen.[10]

Lawyers were also discouraged from settling by the religious orientation of some of the colonies, which was hostile to lawyers and the delays and formalities associated with courts.[11] Until the early 1700s, lawyers were sometimes even banned by law from membership in colonial legislatures.[12] A Pennsylvania resident summed up the dominant feeling in his area:

> Of Lawyers and Physicians I shall say nothing because this Country is very Peaceable and Healthy;

long may it continue and never have the occasion for
the Tongue of the one, or the Pen of the other, both
equally destructive of Mens Estates and Lives.[13]

Though lawyers were rare, litigation was not. A litigant who wanted assistance could consult a friend or
relative, or enlist the services of someone familiar with
courtroom procedures. As litigation became more frequent, the ranks of such practically experienced, but
untrained, advocates grew. A few men, some allegedly of
disreputable reputation, were even able to sustain themselves in this way.[14]

By the early 1700s, public antagonism toward the practice of law had begun to decline, and economically, too, the
colonies were becoming a more hospitable place to trained
attorneys. Domestic and overseas commerce were expanding. The population was growing and with it the
number of legal transactions between people. Litigation
also continued to increase. The colonies were becoming
wealthy and populous enough to support a practicing bar.

The relationship with England also began to change.
Britain came to recognize the importance of regularizing
colonial legal procedures and asserting its ultimate authority over the outcome of important litigation.[15] British
officials, therefore, worked to organize and consolidate
colonial court structures. Judicial appointments also
came under stricter executive control, judges serving
"upon the pleasure of the crown."[16] The goal was to create
supreme provincial tribunals to dispose of litigation efficiently—and, if possible, favorably to the crown.

Lawyers soon arrived to take advantage of the increased opportunities offered by commercial activity and
crown policies. As Botein concludes:

> It was apparent that opportunities for successful
> and respectable legal careers were increasing, as
> mercantile activity became more complex and ad-
> ministrators tried to work out the details of trans-
> atlantic empire.[17]

Men trained at the Inns of Court in London began to
appear throughout the Northeast.[18] At the same time the

sons of colonial planters and businessmen began more
and more often to consider a legal career.[19] These young
men either traveled to England for their studies or, more
frequently, apprenticed themselves to successful colonial
practitioners.

As the numbers of lawyers grew, so did their economic
power and social influence. Land transactions, estate
work, and the law business associated with the growing
overland and overseas trade provided attorneys with
profitable work. Many became wealthy from legal fees
and investment in the business ventures they represented. Lawyers began to be influential in colonial affairs,
less because of their legal training than because of their
wealth and social influence.[20] As historian John Murrin
describes the lawyer's position in midcentury:

> Everywhere the story was similar. From Kittery in
> Maine to Barnstable on Cape Cod, midst the com-
> mercial breezes of Boston, Charlestown and Salem
> or the lordly air breathed by the Connecticut "river
> gods," a strange new man, the lawyer, had convinced
> the community that it needed his services and that
> he should have its respect.[21]

Bench and Bar before the Revolution

The bar also began to develop at an institutional level.
The apprenticeship system allowed the practicing bar to
control entry into the profession.[22] Crown policies aimed
at regularizing court practices also helped the fledgling
legal profession. In Maryland and Virginia, for example,
crown officials introduced legislation to restrict practice
to trained lawyers and to protect fees.[23] The royal gover-
nors in Massachusetts used their powers of appointment
to increase the educational qualifications of judges, who
then shaped court rules to favor lawyers over the untrained advocates the bar derisively described as "petti-
foggers." Some of these appointees were lawyers, but the
rest were at least college graduates; they all sympathized
with the bar's efforts to raise educational standards for
the practice of law.[24] Chief Justice Thomas Hutchinson,

for example, sought to win the favor of the bar (which had opposed his appointment) by restricting access to the court to trained attorneys, requiring gowns and robes in the courtroom, and establishing grades of competence in imitation of the English practice.[25] The Supreme Court of the Judicature in New York followed suit a few years later.[26] Such cooperation between the crown-appointed judiciary and the emerging legal profession was valuable to both sides. The crown got more order and accountability in adjudication, while the bar received an invaluable boost in its effort to control the numbers and qualifications of those who sought to practice law.

The growing authority of the bar over admission to practice encouraged it to attempt to influence standards for appointment to the bench as well. In regions where they had become powerful, lawyers began to argue that judges should be lawyers. Opposition to the appointment of Chief Justice Hutchinson rested in part on the fact that he was not a lawyer. James Otis, Jr., revealed the newfound self-confidence of the Boston bar in his claim that one could take "all the Superior Judges and every Inferior Judge in the Province, and put them all together, and they would not make one half of a Common Lawyer."[27] Virginia lawyers also began to argue for lawyer judges during this period, though without notable success.[28]

Elsewhere, too, the bar seems to have lost the argument that the bench should be restricted to lawyers. Crown officials were not yet willing to concede to the bar the right to set the standards for judicial selection. Instead, political concerns appear to have remained paramount in judicial appointments, despite the increasing assertiveness of the bar.

There is little evidence that the process of adjudication would have changed dramatically if lawyers had won their argument for an all-lawyer bench. Educational differences between nonlawyer judges and lawyers in the latter eighteenth century were not what we might expect. The laymen the crown appointed often were distinguished and well-educated men, while the lawyers sometimes began practice after only brief clerkships. Nor does the evidence indicate that contemporaries (apart from activist lawyers) were particularly concerned about the legal ignorance of judges. Instead, the most frequent complaint was that they were class-biased. Perhaps more significant to the complexion of adjudication in this period was the increasing involvement of the crown and the growing interest of the merchants in a rational, efficient system for enforcing business obligations. Civil process in this period was thus "an uneasy mixture of three basic strands: lawyer's law, merchant's ideals, and the ruler's will."[29]

While practicing lawyers generally benefited from the direction legal development was taking, the growth of the bar was constrained somewhat by economic considerations. Legal business was neither extensive nor profitable enough to support a big, highly differentiated bar. Positions of responsibility in colonial government and administration were also too few to absorb a large number of lawyers—a fact that some scholars believe may have encouraged lawyer sympathies for the revolutionary cause. Edmund Burke apparently even recognized this danger at the time. He warned Parliament that under-rewarding the colonial bar could be dangerous: "When great honors and great emoluments do not win this knowledge to the service of the state, it is a formidable adversary of government."[30]

The economic limitations on the expansionist ambitions of lawyers were particularly obvious in the back country, where lawyers seldom grew wealthy from law practice alone. The economy in rural areas was simply too poor to support lawyers handsomely unless they took up other pursuits as well.[31] As one seasoned attorney advised a young relative trying to choose where to set up his law practice:

> The elements of a successful professional income are population and wealth. Where both are united, in a great degree, there is consequently much business and great demand for members of the profession.[32]

The countryside was also the source of intense anti-professional sentiments. Clergymen and farmers in particular tended to view lawyers as men who sought to gain unfairly from the toil and troubles of others:

> They are plants that will grow in any soil that is cultivated by the hands of others; and when once they have taken root they will extinguish every other vegetable that grows around them. ... The most ignorant, the most bungling member of that profession will, if placed in the most obscure part of the country, promote its litigiousness and amass more wealth without labor than the most opulant farmer.[33]

Legal Education Becomes a Requirement for Judicial Office

Resentment against lawyers, characteristically a rural phenomenon before the Revolution, became more general afterward. The outbreak of hostilities had revealed many lawyers to be loyalists.[34] Lawyers also had made themselves unpopular by representing creditors after the war, and by carrying forward the property claims of British citizens and American loyalists. The prosperity of the lawyers also stirred increasingly widespread resentment. The war—with its hardships and dislocations for many classes—had brought unprecedented financial and political opportunities for the legal profession.[35] As Gawalt notes, "What had appeared to be utopian plans for a large, prosperous, well-trained legal profession before the war became a reality in the postwar period."[36]

Ironically, resentment against lawyers in general did not prevent individual lawyers from achieving important political offices in the aftermath of the Revolution. Lawyers, in fact, were more politically powerful than they had ever been before.[37] They were overrepresented in the Continental Congress, the Constitutional Convention, the first Congress, and, to a lesser extent, in the state legislatures.[38] Nearly half the delegates in both sessions of the

Continental Congress were lawyers, as were thirty-one of the fifty-five delegates to the Constitutional Convention.[39] To historian John Murrin, the predominance of lawyers in important political roles was

> one of the strangest paradoxes of early American history. On the one hand most lawyers were Tories. On the other hand, those who were Patriots won control of the movement and gave it consistent intellectual goals.[40]

Several characteristics of the revolutionary period help explain this anomalous situation. Lawyers were selected for lawmaking bodies in part because they formed a significant proportion of the educated class at this time. Physicians were also overrepresented in these assemblies. Events also helped individual lawyers disassociate themselves from negative images of the profession as a whole. The Stamp Act, which had effectively closed the courts for a year, had encouraged some lawyers to support the revolutionary cause and to shun loyalist colleagues and clients when this became necessary.[41] Republican lawyers had also benefited from the role of their colleagues in three much-discussed cases: the 1761 Writs of Assistance case in Boston, the Parson's Cause in Virginia, and *Forsey v. Cunningham* in New York.[42] Richard Morris concludes that with these cases "lawyers had conspicuously identified themselves in opposition to unconstitutional usurpation, while showing unexpected skill in arousing public opinion on behalf of constitutional principles."[43]

Early Successes in the Campaign to Eliminate Nonlawyer Judges

In at least two states, lawyer legislators used their newfound political power to professionalize the judiciary and to make top judicial posts financially attractive to successful lawyers. The Massachusetts legislature began appointing lawyer judges for the state supreme court right after the war and formally enacted education requirements in 1782.[44] The legislature also raised judicial salaries to encourage prominent lawyers to take these and other judicial positions.[45] Reforms in that state went even further, however: lawyers won the right to preference in all court-related jobs, including clerk, sheriff, registrar of deeds, and even court crier.[46] Lawyer domination in the judicial system, in turn, helped the bar restrict access to practice as it saw fit. The relationship between bench and bar, indeed, proved symbiotic:

> The judiciary reinvigorated the graded seniority system of the profession, and in 1810 they reinforced the profession's institutional autonomy and a high level of educational standards. At the same time, the judiciary looked to the legal profession for defense from common law critics and reformers who sought an elective judiciary, codified law, and an end to judicial interpretation. And together they exercised a strong influence in the state's political life.[47]

In Virginia, lawyer judges began to displace nonlawyers in 1787, with the creation of district courts. Lawyers had proposed and lobbied for the new courts, leading one legal historian to describe the district courts as "the accomplishment of republican lawyers."[48] The new district courts—staffed by lawyers, of course—heard appeals from the county courts, the last significant judgeship open to nonlawyers at that time in Virginia. The district courts encouraged appeals from the county courts with frequent reversals, and they soon eclipsed the county courts in importance.

The political prominence of lawyers in post-Revolutionary politics was not sufficient to win over judicial offices in every state, however. In some areas popular antagonism toward lawyers and the common law was strong enough to keep lawyers out of judicial office for several decades; key nonlawyer judges sometimes encouraged such sentiments. An often-quoted charge to the jury by Chief Justice John Dudley of New Hampshire is illustrative:

> Gentlemen, you have heard what has been said in this case by the lawyers, the rascals! . . . They talk of

law. Why gentlemen, it is not the law we want, but
justice. They would govern us by the common law of
England. Common sense is a much safer guide.... A
clear head and an honest heart are worth more than
all the law of the lawyers.[49]

Especially where the bar was small, as in New Hampshire, Maine, and Rhode Island, nonlawyers continued to
be appointed to top judicial posts into the early 1800s.
Even in these states, however, the most important judicial posts increasingly went to lawyers after the Revolution.[50]

Judicial Qualifications Becomes a Political Issue

The trend toward lawyer judges became a significant
political issue for the first time during Jefferson's campaign for the presidency in 1800. Earlier opposition to
courts and lawyers, such as Shays' Rebellion in 1786, had
raised the judicial qualifications issue only indirectly.[51] In
the presidential campaign, Republicans capitalized on
simmering popular resentment against legal profession
and the increasingly lawyer-dominated courts.[52] Such
antilawyer appeals were particularly appreciated in rural
areas, where opposition to lawyers had always been
strongest. Many of those who exploited antilawyer sentiment most articulately, ironically, were themselves lawyers.[53]

Antilawyer rhetoric during the campaign did not lead to
bills or legislation at the national level directed against
lawyers or lawyer judges. After the election, campaign
arguments against lawyers lost momentum, in part because of dissention between moderate and radical fac-
tions within the party. The two sides divided sharply on
the question of an independent, professional judiciary.
The radicals argued for dramatic changes in the judicial
structure designed to make it more responsive to popular
control—the use of a system of reference or arbitration as
a substitute for courts when possible; election of judges
for short, fixed terms; juries authorized to cross-examine
witnesses and lawyers and to pass on law as well as

evidence. They also favored codification of the common law to end reliance on lawyers who "sport with their client with a parade of wonderful learning and investigation."[54]

The moderates, on the other hand, sought only to end the Federalist monopoly on judicial posts and to reform court organization in certain minor respects. For the moderates, who were generally the more educated, middle-class Republicans, maintaining the rule of law established by a strong, active, and independent judiciary was essential. To better achieve this end, the moderates favored a better-paid, all-lawyer judiciary appointed for life, restrictions on jury power, and publication of court records to make possible an American system of common law.[55]

The moderates viewed the radicals as dangerous levelers. Ellis describes the conflict as one between those that wanted "a cheap, simple, easily available and speedy system of administering justice, one that would ensure equality and provide security with only a minimum of contact with the legal profession," and those who wanted "a technical legal system capable of maintaining order and providing stability, harmony and uniformity, and which would require a well-trained and highly specialized legal establishment."[56]

Moderates dominated national politics after the election. At the state level, however, the conflict between radicals and moderates over whether to bring courts more within the orbit of popular control played itself out in various ways. States like Massachusetts and Virginia remained committed to the principle that judges should be lawyers independent of legislative control.[57] Where the bar had been less successful in promoting lawyer judges, and where radical Republicans were numerous, bills to deprofessionalize the judiciary were sometimes successful, but only temporarily. Such proposals fared best in states where evangelical religious feeling was strong. Evangelical clergymen were hostile to attorneys, whom they considered unchristian, and hostile to law, which they regarded as too rational and complex. These preachers favored the appointment of nonlawyer judges and the establishment of arbitration and other extrajudicial means of settling disputes.[58]

In Kentucky, for example, where both religious fervor and radical Republicanism were widespread, efforts to democratize the judiciary had some success. Radical Republicans persuaded the legislature—a significant fraction of which was made up of nonlawyer justices of the peace—to limit the power of the lawyer judges who sat on major trial courts. The legislature required them to hold court in the county where the defendant resided, where two local lay assistants would share the bench with the circuit-riding lawyer judge. The lawyers complained loudly about the necessary traveling, but they especially resented their co-judges, whom they regarded as incompetent. Moderates succeeded in having the provision for nonlawyer assistant judges repealed in 1816.[59]

In Pennsylvania, radical reformers concentrated on expanding the powers of the justices of the peace. They were successful in getting the legislature to pass a statute that raised the jurisdiction of these courts to cases involving up to one hundred dollars, but the governor vetoed it twice. An account of a meeting between a radical delegation and the governor, moderate Republican Thomas McKean, suggests how the moderate conception of law militated against proposals for expanding adjudication by nonlawyers. Reportedly, the governor took out his watch and asked the chairman of the delegation to repair it. When the chairman protested that he was not a watchmatcher, the governor responded with an analogy to the law:

> The law, gentlemen, is a science of great difficulty and endless complication; it requires a lifetime to understand it. I have bestowed a quarter of a century upon it; yet you who can't mend this little watch, become lawyers all at once, and presume to instruct me in my duty![60]

Governor McKean's sentiments were apparently widely shared. As historian Gary B. Nash reports:

There is little evidence to suggest that these individual attacks on the bench and bar ever became a
great issue, supported by wide majorities. They
were, in part, the pyrotechnics of internecine war-
fare in the Pennsylvania Republican party.[61]

Elsewhere proposals for increasing the jurisdiction of
nonlawyer judges or for replacing lawyer judges with
nonlawyers also failed to galvanize antilawyer sentiments.[62] Radical arguments tended to founder for several
reasons. First, because the national leadership was defi-
nitely moderate in its orientation, moderates in the states
received all the key political appointments. Second, moderates tended to be more articulate and better funded
than the often-rural radicals. Only occasionally did dis-
gruntled attorneys or journalists join the radical cause,
yet such persons were essential for popularizing radical
ideas.

The power of the legal profession in many states was
another significant factor. Lawyers were numerous,
wealthy, and well-connected, which put the profession in
a position to prevent change it perceived as detrimental to
its interests. The bar also had the support of many
businessmen and political leaders on the issue of court
reform. These men agreed with the lawyers' argument for
expertise and independence in adjudication where significant sums were involved. They were also convinced that
a major remodeling of the structure of government so
soon after its establishment was irresponsible and dangerous.[63]

Judicial Qualifications in Jacksonian America

The conflict over lawyer power erupted again in the 1830s
with the rise of Jacksonian democracy. Lawyers, their
political and economic influence obvious to all, were again
an attractive target for egalitarian reformers. The insulation of courts from democratic processes and the
exception-ridden common law were other targets for
reform. This time, however, the attack was directed not so

much at lawyer judges per se as at the ascendance of lawyers in private and public life.[64]

Reformers attacked bar-enforced educational requirements for law practice, and their efforts to open up the legal profession to persons who did not satisfy the strict requirements of the bar associations were often successful. As earlier, lawyers themselves often aroused and encouraged antilawyer sentiment. This time, however, lawyer legislators also sponsored and voted for the necessary legislation. As Burton Bledstein describes these changes:

> In the 1830's the states, with the sanction of the public, began responding to the long-standing grievances against the arrogance of the learned profession by removing the power of certification from the local jurisdictions and investing it in a representative of the state government itself. By 1840 the states had ousted the guild-oriented bar from control of examinations in all of New England except Connecticut. The homogeneity of the older elite group dissolved as white, Protestant, middle-class sons from families of small businessmen, clerks, tradesmen, and artisans began entering the profession in significant numbers.[65]

These developments met surprisingly little resistance from practicing lawyers. Apparently, most successful lawyers were willing to abandon the corporate restrictiveness of the organized bar for the pursuit of individual success. They were not really threatened by the democratization of the bar anyway. By the 1830s elite lawyers had achieved for themselves what Terence Johnson describes as the *sine qua non* of a profession; the power "to impose its own definitions of the producer-consumer relationship."[66]

Outside the ranks of the legal establishment, the influx of new lawyers made the bar more competitive, flamboyant, and resourceful:

> *Formal* restrictions disappeared; but the market for legal services remained a harsh and efficient control.

It pruned away deadwood; it rewarded the adaptive and the cunning. Jacksonian democracy did not make everyman a lawyer. It did encourage a scrambling bar of shrewd entrepreneurs.[67]

Nor did Jacksonian democracy destroy the then-emerging consensus that only lawyers should hold high judicial offices. President Jackson, like presidents before him, showed no inclination to appoint nonlawyers to the federal bench, and the states increasingly emulated the federal government in seeking lawyers for important judicial posts. Lawyers thus retained their near-monopoly on higher judicial office even as the educational standards for admission to practice grew weaker and more uncertain.[68]

Jacksonian reform of the judicial branch went only so far as to make the judiciary directly or indirectly elective in thirty-one states, and to curtail judicial power over juries.[69] The concept of legally qualified judges was apparently so generally accepted by 1830 that reformers did not even challenge it. The idea that only lawyers should be judges has, of course, remained an integral element in the American conception of law and judicial process.

Lawyers and Judgeships: Understanding the Convergence

The obvious answer to the question of why legal education became a requirement for judicial office during the early years of the Republic is that the nation came to realize that judging requires a lawyer's expertise. To this one might add that law itself was steadily becoming more complicated in the post-Revolutionary era. The stakes were getting higher, even in simple disputes, and the impact of judicial decisions was becoming more far-reaching. Important commercial cases involving legally sophisticated counsel on either side seemed to require a more formal and technically trained judiciary.[70]

The English heritage so many Americans carried with them also had an impact on attitudes toward the qualifi-

cations necessary for judicial office. Westminster's dignified barrister judges, for example, may help explain why
the Americans made legal education an implicit requirement for federal judges. Many of the states did the same,
though they also followed the English practice of distinguishing between the higher courts, where they deemed
legal education necessary, and the trial courts of limited
jurisdiction, where they imposed no educational prerequisites for judges.[71]

It is just as important to remember, however, that the
bar itself actively fostered the idea that only lawyers
should be judges, and that lawyers were exceptionally
well-represented in state and federal law-making bodies
after the revolution. Then as now, the structure of legal
employment seemed to offer lawyers certain advantages
over other would-be politicians. Lawyers could arrange
business affairs to accommodate political work, and their
reentry into the private sector was usually not too difficult. Practitioners even stood to gain certain professional benefits from the contacts and exposure public
office brings. Their practical skills in advocacy and negotiation also prepared lawyers for politics.[72]

Once established, the relationship between lawyers in
politics and a judiciary restricted to lawyers was mutually
reinforcing. Prosecutorial offices and minor judgeships
offered convenient stepping-stones for higher political
offices. Higher judicial posts, in turn, provided prestigious
exits from careers in partisan politics. The domination of
judicial administration by lawyers thus helps perpetuate
the overrepresentation of lawyers in the other branches,
while the other branches protect lawyer judges.

The influence of lawyers on ideas and institutions,
however, is more profound than this. A society's legal
profession can help shape its response to social conflict in
ways that the profession is uniquely well-suited to manage. This is what happened in America, according to de
Tocqueville:

> The lawyers of the United States form a party . . .
> which adapts itself with great flexibility to the

exigencies of the time and accommodates itself without resistance to all the movements of the social body. But this party extends over the whole community and penetrates into all the classes which compose it; it acts upon the country imperceptibly, but finally fashions it to suit its own purposes.[73]

Whatever the precise balance between lawyer influence and other circumstances, what is certain is that the American approach to law and dispute resolution changed in the post-Revolutionary period in ways that favored the emergence of a lawyer-dominated judiciary.

Changing Ideas about Law and Courts

The lawmaking incident to litigation was relatively straightforward in the colonies before independence became an issue. Judges and other colonial officials simply had to keep up with the on-going task of shaping the common law borrowed from England to distinctly American purposes. This was an era in which many colonists were friendly to the common law, partly, as Goebel notes, because of ignorance about what it actually entailed: "The common law as an ideal was devotedly prayed for; the law in fact—a tangle of technicalities, was what the lawyers brought."[74] Yet, even on the eve of revolution, the colonists remained optimistic about the role of the judge-made common law, many regarding it as a sanctuary against royal prerogatives.[75]

After the Revolution, which brought with it hostility to everything English, the problems of developing workable legal rules and principles grew acute.[76] Codification, sometimes suggested as a solution to the problems of legal uncertainty and judicial power, proved politically difficult and ultimately unworkable as an alternative to judicial discretion. Law instead was left to grow much as it had before the Revolution. Judicial interpretation remained important, though now it was guided by indigenous statutes and the decisions in American courts rather than frequent references to English practice. This change in the structure of justification made judges and lawyers more creative lawmakers, according to Perry Miller:

> The achievement of the lawyers after the Revolution, the speed with which they vindicated the thesis that a body of legal precepts, such as in 1790 hardly existed, should become declarations of legal reason— this was a truly impressive performance.[77]

During this period of intense growth in American law, the fundamental premises upon which legal justifications rested also began to change. Increasingly, litigation was regarded as important, not simply to resolve isolated disputes but as a means to shape broad legal rules to changing conditions. As Morton Horwitz describes this development:

> By 1820 the legal landscape in America bears only the faintest resemblance to what existed forty years earlier. While the words are often the same, the structure of thought has dramatically changed and with it the theory of law. Law is no longer conceived of as an external set of principles expressed in custom and derived from natural law. Nor is it regarded primarily as a body of rules designed to achieve justice only in the individual case. Instead, judges have come to think of the common law as equally responsible with legislation for governing society and promoting socially desirable conduct.[78]

This conception of law helped support the argument for a lawyer-dominated judiciary, because it recognized the desirability of technical expertise in judicial decision making.

Changes in prevailing conceptions of the role of courts vis-à-vis the other branches of government also favored the emergence of lawyer judges. Before the Revolution, the judiciary held office at the pleasure of the crown, an arrangement the colonists deeply resented.[79] Colonial legislatures constantly sought to limit executive power over the judiciary, and the power of the crown-appointed judiciary itself. Legislative intervention in the judicial sphere even increased immediately after the Revolution in most areas.[80]

Not until Americans had experienced some of the difficulties associated with legislative supremacy in the period between the Declaration of Independence and the drafting of the Constitution did the idea of an independent judiciary begin to take on its modern form.[81] Even then, the concept of separation of the powers of government gained ground only slowly. With it, however, came the view that judges should be lawyers, legal expertise providing the rationale for independent judicial power. Many turn-of-the-century Americans would probably have agreed with Chief Justice Marshall's rhetorical question and the answer he provided:

> Is it not, to the last degree important, that [the judge] should be rendered perfectly and completely independent, with nothing to influence or control him but God and his conscience? ... I have always thought that the greatest scourge an angry Heaven ever inflicted upon an ungrateful and a sinning people, was an ignorant, a corrupt, or a dependent Judiciary.[82]

Some turn-of-the-century Americans, however, deeply opposed the legal profession's growing authority over adjudication. For the most part, opposition was centered in rural areas, where a more tradition-based vision of the role of courts and law continued to prevail. This vision could not readily accommodate the modernization of law associated with the rise of lawyers and lawyer judges. As Roeber analyzed the conflict in Virginia:

> The Country's vision of the law was one that saw law tied to tradition, to religious beliefs that proclaimed that man's laws should reflect God's. The pragmatic arguments in favor of instrumental law ... failed to take seriously the depth of the older, Country convictions. Law had operated in prerevolutionary Virginia as a forum where formal authority and familiar custom met. The rise of print culture, of a legal

profession, and of an expanding economic and social horizon wrenched apart that union.[83]

Conclusion

There are echoes of the tension Roeber describes—between rural traditionalism and the spirit of innovation and professionalism—in twentieth-century legal arrangements. Lawyers continue to be relatively scarce outside the cities, which helps limit their influence.[84] Rural areas are also more likely to rely on nonlawyer judges and to offer them political support. These differences, however, no longer imply geographically determined differences in popular conceptions of law, as they may have in the period Roeber studied. The concept of law as a secular social instrument is now firmly entrenched everywhere.

Recognition that law is, in Max Weber's words, "a rational technical apparatus . . . continually transformable in the light of expediential considerations and devoid of all sacredness of content"[85] suggests important roles for experts in lawmaking and adjudication. Where law is plentiful and disputes over its application are frequent and involve large sums, as in the United States, legal experts are particularly valuable. As roles for lawyers become more important, though, the legal ignorance of lay persons inevitably increases. Law and adjudication become matters for experts. Legislation restricting legal practice and judgeships to professionals hastens and reinforces these tendencies.

The transformation in thinking about law and adjudication early in this nation's history and the economic, political, and social changes that came with it thus produced a judiciary dominated by lawyers. The movement toward an all-lawyer upper-court judiciary, however, involved only qualified devotion to profesionalism in adjudication. Even at the higher levels in the judiciary where lay persons disappeared early, the process of professionalization was, and remains, incomplete. America never made the judiciary into a true specialist's domain, requiring technical training geared to the responsibilities of office. Practitioners whose education is for law practice, not adjudication, are our "professional" judges. We also have kept alive the arrangements established long ago, whereby these "professional" judges are popularly elected or appointed by political officials employing frankly political criteria. The means we have settled upon to choose our judges implicitly acknowledge the reality of the judiciary's power to make policy, and the limits of professional expertise in satisfying demands for court-room justice.

Political considerations in the selection of law-trained judges, not surprisingly, remain a sore point for reform-minded lawyers comparable to the survival of lay judges. On both fronts, lawyers press for judicial selection criteria more responsive to legal expertise and professional judgment. The next chapter describes the efforts directed against lay judges in limited-jurisdiction courts, the most obvious legacy of an earlier era.

2 TWENTIETH-CENTURY COURT REFORM AND THE LAY JUDGE

Confined to the bottom rungs of the judiciary, lay judges coexisted with the legal profession more or less without incident until early in the twentieth century, when leaders in the profession for the first time became actively concerned about the quality of adjudication in the lower courts. The leading lawyers and legal educators who spearheaded the reform movement blamed many of the problems they saw in the lower courts on the lack of legally educated judges at this level. Progressive ideology, the growth of the cities, and the development of national associations of lawyers all fostered the effort to reorganize these courts and eliminate judges without professional credentials.

This chapter considers the twentieth-century movement to make legal education a prerequisite for judicial posts traditionally open to lay persons. The arguments reformers have used reveal their presuppositions about professional education and about the process of adjudication in the lower courts. The obstacles they have encountered indicate the tenacity of the judicial status quo. The effort to eliminate lay judges thus pits professional ideals against institutional realities, but it also reveals inconsistencies in the demands reformers and the public place on the judicial system.

24

Reorganizing the lower courts to eliminate lay judges, this chapter demonstrates, has been much more difficult than eliminating lay persons from the appellate level, where they were never firmly entrenched. Our limited-jurisdiction courts, in contrast, represent a singular form of judicial organization designed to use lay persons to overcome geographical isolation and a scarcity of lawyers. Part-time, highly dispersed, locally financed lay courts provided inexpensive, accessible adjudication for minor civil and criminal cases where it would not otherwise have existed. The changes necessary to attract lawyers to these offices, particularly in rural areas, have provoked resistance, in part because they threaten to destroy the attractive features of traditional arrangements. Within the court reform movement, too, tensions between famil-iar reform goals—professionalism, centralized control, cost-effectiveness, and accessibility—have proven diffi-cult to resolve. As a result, the war against nonlawyer judges tends to be slow, inconclusive, and, occasionally, ironic.

The Context in Which Lay Adjudication Proceeds

Nonlawyer judges serve in district, town, village, county, city, municipal, traffic, police, alderman's, mayor's, mag-istrate's, common pleas, surrogate's, orphan's, probate, and justice courts, depending on the state.[1] The variety of titles reflects the independence with which states arrange and refurbish their judicial systems, but it masks the underlying similarity among lay courts. Most still bear a strong resemblance to their common ancestor, the justice of the peace. States have obviously found it easier to change the names of their courts of limited jurisdiction than their organization and character.[2] Few have moved very far from the model of lay adjudication in the lower courts borrowed from England and revised to fit Ameri-can needs two centuries ago.

Those who criticize lay judges as unqualified also criticize justice-of-the-peace-style adjudication as inadequate and unfair to litigants. The local financing and part-time organization of these courts are nearly as dismaying to these observers as judges without professional credentials. To appreciate the case against non-lawyer judges, therefore, it is important to understand the type of courts in which they serve. The first section of this chapter outlines the origins and evolution of the justice of the peace and describes the relatively successful Progressive-era campaign to abolish this office from our major cities. The section concludes with an analysis of how and why lay justice survived in the countryside in the face of determined opposition from idealistic lawyers.

The Justice of the Peace in Early America

The colonists borrowed the office of the justice of the peace from England, where it had originated several hundred years earlier during the Edwardian drive to consolidate state power in the crown. Lay persons dominated the office from the beginning, though not without some opposition from high crown officials, who preferred to staff these positions primarily with lawyers, a group that tended to be more favorable to crown policy.[3] As an English institution, the office waxed and waned in authority over the centuries, yet its basic organization remained surprisingly constant. The justice, a member of the local aristocracy, was always appointed, at first by Parliament, later by the King. The post was invariably part-time and unsalaried. Tenure was indeterminate, though in practice removal was infrequent and was employed only to punish misbehavior in office. Justices of the peace resolved minor criminal cases and exercised preliminary jurisdiction in felonies; their jurisdiction, however, never extended to civil cases or those involving the right to a jury.

When it was most powerful, the duties of office were administrative as well as judicial. Justices supervised tax collection, road building, schooling, and police work. John Dawson reports that by the end of the seventeenth century the justice of the peace had become the primary organ of local government:

> The justices of the peace became in the fullest sense the "rulers of the counties." Most of their work was still done under judicial forms but almost all were laymen. Their wide powers and more flexible procedures enabled them to control the machinery of local government and gradually to displace such older institutions as the county leet, which had a wider base of popular participation. And so, until the nineteenth century, in all but strictly national matters England was ruled increasingly by "little knots of squires and parsons."[4]

During the eighteenth century, as the judicial duties of the justice of the peace took on more importance. It became customary for these courts to employ law-trained clerks, generally local solicitors. The justice of the peace, however, remained an honorary office, though justices did collect fees for some services. In urban areas the fee system eventually proved remunerative enough to create an overpopulation of justices and competition for cases. England finally eliminated fee-supported justices of the peace in London in the mid-nineteenth century in favor of salaried, or stipendary, magistrates, most of whom are law-trained. It has retained unpaid nonlawyer judges outside the major cities to decide minor cases.[5]

Americans transplanted most characteristics of the English justice of the peace, but not all of them. From the first, American justices of the peace exercised civil as well as criminal jurisdiction and held jury trials. As in England, however, jurisdiction was always limited to minor cases, appeal was usually by trial de novo before a three- (or more) judge bench, and the collection of fees from litigants helped support the system. The resemblance between the two systems was closest in the early years of the Republic, when selection was still by appointment in the new states and territories.[6]

Here, as in England, the office was established as a means of bringing government to outlying areas without the expense of a public bureaucracy; for most judges, the office was honorific, carrying with it significant prestige and power.[7] In both countries, too, the office remained the preserve of lay persons rather than lawyers, even after lay persons lost the right to hold higher judicial office. Lawyers were scarce in most areas, and the office did not attract those who might have been available.

Surviving court records are few, but those that are available suggest that many of these early justices of the peace, like the lay judges in higher state appellate courts described in the last chapter, tried hard to establish and follow regular procedures.[8] Julius Goebel and Raymond Naughton wrote of colonial justices of the peace in New York:

> No one who has examined the now fragmentary records of how the body of justices applied themselves to their duties can fail to marvel at the pains taken by so many of them to discharge their office. Indeed, these papers disclose a devotion to public service for little recompense that no longer exists. To view the warrants or examinations, laboriously penned by some Dutchess Dutchman fumbling with his English, or to read how a dozen Ulstermen would assemble from the ends of a huge county in the dead of winter to inquire into some petty crime inevitably stirs some feeling of admiration. The city lawyers who inveighed against the country magistrates and their proclivity for holding court in taverns rarely frequented country Sessions, although they did not themselves hesitate to confer on their cases over the comfort of a bowl.[9]

Jackson's presidency and the movement of the justice-of-the-peace system westward to the new states and territories brought changes in the institution. The post became elective, with a short term of office and no formal or informal qualifications beyond local residency, adulthood, and, sometimes, literacy.[10] America, however, never adopted the then-growing English practice of employing law-trained clerks to assist the justices. The elective system helped maximize local control over the office, which had always been quite strong anyway because of the difficulty of communications and the infrequency of appeal. At the same time, the availability of the post to all classes also helped make the fee system more prominent, fees becoming a significant source of income for some judges.

These developments, according to critics, reduced respect for the office and made it inferior to its English ancestor.[11] Others disagree, citing the education and social background of some justices and the adherence to correct legal forms revealed in surviving court records from the western territories and new states.[12] De Tocqueville's contemporary impression was that the justice of the peace was an important mediator between the formalism of the higher courts and the citizen:

> The justice of the peace is a sort of middle term between the magistrate and the man of the world, between the civil officer and the judge. A justice of the peace is a well-informed citizen, though he is not necessarily learned in the law. His office simply obliges him to execute the police regulations of society, a task in which good sense and integrity are of more avail than legal science. The justice introduces into the administration, when he takes part in it, a certain taste for established forms and publicity, which renders him a most unserviceable instrument for despotism; and, on the other hand, he is not a slave of those legal superstitions which render judges unfit members of a government.[13]

The combination of judicial and administrative powers justices of the peace enjoyed made them powerful in the pre–Civil War era. In Kentucky, for example, they performed most of the duties associated with governing the counties along with their judicial functions. They also comprised one-fourth of the state House of Representatives and one-fifth of the Senate.[14] Historical research indicates that in Nevada, too, the justice of the peace was the most important county official in the territorial and early statehood period.[15]

Justice-Court Reform: The First Wave

As communities continued to grow during the nineteenth century, justices of the peace either began to lose their administrative responsibilities or started to share them with other local officeholders. Their judicial responsibilities, however, tended to remain the same. Some state legislatures simply increased the number of justices as urban populations grew; others created mayor's, alderman's, or police courts.[16]

During the first decades of the twentieth century, the multiplicity of courts in the cities, their informality and lack of dignity, the competition among justices for fees from cases, and the vulnerability of these offices to patronage politics, brought calls for their elimination. Activists succeeded first in reforming the court system in Chicago, replacing a welter of over two-hundred justices of the peace and specialized courts with a unified metropolitan court system staffed by full-time lawyer judges in 1906. The first indications of success in Chicago encouraged reform efforts in other cities.[17]

The times also favored court reform. Lawyers, increasingly educated in law schools rather than individual law offices, had begun to organize nationally. Even outside the schools, however, attitudes had begun to reflect what Burton Bledstein has called "the culture of professionalism." The public seemed increasingly willing to defer to the bar's claims of expertise concerning legal institutions.[18] The bar, in turn, was responding to the new mandate it had helped create. Roscoe Pound galvanized the American Bar Association with his famous 1906 speech criticizing the bar's complacency about court organization and trial practice.[19] The American Judicature Society, which made court reform its goal, was founded in 1913.[20] About the same time, appellate judges in both state and federal court systems began to form councils to discuss common problems.

Progressivism, with its sometimes-conflicting impulses toward social justice, accountability, and efficiency in government, also nourished the bar's awakening interest in court reform. Lawyers called for modern courts which would articulate as a unified, efficient system.[21] Justice in such courts required trained administrators and sound management. Popular democracy, even if shorn of patronage politics, was not the appropriate means to select the judges to manage courts at any level in the judicial pyramid. Lawyers instead favored lifetime appointment based on merit, as determined by professional criteria.

In emphasizing expertise and efficiency in the management of disputes, the legal profession subtly shaped the broad Progressive mandate for governmental reform away from popular democracy where courts were concerned and toward a restrictive and elitist view of qualifications for judicial office. Part-time lay judges, especially those with little formal education, obviously could not cope with the demands of modern judicial administration, but reformers seemed oblivious to the class bias in their reasons for eliminating these judges:

> When we have a highly technical and specialized body of law by means of which and through which we demand that justice be administered, what confidence in our judicial organization can we hope to develop when we elevate farmers, blacksmiths, carpenters, shoemakers, plumbers, and every conceivable kind of laborer and tradesman to the bench of a court of justice?[22]

Such arguments met with no outcry from educated Americans outside the profession. The attentive public linked lay judges to the justice-of-the-peace system, which it had begun to view as an amateurish holdover from an earlier era. No one tried to defend the justice of the peace courts in ideological terms as an important route to popular participation in the resolution of disputes. The U.S. Census even refused to take justices of the peace seriously as judicial officers. It listed them with fortune tellers, spiritualists, and healers in its 1915 categorization of pursuits.[23]

Some lawyers claimed that lay judges tended to be not just ignorant or illiterate but corrupt. J. M. Levine called them "a public menace which had to be resisted with grim determination."[24] Without professional standards, reformer W. F. Willoughby charged, these judges were "moved in the performance of their duties by political and other improper considerations." In retaining "this archaic survival" government discriminated against the poor, who deserved the quality of adjudication available to "those better provided with the goods of this world."[25] The role of the poor, in this conception, was clearly to consume justice, not to administer it. (That responsibility was to be reserved for legal professionals from the comfortable classes.) The poor had no reason to complain of their disenfranchisement because legal professionals greatly improved the quality of the product (justice) available in the lower courts.

Installing legally educated judges would not solve every problem associated with adjudication in the lower courts, reformers realized. The agenda for better courts included changes in administration as well as changes in personnel. The municipal courts, increasingly staffed by lawyer judges, but often administratively archaic and inefficient, illustrated the scope of the problem. The dividing line between problems created by inadequate judicial training and inadequate administrative structure nevertheless remained obscure. Reformers apparently saw no need to consider the impact of court reforms item by item.

Though unconcerned with the precise relationship between items on the reform agenda, legal activists were very articulate about the urgency of the need to adopt it. Every citizen, they argued, should be concerned about the quality of adjudication in the lower courts, even those who had little occasion to rely on these courts themselves. The attention of the propertied and professional classes was warranted because lower courts handle huge numbers of cases and provide the only experience with adjudication most ordinary citizens have. Inadequate courts at this level, therefore, bred dangerous disrespect for law and government. Thus Chief Justice Charles Evans Hughes condemned the "petty tyrant in a police court" and warned lawyers that the incompetence of such judges "will daily breed bolshevists who are beyond the reach of your appeals."[26]

The campaign for professionalism in adjudication sometimes conflicted with efforts on behalf of another Progressive-era concern: access to courts for small disputes as well as large. For many lawyers, the desire to make adjudication more accessible and economical in minor civil cases, while a laudable goal, could not justify departure from legal standards and lawyer judges. When Kansas established Small Debtors' Courts to provide quick, inexpensive resolution of disputes over small sums and relied on nonlawyers to staff these courts, Reginald Heber Smith, a well-known reformer and highly respected lawyer, charged that the state legislature had attempted "to secure justice without trained judges and without law." To Smith, this was "justice according to individual conscience after the manner of an eastern cadi."[27]

Justices of the peace and other nonlawyer judges began to disappear from the major cities during the first three decades of the century, a period of widespread governmental reforms. By 1930, municipal courts had been reorganized to eliminate nonlawyer judges in Cleveland, Detroit, Milwaukee, Pittsburgh, New York, Philadelphia, Atlanta, and other large cities.[28]

In many areas, reform proved relatively easy because the volume of business was high enough to permit full-time, salaried judges. Lawyers were available to take judgeships under these conditions. Judicial specialization, another watchword of the early court reform movement, was even possible in the largest cities. Chicago, for example, created juvenile, domestic relations and small claims divisions.[29]

The U.S. Supreme Court contributed indirectly to this first wave of reform with its 1927 decision in *Tumey v. Ohio*[30] which declared unconstitutional Ohio's fee system for supporting its limited jurisdiction courts. The Court pronounced the fee arrangement—by which judges received "costs" only if they found defendants guilty—a violation of the Constitution's due process clause. The immediate impact of this decision varied from state to state. In some, legislatures hastened to make the fee system neutral regarding guilt. Other states did not respond at all for years.[31] State courts and the Supreme Court contributed to the confusion by subsequent decisions construing *Tumey* narrowly.[32] The Ohio Supreme Court, for example, read *Tumey* to make decisions in the unconstitutionally financed courts void only if defendant objected to their jurisdiction at the earliest opportunity in the proceedings.[33]

Nevertheless, the Court's recognition in *Tumey* that the evils of fee-maintained courts could rise to constitutional proportions provided welcome support in the campaign to establish modern municipal courts.[34] For the first time, the Court had explicitly recognized that judges at this level were part of the state judicial system, not simply an agency of local government:

> The field of jurisdiction is not that of a small community engaged in enforcing its own local regulations. The court is a state agency, imposing substantial punishment. . . . It is not to be treated as a mere village tribunal for village peccadilloes.[35]

Reforming Rural Justice

Outside the cities, the impulse for revamping the justice-of-the-peace system was weaker, and the obstacles to change were greater. The elimination of part-time, fee-maintained, nonlawyer-judge courts required the abolition of courts in towns and villages long accustomed to having their "own" judge. Modernizing the justice-of-the-peace system also posed financial and logistical problems. Full-time lawyer judges would be much more expensive to maintain than justices of the peace, even with drastic reductions in the number of judges. "Professional" judges would require suitable courtrooms, facilities, compensation, and staff—costs traditionally minimized or ignored in many rural areas, where the fees of litigants sometimes financed the local court. To create adequate caseloads in areas of low population, judicial districts would have to be large, or else judges would have to ride circuit. None of these changes were likely to be popular among the rural constituents of the state legislators.[36]

Nor were lawyers in rural areas nearly as enthusiastic about reform as their urban counterparts. Bellamy Partridge, for example, describes the incompetence of the local justices in Phelps, New York—including one that arranged the sale of a neighbor's wife—with bemusement rather than indignation in his 1939 book, *Country Lawyer*.[37] The rural lawyer's willingness to work around the inadequacies of justices of the peace, or exploit them if necessary, angered Roscoe Pound, who saw these judges as "a humiliating anachronism."[38] Pound noted that the impulse for reform was an entirely urban phenomenon:

> The demand for organization of justice and improvement of legal procedure comes from our cities. It is a significant circumstance that in the debates upon this subject in the past six years in our bar associations, national and state, the city lawyer has asserted that reform was imperative, while the country lawyer has contended that the evils were greatly exaggerated and that grave changes were wholly unnecessary; the city lawyer has been urging ambitious programs of reform and the country lawyer has been defeating them. A modern judicial organization and a modern procedure would, indeed, be a real service to country as well as to city. But the pressure comes from the city.[39]

State constitutions also protected justices of the peace by providing for the existence of these courts, and sometimes even describing their powers. Forty-seven of the forty-eight states listed justices of the peace in their state constitutions in 1915, and in these states the legislature could not simply abolish the office by statute.[40] To eliminate the office, a constitutional amendment was necessary, unless the legislature took the legally questionable path of eliminating the jurisdiction of its justices of the peace.[41] Provision for home rule, a key to success in Chicago and other cities, was not usually available to help legislators eliminate nonurban justices of the peace.

Such impediments kept the pace of change slow outside the major cities, despite unanimity among reform-minded lawyers and other advocates of court improvement that the justice of the peace was an undesirable anachronism in American jurisprudence, "a cog in the wheels of justice" and a "barnacle of jurisprudence" in the colorful rhetoric of pre–World War II court reform.[42] One writer doubted whether "a more striking example of cultural lag can be found in the political field than the attempt which is made in most of our forty-eight states to serve the ends of justice in the twentieth century by a medieval English instrument."[43]

To these critics, the survival of the rural justice of the peace represented not just tolerance for amateurishness and traditionalism, but also a challenge to the concept of a unified and centralized court system dispensing the same justice for all citizens. Legislation restricting non-lawyer judges to rural areas created "a discrimination between urban and rural populations which no argument can justify."[44] Urban courts were presumed to provide "that certainty and security in legal transactions which comes only with justice according to law." Rural residents, on the other hand, were "still compelled to gamble with the chance caprice of the lay magistrate whose compensation depends on fees." The survival of the justice of the peace outside the cities thus meant that "the rural population is absolutely denied justice according to our highest conception thereof, and is accorded no certainty whatever in legal transactions involving small sums."[45]

Although informality per se was not necessarily disturbing, the undignified settings of many justice courts did upset many reformers, themselves often successful urban lawyers:

> Have you ever visited a justice's court? You usually find it in some dingy basement or up a rickety flight of stairs, or in a dirty, ill-smelling place such as you would associate with some cheap, tawdry business. It is not such a place as you would care to be caught

in; your presence there would call for explanation and apology. You would not wish your wife or daughter to go there even as a witness. It is not the environment of justice.[46]

Such critics saw no redeeming value in the rural justice of the peace, who survived only for the worst reasons. "The system," one writer charged, "has no defenders and few apologists. The only persons actively desiring its continuation are those who profit from its operation in some way."[47]

Empirical evidence hardly seemed necessary to bolster the profession's case against this "universal, and universally condemned, American institution,"[48] and little was undertaken before the 1930s. Even at that point, scholars sometimes apologized about actually investigating the justice-of-the-peace system. T. L. Howard, for example, felt compelled to justify his 1934 study of the justice of the peace in Tennessee:

> It may be objected that statistics are not necessary to prove that the justice of the peace system is a failure; it may be said that when a piece of meat smells to heaven it is not necessary to make a chemical analysis in order to know that it is spoiled. And this criticism may be conceded to have some merit, without surrendering the view that accurate information about the justice situation is a desirable and necessary prelude to reform.[49]

Others studied justices of the peace in Ohio, Illinois, West Virginia, North Carolina, and Michigan during the 1930s and 1940s.[50]

The pattern these studies revealed was consistent. Caseloads consisted primarily of civil cases in rural areas, particularly overdue debts and bad checks. Criminal cases included public intoxication, assault, other minor breaches of the peace, and motor vehicle cases. Lawyers seldom appeared to defend these kinds of cases. Prosecuting lawyers also avoided these courts, sometimes leaving police officers to carry forward the state's case when trial was necessary. Court might be in the judge's home or

place of business. A study of justice courts in Hamilton
County, Ohio, for example, showed that nine of the
twenty-six judges surveyed held court at home.[51] Many
had few law books, and a significant proportion were
without even a copy of the motor vehicle code, according
to another report.[52] Terms were short in most states, and
turnover tended to be rapid, although a small percentage
of judges held office twenty years or more.[53]

Everywhere large numbers of judges were virtually
inactive, while a few handled nearly all the cases. In
Illinois, for example, where each justice had countywide
jurisdiction, only thirty-two of 163 judges authorized for
a six-county area had any cases at all, and the nine judges
in the county seat handled nearly all of these.[54] In general, the justices nearest the county seat enjoyed the most
business and tended to be most expert in handling their
work.

Judges without caseloads complained of forum shopping by police officers and plaintiffs' lawyers. Where con-
stables shared in court fees, the practice in some areas
apparently was to bring in cases—through speed traps
and other stratagems—so that both officials would benefit.[55] Some judges reportedly abused the fee system on
their own, serving as collection agencies in private life and
using their part-time judgeships to hasten payment of
overdue debts.[56] Plaintiff-oriented judges, therefore, allegedly enjoyed the lion's share of the judicial business
and the fees that went with it. According to some observers, this meant that the familiar abbreviation "j.p."
should be translated as "judgment for the plaintiff"
rather than "justice of the peace."[57]

Whether or not large numbers of these justices were
actually biased or corrupt, however, is unclear from the
data investigators collected. It does seem clear that for
most judges fees were not a major source of income.[58] As
Bruce Smith noted in his 1932 book on rural justice:

> Many justices have now ceased altogether to per-
> form their judicial functions because there is no real
> need for their services; others receive but a mere

pittance in compensation for the few cases which they do hear; a few who secure a considerable volume of judicial work, sometimes by active solicitation, find that their fees provide a welcome supplement to their regular incomes; and a mere handful are placed upon a fixed salary which, in rare instances, is generally consistent with the abstract dignity of the judicial office.[59]

Seldom, however, did investigators systematically observe case processing in these courts. Douglass, in his research on the justices of the peace in Hamilton County, Ohio, probably visited the most actual court sessions and was, perhaps in consequence, the most sympathetic to justices of the peace. He reported in 1932 that the justices he observed

perform a significant function in being impartial and patient listeners to tales borne by excited principals, interested relatives, and officious intermeddlers ... he effects a catharsis by calming emotions and analyzing the facts of a situation. In civil as well as criminal difficulties he acts as a sort of foster father to a portion of each community.[60]

Most researchers concentrated on the information they could gather from docket books and personal interviews. Such investigation showed that plaintiffs in civil cases won their cases in overwhelming proportions, and defendants seldom appealed. Critics, however, disregarded the infrequency of appeals as an indication of the success of these courts. Appeals were infrequent, they contended, because cases were small, and trial de novo in a distant court of record (the usual method of review) was time-consuming.

Studies undertaken in this period also showed that justices of the peace were, for the most part, older men. They tended to be farmers, independent businessmen, craftsmen, and retirees from such occupations. As one observer noted:

The tradesman and the manual worker in this country have for so long been closely identified with the justice of the peace system as to have become a distinguishing characteristic of that system. No one can visit the rural justices without being impressed with this fact.[61]

Most also appear to have had limited educations and limited incomes. Nearly half of those surveyed in North Carolina and Ohio, for example, had not graduated from high school, and fewer than 10 percent had college degrees. It should also be noted, however, that in each state a few justices of the peace were lawyers.[62]

From the perspective of the court-reform movement, of course, such backgrounds could hardly produce adequate judges. The emphasis on expertise in adjudication that characterized the court-reform movement in its early years had not diminished. "Modern justice," as Robert Keebler explained in a 1930 article "demands trained minds, ripened by experience, free from interest or bias, devoted exclusively to the business at hand, with no cross currents or distractions, operating in an atmosphere of justice."[63]

Other critics of the period went even further. George Warren argued, in an often-cited report prepared for the National Committee on Traffic Law Enforcement, that the traffic judge must have more training and expertise than law school and law practice provide:

A traffic judge must have more than merely a legal background. A knowledge of traffic policing and engineering, and an understanding of the safety field, must go with his legal training and his knowledge of human nature. It is extremely important for the proper man to be on this bench.[64]

The inefficiency and lack of accountability inherent in the office also remained a popular source for criticism and proposed reforms.[65] In 1938, for example, the American Bar Association recommended centrally accountable municipal or district courts staffed by full-time judges in a series of unanimous resolutions that became known as the Parker-Vanderbilt standards.[66] The emphasis in these standards was upon efficiency rather than educa-

though it was assumed that all judges would be lawyers. Neither the justice of the peace nor nonlawyer judges had any place in this program for institutional modernization and efficiency. As a Wickersham Commission noted in its 1931 report on the lower courts:

> The old-time country squire, a leader in his community, exercising a sort of patriarchal jurisdiction, is as much in the past as the conditions in which he administered justice.[67]

Time, legal writers agreed, had passed by this "lay and inexpert arm of the law."[68] Communities had grown too big for personalized adjudication free of proper procedures and legal accountability. Whether proper procedure and high professional standards actually prevailed in the urban trial courts where the reform program had been successful was a matter for speculation. No one had studied adjudication in the reformed courts of limited jurisdiction systematically, and no one had compared the process of adjudication in lay and lawyer courts. Reform arguments hinged on assumptions about the impact of judicial credentials and structural reorganization, not on data about court operations, which remained scarce for some time. The lawyers who addressed themselves to court reform in this period believed its goals to be self-evident. As they saw it, the responsibility of the bar was simply to make the necessity for modernization clear to the public. "Some day," the eminent reformer Arthur T. Vanderbilt mused in introducing the 1938 American Bar Association recommendations for court improvement, "a more enlightened generation will look back on these reports and wonder that it should have been necessary to write them, necessary to agitate for the recommendations set forth in them, and necessary, perhaps, in some states, to invoke the aid of enlightened and farseeing laymen to bring about their adoption."[69]

In the meantime, reformers relied on their sense that progress in professionalizing the lower courts was almost inevitable:

Every advance must be a personal sacrifice and over heated opposition. But it is the proud heritage of the legal profession that there have never been lacking those who were willing to make the sacrifice and able to win the day. For the stars are on the side of justice and progress; and in due season all the ancient institutions which stand in our pathway must topple down. One of these is the justice of the peace system. Its day is done, and it must give way to an orderly, economic and efficient administration of justice.[70]

Nonlawyer Judges: Recent Themes and Trends

The fundamental themes of the court-reform movement have remained remarkably consistent since World War II. The emphasis is still on efficiency, clear lines of authority, properly allocated expertise, and merit selection of judges.[71] The lower courts—where jurisdictions often overlap and court personnel tend to be politically accountable— are still a primary focus for concern. The part-time, decentralized, unsupervised, untrained, and often fee-supported justice of the peace is particularly to be condemned.[72] Periodically the ABA, other professional organizations, and individual lawyers and judges have repeated the call for eliminating these courts and replacing them with a district or circuit-court system presided over by a full-time, all-lawyer bench.[73]

These calls for reform have met with mixed success. Some of the most-often criticized features of the now largely rural justice-of-the-peace courts, such as their near total independence from state-level supervision, have been eliminated or mitigated. Nonlawyer judges, on the other hand, are still common outside metropolitan areas, though they are not as plentiful as they were earlier in the century. The changes that have occurred in the past four decades have been incremental, not wholesale.

The primary constituency that promotes reforms at this level remains successful urban lawyers and, increasingly, law professors, law students, and professionals in court administration, but not elected politicians or the social scientists who study the process of adjudication in the lower courts. Evidence of how the lower courts actually operate, which has begun to accumulate in the past two decades, plays no more than a supporting role in efforts to improve lay courts. Most reform proposals still flow deductively from professional presuppositions about credentials and court organization.

The court reform movement also continues to struggle with the problem of access to courts for small disputes. During the past two decades this concern has focused particularly on the capacity of the courts to resolve conflicts between individuals embedded in long-term relationships with each other.[74] Those who advocate more informal, easily accessible, consensus-oriented institutions for the resolution of such conflicts have won considerable financial and foundation support. Neighborhood justice centers and other institutions for mediating minor civil and criminal disputes began to appear in the 1970s. Bar associations and other professional groups have been enthusiastic about these centers, even though nonlawyers often serve as mediators.

Clearly, professional attitudes toward dispute resolution by lay persons have become more complicated. It also seems clear that the public-spirited lawyers interested in court reform now are less confident than their predecessors were about the structural reforms necessary to bring the performance of the lower courts up to professional standards. Optimism about straightforward "solutions" has faded as our experience with reform has become more extensive and the process of adjudication at this level is better understood. Professional opposition to permitting nonlawyers to be full-fledged judges, nevertheless, remains strong.

This section considers contemporary legal writing about nonlawyer judges and relates it to concern for controlling court costs and expanding dispute-resolution alternatives. The final part of the chapter addresses the success of the post–World War II court-reform movement in eliminating lay judges, and assesses the political strategies lawyers have relied upon in advising government about judicial credentials.

Lay Judges and the Justice-of-the-Peace System: The Case for Reform Revisited

Renewed interest in making dispute resolution convenient and inexpensive for both citizens and the state has not preserved nonlawyer judges or the justice-of-the-peace courts from professional criticism. Lay authority over the progress and outcome of litigation has always rankled lawyers, despite its advantages of low cost and convenience. Neither the arguments critics use against lay justice nor the means by which they arrive at their conclusions have changed appreciably since the Progressive era. Consider, for example, the best known and most influential assessment of justices of the peace and lay judges since World War II, that prepared by the Task Force on the Courts, a prestigious, presidentially appointed commission composed primarily of law professors, high-level staff from the Department of Justice and other federal agencies, and attorneys from major firms.

The commission's 1967 report on the lower courts denounced justice-of-the-peace courts as anachronistic and recommended their prompt elimination.[75] The commission was only slightly less hostile in its evaluation of statutes opening the lower court judiciary to nonlawyers. On-the-job judicial training could mitigate the evils of this misguided legislation, but courses for nonlawyer judges were only a palliative:

> While such courses may prove beneficial, to ensure a better quality of training and higher interest in the work performed, it is far preferable that judicial officers be lawyers.[76]

The Commission, which supported its recommendations regarding metropolitan courts with an extensive series of empirical studies, indicated no similar respect for the nonmetropolitan justice of the peace. The only evidence for its recommendations concerning justices of the peace were anecdotes and complaints supplied by miscellaneous detractors. The commission reported, for example, that in a justice court "questionable practices may often go unchecked," citing an unidentified Maryland judge for support. The commission even quoted this judge's remarks to a local newspaper:

> [They have] treated some good, decent citizens like common criminals. . . . The justice of the peace system is completely outmoded. . . . If things keep going like they've been going, some of these people are going to get us into serious trouble. . . . Many of the J.P.'s are just plain nasty to people. There have been all sorts of instances where they have been rude to people, and when the person complains they tell him to "go to see your congressman."

In support of its conclusion that courtroom facilities are often inadequate, the commission quoted two incidents reported in Montana: "One justice reportedly tried a case while repairing an automobile; another justice disposed of a case while sitting on a tractor during a pause from plowing his field." To justify its conclusion that localism "colors the quality of justice dispensed in these courts," the commission repeated without further evaluation this conclusion from an earlier anti–lay-judge invective: "It has often been noted that local offenders have many cases, usually traffic offenses, fixed in advance, while out-of-State defendants must pay the full fine or penalty."[77]

That such off-the-cuff opinions from practicing lawyers and (lawyer) judges could be used to support the recommendations of a presidentially appointed panel of influential lawyers will be surprising only to those unfamiliar with the profession's long-standing opposition to the justice of the peace. Characterizations of the justice of the peace in the professional literature remain patronizing at best.[78] As Jack Kress and Sandra Stanley found in a 1976 review of the literature:

> It was startling to learn that academic and commission studies and recommendations have almost uni-

formly been based upon speculation and imitation rather than upon factual information and actual observation.[79]

The rural justice of the peace, in short, still has no admirers among reformers. So consistent is this antagonism in legal commentary that one magistrate could assert in 1968 that "there seems to be no recorded instance of a magistrate . . . being drawn as anything better than a buffoon, and sometimes the portrayal is much less flattering."[80] Harry Lawson, a long-time observer of court studies and reform proposals, came to the same conclusion, claiming that "if justice of the peace courts did not exist, court reformers would have had to invent them."[81]

The dearth of law degrees among justices of the peace—even more than the fee system, excess numbers of judges, and other structural aspects of the post—remains the most potent criticism of these judges among lawyers. A poll of practitioners conducted by Edson Sunderland revealed, for example, that lack of a legal education was "the most serious and widespread complaint about the justice of the peace courts."[82] Even scholars not directly concerned with courts and court reform sometimes simply assume the desirability of law school education for all judicial posts. Paul E. Dow's 1981 survey of American court systems, for example, describes lay judges as "an abomination" and "an insidious custom." The author draws an analogy between surgery patients who "no doubt expect the surgeon to be a qualified doctor," and defendants who, "brought before a court in which often complex legal issues must be adjudicated, expect the presiding authority to be a 'judge.'" To be a real judge, Dow argues, "should require no less than a law degree, a license to practice, and trial experience."[83] This medical metaphor appears over and over in lawyer criticisms of nonlawyer judges.[84]

Probative evidence of the significance of law school education to judicial office seems no more necessary than it did to an earlier generation of reform-minded lawyers. The incompetence of nonlawyer judges follows ineluctably, as it always has, from certain self-evident truths about adjudication and lay capacities. The intuitive case against lay judges has actually grown stronger as constitutional standards in criminal cases have become more comprehensive.

The deductive approach is particularly evident in the law reviews, which became involved in the question of judicial credentials in the 1970s, when litigation increasingly challenged the constitutionality of nonlawyer judges. It is in the law reviews, not surprisingly, that the rhetoric opposed to untrained judges is most strident. The typical chain of reasoning begins with the assumption that the cases in limited-jurisdiction courts frequently contain technical evidentiary questions wholly beyond a nonlawyer's grasp:

> In handling criminal and civil cases, it is reasonable to assume that they will involve technical evidentiary questions which the untrained person will not even recognize, let alone make accurate and just rulings on, based on the ever-changing case law.[85]

Counsel's arguments before such a person are "of no conceivable value," according to another law-review author, who complained that "the probability of a legally correct judgement might be improved by flipping a coin or casting dice against the courthouse steps."[86] Clearly, if legal decisions are to be correct, the "professional excellence of the specialist" is necessary in judges at this level. The pressure of high caseloads creates additional demands. The workload requires "a man of first rate capacity" who can render correctly "split-second decisions on questions of criminal law and procedures" and at the same time "exercise sentencing responsibilities thoughtfully and wisely under exhausting pressures of time."[87]

Lawyer critics of nonlawyer judges remain convinced, as they have been from the beginning of the court-reform movement, that professional credentials promote not just technically correct decisions but fairness. Legal education helps insulate judges against those twin enemies of justice, prejudice and bias. Common sense is no substitute for this protection:

> A judge without legal expertise can become biased easily. If he relies on his common sense to solve legal issues, his personal prejudices and biases will likely affect his decisions.[88]

The consequence is that lay judges tend to favor local residents over out-of-towners and that "too many cases are decided on personal considerations rather than the evidence presented."[89]

Only occasionally do commentators try to explain just how legal education and practice protect lawyer judges from prejudice and bias. James J. Cavanaugh, however, undertook such an explanation in his 1963 book, *The Lawyer in Society*. "It is sometimes asked by laymen," Cavanaugh noted, "why judges have to be lawyers." He went on to cite three "very strong reasons," including experience with legal arguments and practice in responding to them. Most important, though, is the impartiality a lawyer develops in the course of a legal education and career:

> The lawyer is far more likely—on the average—to be impartial than his fellow citizens. He has seen too many of his own arguments broken up by the painstaking analysis of the opposition to carry very many strong preconceptions into a given case or to be too impressed with the apparently invincible argument, or to too unimpressed, for that matter, with a weak but plausible argument.

"Whether the man chooses the profession or the profession chooses the man," Cavanaugh concluded, "the instincts of a judge, with his open mind and conservative will, are to be found in most lawyers."[90]

Practical Exceptions to the Lawyer-Judge Ideal

Evidence about the day-to-day work of courts of limited jurisdiction has only occasionally figured in professional debate over qualifications for judicial office. Sensitivity to the practical burdens of moving cases through these courts, however, suggests at least a limited role for nonlawyers as adjudicators. During the past twenty years or so, students of judicial administration have more and more often sought to define such a role by differentiating between routine and complex functions in the lower courts. Lawyer judges are reserved for the more difficult tasks, of course, but nonlawyers may be able to help them with more mundane work. As the conferees at the second national Conference on the Judiciary agreed: "The challenge is to distribute disputes among dispute resolution methods in some rational manner that will contribute to the overall performance of the justice system."[91]

Some consider nonlawyers capable of handling certain routine matters, like arraignments, bail hearings, and simple traffic cases.[92] Current proposals for revamping the lower courts, therefore, sometimes recommend lay referees or lay-staffed administrative bureaus for traffic cases,[93] or lay screening of small claims cases.[94] Some have also suggested that nonlawyers might be capable enough of judgelike functions to be parajudges—appointees who carry out routine judicial functions under the supervision of a lawyer judge.[95] Such proposals are designed to preserve the benefits of lay participation in adjudication: low cost and relief for lawyers from routine tasks, without the presumed disadvantages of autonomous nonlawyer judges.

Proposals for lawyer-supervised adjudication by nonlawyers have become more popular as lawyer judges have let it be known that they do not enjoy handling petty cases. A 1971 ABA-sponsored study of lawyer judges in California found, for example, that:

> Many of the judges felt it would be a waste of judicial expertise to handle typical municipal court cases. And many municipal court judges expressed concern over the use of trained judges to handle minor traffic matters and small claims. Fifty-one percent of the municipal court judges ... indicated that they least

preferred to handle traffic, and 41 percent least preferred to handle small claims.[96]

The costs and distances involved in providing full-time lawyer judges have also encouraged some observers to recommend retaining nonlawyer judges in isolated areas, albeit with improved training and supervision.[97] A 1974 study of Oregon's justice-of-the-peace system by area law students, for example, noted "the continuing viability of the J.P.'s historic function of furnishing prompt and economical justice in rural areas."[98] The Temporary Commission on the New York State Court System was more dubious about the capacities of nonlawyer judges, but it also recommended permitting them in counties below 145,000 in population.[99] The commission was unwilling, however, to give these nonlawyers the traditional powers of a lower-court judge, suggesting that jurisdiction for misdemeanor trials, preliminary hearings in felony cases, and civil actions over $500 be confined to full-time lawyer judges.[100]

The most extensive analysis of adjudication by non-lawyer judges in recent years, a 1979 book-length report issued by the Institute for Judicial Administration and the National Center for State Courts, adopted a similar stance. In a companion article, one of the principal investigators, a New York University law professor, supported a limited role for nonlawyer judges:

> ... for those states in which financial or demographic constraints necessitate the use of non-attorney judges. Non-attorney judges can successfully resolve some controversies, thus eliminating the need in those cases either for extensive travel by the litigants, or for adjudication of simple matters by attorneys from outside the community or by part-time attorney judges who might have serious conflicts of interest.[101]

She concluded nevertheless that "non-attorneys should not be authorized to act as judges when attorney judges are a viable option."[102] The report recommended sharp limitations on nonlawyer judge jurisdiction in both criminal and civil cases, even though the researchers' own on-site investigation of limited jurisdiction courts in seven states had revealed no significant differences between lay and lawyer judges.[103]

The Informal Justice Movement

The recent wave of enthusiasm among bar associations and other professional groups for mediating minor civil and criminal disputes with personnel not necessarily trained as lawyers might seem to signal a fundamental shift in the bar's traditionally negative assessment of lay decision making. The mediators and facilitators in the neighborhood justice centers and analogous community-based institutions that began appearing in the 1970s do apply themselves to disputes that might otherwise move through courts. The program in Columbus, Ohio, for example, has absorbed one-third of the minor criminal cases that would otherwise have gone through the municipal courts.

Lawyers accept lay mediators as agents for the disposition of minor criminal and civil cases because mediators do not have the legal authority judges do. The concept of mediation depends on voluntary participation from disputants who are supposed to create their own resolution of the difficulties between them. The mediator has no power to bind the parties as a judge does.[104]

The coerciveness of the courtroom, however, is not entirely absent in most community mediation programs. Those who promote this form of resolution envision lay persons performing time-consuming counseling functions, with lawyers in the crucial backup roles that might involve coercion:

> Victims meet victimizers in the presence of neutral moderators or mediators, themselves community residents, volunteers who attempt to reach beneath the surface "right-wrong" aspects of the conflict in an effort to discover a mutual acknowledgement of the problem and to craft a solution that is meaningful in human terms to each of the disputing parties.

To ensure that such justice does not become tribal, decisions reached by such proceedings are thereafter reviewed and approved by lawyers and judges.[105]

The movement toward this type of informal dispute resolution offers a fresh route to a goal reformers set early in this century: provision for inexpensive, convenient fora for small cases.[106] The sources of inspiration for this particular approach to the problem of access are disparate. They include neighborhood moots from West Africa, East European comrades' courts, and domestic arbitration and mediation.[107] What unifies the proponents of informal dispute resolution alternatives to U.S. courts is the conviction that traditional adversary processes are inappropriate and ineffective in many cases. Adjudication where two individual antagonists are involved simply turns over the undigested differences for third-party processing, in which the assignment of blame and penalty tends to be the most prominent feature. A mediative approach is better in such circumstances because it may permanently resolve the underlying dispute:

> The people who can understand the defendant's problem, secure his confidence, and possibly assist him towards finding a solution are those in his own community, sharing many of his experiences. The power must be transferred to the source of the solution.[108]

The interest in implementing informal dispute resolution theory has been broad-based. The *Yale Law Journal* reported enthusiastic support from "a surprising array of proponents, ranging from Chief Justice Warren Burger to consumer advocate Ralph Nader."[109] The Ford Foundation, Department of Justice, American Bar Association, scholarly journals, and the popular press have also endorsed such efforts. The federal government has encouraged local, informal dispute resolution programs with implementing legislation and financial support.[110] Existing court systems have also provided crucial support by referring cases to neighborhood centers. For most centers, in fact, referrals from courts, prosecutors, and other government agencies are the primary source of cases.[111]

Some of this enthusiasm for informal dispute-resolution institutions arises from their potential for helping control the ever-growing costs of processing lower-court case-loads. Economic considerations were prominent, for example, in Chief Administrative Judge Lawrence Cooke's description of New York's new Community Dispute Resolution program:

> These local dispute resolution centers will provide their communities with an economical and simple alternative to expensive and complex formal court proceedings. The use of local resources, including volunteers and available building space, will provide accessible, cost-effective resolution of minor disputes that would otherwise drain upon limited and hard-pressed judicial resources.[112]

Critics of the informal justice movement argue that the new dispute resolution centers rest on two myths: (1) "that a stranger with minimal training can, in the course of an hour's meeting, resolve deep-rooted, long-standing conflicts between intimates"; and (2) "that an intermediary without coercive authority can secure redress for a grievant against a powerful adversary."[113] They argue that proponents of the new institutions also downplay the coerciveness implicit in court-ordered referrals to a setting that relaxes or abandons procedural guarantees usually associated with state-backed dispute resolution.[114] The disproportionate degree to which the poor are the clients of these new agencies has been another focus of criticism.[115] To date, the middle class has been more involved in administering dispute resolution centers than in using them to resolve their own disputes.

That mediators are not necessarily lawyers has not been a source of concern either to proponents or opponents of the neighborhood justice center concept. McGillis and Mullen, who favor neighborhood justice centers, see reliance on lay personnel as "a particularly appropriate and timely model viewed in the context of the broad goal of citizen participation in the resolution of community disputes."[116] Even critics of neighborhood justice, however, seem relatively uninterested in legal qualifications per se. They have been more concerned that the position of mediator might become professionalized, credentials in social work or counseling becoming qualifications for the position.[117]

Nor has anyone devoted much attention to the obvious kinship between the modern concept of a community-oriented mediator free of procedural constraints and the justice of the peace, who allegedly decides cases with reference to local values and little attention to legal procedure.[118] Lewis R. Katz, in promoting a lay council for minor criminal cases, even denies that any parallel exists with "the outdated counterpart of the urban municipal court—the justice of the peace court."[119] To social scientists Roman Tomasic and Malcolm Feeley, on the other hand, the enthusiasm with which reformers have greeted lay mediation after decades of opposition to lay judges is rather odd:

> Indeed, it is ironic to note that just as it is completing its more-or-less successful campaign against the justice of the peace and other forms of lay-administered justice, the organized legal profession in America is coming to embrace another type of informal justice in the neighborhood justice centers.[120]

Lay-staffed neighborhood justice centers are respectable, while the traditional justice of the peace is not, probably because the centers are subordinate to and supervised by local (lawyer judge) metropolitan courts and social service systems.[121] That mediation—ostensibly at least—is voluntary also helps make informal dispute resolution institutions more acceptable than nonlawyer judge courts. This rationale is weakened, of course, with growing evidence that many centers cannot operate without court referrals and the threat of judicial sanctions upon the failure of mediation. The relationship between neighborhood justice centers and supervising metropolitan courts and social agencies may, in fact, be symbiotic.

The centers rely on the courts for cases, while the courts use mediation centers, in Geoff Mungham and Chris McCormick's words, as "a depository for work other [professional] agencies find distasteful, demeaning, or unimportant."[122]

The Politics of Court Reform

The growth of neighborhood justice centers and other lay-staffed modes of informal dispute resolution has occurred, as Tomasic and Feeley noted, in the face of a gradual decline in the traditional justice-of-the-peace court financed by fees and virtually unsupervised from the state level. By the mid-1970s, most states had reformed these courts significantly, reducing excess judges, instituting training programs and qualifying exams, usually with federal funding from the now-defunct Law Enforcement Assistance Administration (LEAA), eliminating the worst aspects of the fee system, and sometimes providing salaries for justices traditionally supported by fees.[123] Some states have even moved to appointive systems to better control the qualifications of their nonlawyer judges. One 1975 report claimed that thirty-one states had "made progress" toward eliminating the justice of the peace.[124]

Nonlawyer judges have proven more resiliant than traditional court structures, but here too important changes have occurred in the past four decades. A few jurisdictions have eliminated nonlawyers entirely from their judicial ranks, and many others have reduced their authority. Most now restrict lay judges to jurisdictions where lawyers are scarce. The federal government has moved in the same direction. Congress revised the U.S. commissioner system in 1968 to close the federal judicial system to nonlawyers. Under the old system, almost one-third of the 731 commissioners had been lay persons. Their duties were much like those of the state-level justices of the peace.[125]

A few states, it should be noted, have moved in apparently contradictory directions, reducing the numbers of nonlawyer judges and their autonomy from state-level supervision but increasing their authority. New York, for example, has increased the monetary jurisdiction of its nonlawyer judges in recent years. Only six states and the District of Columbia have actually abolished nonlawyer judges, though in several other states their duties are minimal.[126] The pace of reform seems to have slowed in the past decade as interests in the court-reform movement have shifted and the states have eliminated the most-criticized aspects of the justice-of-the-peace system.

Given the vehemence of the legal profession's rhetoric about lay judges, it may seem surprising that its almost century-long campaign to eliminate these "unqualified" judges has not been more successful. Americans concede to the legal profession authority for managing legal affairs, and they elect large numbers of lawyers to the legislative bodies that determine judicial qualifications. Why hasn't this political power enabled the bar to control access to the judiciary? What explains the relative weakness of the twentieth-century court-reform movement?

One problem has been that the bar as a whole has never been whole-heartedly behind most reform proposals, including those for eliminating lay-judge courts. For the most part, active concern about court structure and performance has been limited to the elite segment of the urban bar and legal educators, groups that also tend to dominate national bar organizations like the American Bar Association.[127] While these lawyers are powerful within their own organizations, they tend to be much less influential in party politics and among state legislatures, where they usually operate as outsiders.[128] Their isolation helps make them insensitive to the political dimensions of institutional change. J. Willard Hurst calls court reformers "crude amateurs" as lobbyists, who work for changes "in isolation from the social context."[129] Peter Fish, an authority on reform politics in the federal court system, stresses their tendency to see reform in terms of efficiency in the management of cases. "Politics," he notes, "is perceived as playing little or no part in setting or realizing this goal." In fact, it is "political encumbrances" that prevent courts from dispensing justice as they should.[130] The essential problem with this approach, Beverly Blair Cook has argued, is that it ignores the interest legislators and the executive have in maintaining patronage and the necessity for some kind of quid pro quo for the bench and bar, parties which must be involved in reforming the lower courts:

> The numerous city, county and township judges have close political connections with their city, county, and state representatives and so are able to veto reforms, unless the change takes into account their needs and interests. The local bar, law enforcement officers, and local businessmen also have a stake in changes in lower courts. Traffic officers want a convenient court for week-end offenders; businessmen want a court of limited jurisdiction for collection cases; lawyers want inferior courts where costs are not too expensive in relation to the value of the case.[131]

Nonlawyer judges themselves have also played a significant role in preserving their judgeships. Often associated with local government lobbies, state organizations of judges not only work to protect their jurisdiction but also to make the office less subject to criticism.[132] The lay-dominated New York State Association of Magistrates, for example, has consistently promoted mandatory judicial training. This association has also fought off challenges to nonlawyer judges. It commissioned a comprehensive report on lay courts in New York, for example, and it filed a friend-of-the-court brief in the one Supreme Court case that considered the constitutionality of nonlawyer judges.[133]

Political support for nonlawyer judges, institutional inertia, and the weakness of the court-reform movement thus all keep the pace of reform slow. Arthur T. Vanderbilt was right when he warned that "court reform is no sport for the shortwinded."[134] Typically, the effort to eliminate nonlawyer judges begins decades before it succeeds.[135] In Illinois and Connecticut, for example, the effort to remodel the court system began in the 1920s and resulted in the abolition of nonlawyer judges only in 1959 in Illinois and 1962 in Connecticut. In both states it was only after the governor, the press, and citizen groups joined reform-minded bar leaders that court reorganization occurred.[136]

Conclusion

The bar's nearly century-old effort to eliminate non-lawyer judges reveals much about the profession's conception of justice in adjudication. The reform-minded bar obviously puts professional knowledge at the center of the judicial process in the lower courts. The impossibility of creating a fair system with judges not trained in the law is, accordingly, almost too obvious to require investigation, or even extensive discussion. Nonlawyer judges are bound to make technical mistakes, and they lack the professional detachment to stay wide of prejudice, bias, and corruption. Election to office only exacerbates these problems:

> Any citizen twenty-one years of age may offer himself for election; and in order for the job to be attractive to any citizen nowadays, it is a reasonably safe assumption that he has a keen taste for petty politics, that he has little education and no legal training whatsoever, and that he is a misfit in the world of business and affairs. The exception to this generalization is rare enough to be worthy of a Congressional medal.[137]

Running through arguments like these is a profound distrust of the impact of democracy on the judicial branch. Popular elections are anathema to court reformers, and sensitivity to one's community in a judge is to be viewed with distrust. The influence of the community is described in the rubric of prejudice and bias. Representation on the bench for the classes and groups served by these courts is of no particular concern, for the professional conception of adjudication is divorced from the particularity of individual communities.

Legal rules and procedure, and the technical problems that arise with their application thus loom large in adjudication. Even the exercise of judicial discretion should be guided by considerations understood best by those with professional training in law. The citizen can rightfully be concerned with the professional competence of the adjudicator, but not with the representativeness of the lower-court bench or its sensitivity to the mores of the community.

Neighborhood justice centers and other mediation-focused institutions have emerged as something of a qualification on this conception of justice in adjudication. Community attitudes have taken on a legitimacy they did not enjoy before the informal justice movement. Reformers acknowledge no conflict here, because informal justice, in theory at least, is a voluntary enterprise. It also absorbs the cases professionals have found least satisfying to handle. The informal justice movement, in fact, may finally have solved the paradox created by a history of widely dispersed lay courts: providing cheap, accessible justice in small cases while not abandoning the ideal of professional standards in adjudication. This recipe for coexistence arguably removes any justification that might otherwise exist for lay courts.

"Institutional toughness," however, is a characteristic of the American judicial system. American judicial systems, in fact, may be tougher than most. According to legal scholar Mirjan Damaska: "It is not an exaggeration to state that nowhere else in the Western world have legal arrangements stemming from traditional, preindustrial society survived with as little change as in modern America, technologically the most advanced country in the world."[138]

History helps preserve lay courts, but history has also made lay judges more unpopular than they might otherwise have been among lawyers, for reformers tend to evaluate judicial credentials in terms of their attitudes toward the justice-of-the-peace system. At no point in the long history of agitation against lay judges have their critics sought to differentiate carefully between educational background and other characteristics of these courts, such as limited staff and facilities.

The failure to look more carefully at the issue of judicial credentials is particularly unfortunate, given our experience with criminal trial courts staffed by full-time lawyer judges. Many of the complaints observers have made about these courts—inattention to procedural safeguards, proprosecution bias, improper use of bail—are the same as those attributed to lack of legal education in lay-judge courts. The court-reform movement may have focused on judicial credentials because professional sensibilities are offended by amateur authority in the administration of law, but the deeper, still unarticulated problem for these lawyers and the organizations that support them may be in accepting the routinized, nonadversarial, informal process of adjudication so characteristic of our lower courts.

3 LAWSUITS OVER NONLAWYER JUDGES

The presence of lay judges in our law-conscious and highly lawyered society has spawned many lawsuits. These suits generally proceed from the same premise that inspires legislation to eliminate nonlawyer judges—that lay persons are incapable of adhering to legal rules in rendering judgment. As the American Judicature Society argued in *North v. Russell*, a 1976 case that challenged the constitutionality of nonlawyer judges in criminal cases: "All the safeguards of the law are useless when placed in the hands of a judge untrained in the law"; a lawyer judge, in contrast, "is, in many instances, the best safeguard against arbitrary deprivations of liberty."[1]

Lawsuits aimed at eliminating lay judges typically argue that state and/or federal constitutional guarantees should be construed to prohibit them. Couching reform issues in these terms offers the possibility of an end run around the legislative inertia described in the last chapter. The reform-minded litigant need only convince the reviewing court that lay courts put a defendant's constitutional rights in jeopardy. The power of judicial review thus makes the all-lawyer appellate courts a potential arbiter of institutional reform, and an available battleground for policy-minded challenges to lay judges.

Litigation attacking nonlawyer judges, however, exhibits little of the coordination or planning one would expect in a campaign to enlist courts as policymakers.[2] No organization has sponsored a series of suits, nor have individuals or organizations cooperated in creating conflicts within the appellate structure to precipitate Supreme Court review.[3] Nor have the lawyers or groups most active in the effort to eliminate lay judges through legislation or constitutional amendment been prime movers in this type of litigation. Reform groups tend to become involved only late in the progress of lawsuits, submitting supplementary briefs as *amici curiae*, or friends of the court, in cases well on their way through the appellate courts.

The cases themselves are typically filed and managed by individual defense lawyers or legal aid groups who become involved in this species of constitutional litigation in order to reverse the convictions their clients suffer before nonlawyer judges. These attorneys borrow arguments from the court-reform literature, but, for most, their interest in reform is primarily instrumental: they litigate to help clients in trouble. Even the minority of litigants who are more concerned with legal change than remedies for individual defendants have pursued constitutional litigation episodically rather than systematically. The development of constitutional law concerning adjudication by nonlawyers reflects this characteristically ad hoc, individualistic pattern of case filing.

Judicial responsiveness to constitutional arguments for the elimination of lay judges has varied considerably. Some courts have been reluctant to generalize from particular errors by nonlawyer judges to their incompetence as a class, while others have not. Nearly every court that has considered the constitutional issues, however, has been alert to the practical difficulties involved in rearranging the courts of limited jurisdiction by judicial fiat. Appellate judges, like state legislators, are reluctant to disrupt the traditional system of lay courts because replacing them with salaried, lawyer judges would be expensive and complicated. Lay judges survive constitu-

tional attack, in short, because they are difficult to eliminate, not because appellate courts regard them as the
equal of lawyers.

The Constitutional Significance of Legal Learning

Challenges to nonlawyer judges in the courts predate the
court-reform movement; the cases began over a century
ago. The earliest challenges relied on the requirement in
many state constitutions and occasional statutes that
some or all of the state's judges be "learned in the law," or
some analogous phrase.[4] Such requirements supersede
the assumption under common law principles that a judge
need not have any legal experience to be qualified to
serve.[5] The cases often came up at election time, when
interested parties sued for a definitive construction of
constitutional and statutory requirements.[6]

Courts have varied in interpreting these requirements,
but the dominant view is that to be "learned in the law"
a judge must be a duly-licensed attorney.[7] This construction is particularly likely when a nonlawyer seeks to be
elected to a judicial post ordinarily occupied by lawyers.
When lawyers have tried to use such language to close
judgeships traditionally open to lay persons, on the other
hand, courts have tended to protect the status quo by
declaring the requirement of legal learning to be advisory
only.[8]

Not until the late 1960s did litigants begin to reformu-
late the old "learned in the law" argument against
nonlawyer judges in terms of the broader constitutional
guarantee of procedural due process. The time was ripe
for such a shift, given the Warren Court's concern with
due process issues in other contexts. Litigation soon
challenged every species of lay authority in misdemeanor
courts on due process grounds. Couching the challenge to
judicial credentials in these terms made courts that had
been specifically exempted by statute from "learned in
the law" requirements newly vulnerable to constitutional
attack.

At first, reviewing courts rejected all of these due process arguments. Courts turned down claims that nonlawyer judges could not constitutionally instruct juries,[9] act as magistrates in nuisance prosecutions,[10] conduct preliminary examinations in felony cases,[11] and carry out other duties typical of misdemeanor-level judges.[12]

In none of these cases was the constitutional issue even close, the continued existence of nonlawyer judges occasioning neither extensive judicial discussion nor dissents. The approach the court took in *Melikian v. Avent*, a 1969 federal district court case, is typical. Describing the constitutional claim as "unique and of no merit," the court seemed surprised that it had even been raised:

> To assert that the Justice of the Peace Court, which has a limited civil jurisdiction of $200 and final criminal jurisdiction of misdemeanor cases only, must be presided over by a person trained in the law, if it is to meet constitutional standards is novel indeed. The Court can find no justification for such a determination.[13]

Nor was the U.S. Supreme Court moved to declare nonlawyer judges unconstitutional when it had an opportunity to examine their authority in 1972 in *Colton v. Kentucky*, a case involving a conviction before a lay judge.[14]

The Supreme Court having implicitly accepted nonlawyer judges in *Colton*, inadvertently resurrected the issue of judicial qualifications in *Argersinger v. Hamlin*, a case it handed down the same day.[15] *Argersinger* extended to the misdemeanor level the right to counsel principle the Court had developed in felony and juvenile cases. The case was important to the issue of judicial qualifications for two reasons. One is that it acknowledged the potential legal complexity of the so-called petty cases decided by nonlawyer judges:

> We are by no means convinced that legal and constitutional questions involved in a case that actually leads to imprisonment even for a brief period are any

less complex than when a person can be sent off for six months or more.[16]

The case is equally important, however, for its perspective on lay legal capacities. Even the well-informed (lay) defendant, the Court decided, was ill-equipped to manage a defense.[17] In support of this view, the Court quoted *Powell v. Alabama,* the 1932 landmark that established the right to counsel in capital cases:

> Even the intelligent and educated layman has small and sometimes no skill in the science of law. If charged with crime, he is incapable, generally, of determining for himself whether the indictment is good or bad. He is unfamiliar with the rules of evidence. Left without the aid of counsel he may be put on trial without a proper charge, and convicted upon incompetent evidence, or evidence irrelevant to the issue or otherwise inadmissible. He lacks both the skill and knowledge to adequately prepare his defense, even though he have a perfect one. He requires the guiding hand of counsel at every step in the proceedings against him. Without it, though he may be not guilty, he faces the danger of conviction because he does not know how to establish his innocence.[18]

Argersinger's emphasis on the complexity of misdemeanor adjudication and the legal ignorance of lay persons made it a valuable precedent in litigation challenging the constitutionality of lay judges in misdemeanor courts. The state courts soon faced a variety of suits likening nonlawyer judges to criminal defendants in legal skills, and arguing from this premise that due process required lawyer judges. Some litigants even stood *Argersinger* on end, suggesting that before a lay judge a defendant could never have the effective assistance of counsel, because such a judge could not comprehend counsel's arguments.[19] Litigants also argued that states which had both lay and lawyer judges denied equal protection, *Argersinger* suggesting the second-class treatment defendants endured before the nonlawyer judges.[20]

Most state courts rejected these arguments for extending *Argersinger* to nonlawyer judges. *Ditty v. Hampton*, a 1972 Kentucky case, illustrates how one court handled the constitutional issues.[21] Faced with the Harlan County Circuit Court's decision that lay judgeships deny criminal defendants due process and equal protection, the Kentucky Court of Appeals critically examined the parallel between the judge's role in adjudication and counsel's:

> The function of the court [judge] is not to defend the accused, or to represent him, but to decide fairly and impartially. An accused needs counsel to defend him. . . . But the judge is not one of the accused adversaries and is not there either to defend or to prosecute him. So the fact that the accused needs a lawyer to defend him does not mean that he needs to be tried before a lawyer judge.[22]

The Court also refused to simply assume that lay judges disadvantage defendants, absent evidence comparing them to similarly situated lawyer judges:

> There has been no showing in this case that nonlawyer police judges, proportionately, convict more defendants, impose higher sentences, or are reversed more on appeal, than lawyer judges. There is no basis for any finding that they are less fair and impartial . . . or that their ignorance of the law harms the accused more than the government. There is no support for the assertion that the non-lawyer judge, generally, will accept the prosecutor's version of the law rather than that of defense counsel.[23]

Not every court, however, refused to assume the inferiority of nonlawyer judges. The exception to the general rejection of the *Argersinger* argument was the California Supreme Court's decision in *Gordon v. Justice Court.*[24] *Gordon* immediately became a highly visible case on the constitutionality of nonlawyer judges in criminal cases, not just because it stood alone legally but because it came from an important state court. Attention from the law reviews also helped make the case prominent in the literature. Law review note writers read *Gordon* as a bellwether, pointing toward the elimination of archaic and highly undesirable lay courts through imaginative constitutional interpretation.

Gordon v. Justice Court and Its Impact

Gordon v. Justice Court has the earmarks of a test case. Defendants Gordon, charged with disorderly conduct, and Arguijo, charged with driving under the influence of alcohol, seem ordinary enough, but the legal development of their consolidated case is unusual. The proceedings began, not with trial or guilty pleas, but with pretrial motions challenging each presiding nonlawyer judge's authority. The case then proceeded as a class action, thus maximizing its scope, and eliminating possible problems of mootness. Petitioners were represented, not by individual attorneys but by law-reform-oriented Rural Legal Assistance. Amici curiae participated in both state appeals, and all parties were well-prepared with statistics on the numbers, education, and caseloads of the lay-dominated justice court bench. The State Judicial Council even commissioned a study on the nonlawyer judges it certified (its authors concluding that they should be eliminated).[25]

The California Court of Appeals unanimously rejected all of the petitioners' constitutional arguments, but the California Supreme Court unanimously reversed, holding that defendants charged with crimes punishable by jail sentence have a due process right to demand trial before a lawyer.[26] The California Supreme Court relied heavily on *Argersinger* as evidence of legal complexity at the misdemeanor level and as evidence of legal ignorance among nonlawyers. From these general propositions, the court concluded that the nonlawyer would have difficulty performing many specific judicial duties, such as recognizing and resolving constitutional issues, deciding evidentiary matters, handling juries, deciding the voluntariness of guilty pleas, and making proper sentencing decisions.[27] The availability of appeal, the court decided, was insufficient protection against mistakes.[28] Nor did

California's requirement that nonlawyer judges pass a three-hour examination adequately guarantee their competence, because it was not nearly as rigorous as the state bar examination:

> We have scrutinized the most recent Judicial Council examination and, although it extends over a wide area of the law, the examination is far less rigorous than the two-and-one-half day State Bar examination required of one seeking to become an attorney.[29]

The court measured the constitutionality of adjudication by nonlawyer judges according to whether "a *reasonable likelihood* exists that a fair trial cannot be had."[30] But "reasonable likelihood" was not an empirical test. The court had before it no comparative evidence indicating that defendants were disadvantaged by nonlawyer judges. It had only selected examples of nonlawyer judge mistakes and opinions from litigants and professionals opposed to nonlawyer judges.[31] The three-man intermediate appellate court below had found none of this persuasive.

The California Supreme Court, however, had approached the issue deductively, reasoning from its own assumptions about misdemeanor adjudication and lay capacities. This approach was evident, too, in the way the court interpreted petitioner's right-to-counsel argument. The court simply assumed that the absence of a law degree disables a judge from understanding counsel:

> Since our legal system regards denial of counsel as a denial of fundamental fairness, it logically follows that the failure to provide a judge qualified to comprehend and utilize counsel's legal arguments likewise must be considered a denial of due process.[32]

The outcome in *Gordon* encouraged the California legislature to redesign its lower-court system to prevent nonlawyers from assuming judicial posts after January 1975. The decision also made *Gordon* a popular decision in the nation's law reviews. Every case note was favorable, the student authors sometimes endorsing *Gordon* with their own opinions about the incompetence of nonlawyer judges. Typical was this line of argument:

> The due process clause requires judges to be impartial and capable, and it is submitted that judges who lack formal legal training are generally lacking in these characteristics.[33]

This author likened nonlawyer judges to jurors in their inability to spot legal issues crucial to due process. A Harvard *Civil Rights–Civil Liberties Law Review* student note was more specific:

> A judge untrained in law would have to rely on the advice of others to resolve legal questions. Self-reliance would not suffice. Some simple matters, such as maximum and minimum sentence or determination of the amount of bail, might be within the lay judge's grasp, perhaps with the help of form books and step by step guides.[34]

To these observers, *Gordon* was an exciting case because it had laid to rest an archaic judicial institution tolerable only in an era when transportation was difficult and law was simple: "The non-lawyer judge, a product of closely-knit agrarian society, is an anachronism in a largely decentralized urban community."[35]

Although some law reviews qualified their views about the impact *Gordon* would actually have,[36] none criticized the opinion for the inadequacy of its evidence of lay inferiority. The case notes, in fact, were as casual as *Gordon* had been in their approach to evidence. One supported its assertion that "studies indicate that lay judges sometime disregard or do not understand the jurisdictional limitations of their courts" with a footnote to a 1927 article condemning nonlawyer judges and the 1967 President's Commission report discussed in the last chapter. Neither source contains any probative evidence.[37] Another used Henry Fielding's sarcastic analysis of the eighteenth-century English country squire to condemn nonlawyer judges.[38]

Nor did most of these articles mention that lawyer

judges in the lower courts sometimes violate due process standards. Problems endemic to misdemeanor courts generally were barely noted, although one author did at least acknowledge that "legal expertise and training do not guarantee complete fairness."[39]

Gordon and the enthusiasm with which it was received in the law reviews made an impression in trial and appellate courts outside California, though the impact proved less than some note writers had predicted.[40] A Utah District Court relied on *Gordon* to declare that state's use of nonlawyer judges unconstitutional.[41] The state supreme court reversed, however, citing practical problems and judicial self-restraint as reasons for its holding.[42] *Gordon* also figured in dissents from denials of constitutional relief in Tennessee and Wyoming.[43] Wyoming's Justice Rose, for example, agreed with the California Supreme Court that lay persons cannot grasp legal argument:

> It would have done Einstein no good to have explained his theory of relativity to me. I would not have understood it. I am not *equipped* to understand it. The same, I feel, applies to a layman justice of the peace.[44]

Gordon may have had its greatest impact in Indiana, where the Supreme Court, on its own motion, declared a statute permitting nonlawyer judges unconstitutional:

> We cannot in good conscience concede, as this Act in question does, that less legal ability and knowledge is required of a judge than of the lawyers practicing before the judge.[45]

Courts elsewhere considered and rejected the *Gordon* rationale.[46] During this period, the U.S. Supreme Court avoided becoming involved in the issue. It denied certiorari in *Gordon v. Justice Court* and dismissed an appeal in *Ditty v. Hampton* as moot when the defendant was fatally stabbed in jail.[47]

An appeal it received in another Kentucky case, *North v. Russell*, proved harder to avoid. In *North* the Court for

the first time confronted squarely the argument that a
system permitting nonlawyer judges in misdemeanor
cases violates constitutional guarantees. *North*, decided
in 1976, has also been the Court's last word on this
subject.[48] The case, therefore, merits detailed attention.

The U.S. Supreme Court Considers
the Constitutional Issue

Lonnie North was convicted of driving while intoxicated
in Lynch, Kentucky, a city small enough to have a
nonlawyer judge under then-current Kentucky law.
North came before Judge C. B. Russell, newly appointed,
and apparently ignorant of the penal and procedural law
applicable in drunk driving cases. Judge Russell declared
North guilty after questioning him and sentenced him on
the spot to thirty days in jail. North later secured bail and
telephoned attorney Eugene Goss to complain that he had
had no trial nor any opportunity to consult a lawyer.[49]

Judge Russell's manifest errors in handling North's
case gave Goss ample grounds for an appeal. The judge
had failed to advise the defendant of his rights, had
refused defendant's request for a jury trial, and had even
sentenced North improperly, sending him to jail when
only a fine was permitted. The very egregiousness of the
judge's behavior, however, encouraged Goss to look beyond North's individual plight to a constitutional challenge to lay adjudication. Goss, therefore, filed a habeas
corpus petition to focus upon the nonlawyer judge issue,
forgoing North's right to trial de novo before a lawyer
judge.

The habeas corpus petition came before Judge Edward
G. Hill in the Harlan Circuit Court, the same man who had
declared nonlawyer judges unconstitutional a few years
earlier in *Ditty v. Hampton*, only to be reversed later by
the Kentucky Court of Appeals. Judge Hill issued the writ
and held a hearing but reluctantly denied relief on the
basis of *Ditty v. Hampton*.[50] The Kentucky Court of
Appeals, as all concerned with the case had expected,
affirmed this interpretation of the law.[51] Goss then took

North's appeal to the U.S. Supreme Court, anticipating that the Court's liberal members would note probable jurisdiction.

The Court, however, was eager to avoid deciding the constitutional issues Goss was pursuing. The Court, therefore, remanded the case for further consideration when the state's attorney general suggested that it could be resolved on procedural grounds.[52] But the Kentucky Court of Appeals was unwilling to let the Supreme Court off that easily. To the Supreme Court's remand "for further consideration in light of the position presently asserted by the Commonwealth," the Kentucky court replied:

> We find ourselves performing an unwilling and not altogether felicitous role in a judicial fan dance. . . . The blunt fact is that this appellant wants only to test the constitutional status of lay judges in criminal cases, whereas the Attorney General has no appetite for that particular field of battle. We fully appreciate the absurdity of having a lawsuit—any lawsuit—presided over in this day and age by a person without legal training or experience. Nevertheless, it was our conclusion in Ditty v. Hampton that the federal constitution does not deny the people the right to have it that way if they so desire. . . . The constitutional issue was and is the only issue before us, and we have decided it adversely to the appellant. So again, the judgment is affirmed.[53]

Thus rebuffed, the Supreme Court finally noted jurisdiction.[54] To have exercised any other option—dismissal or summary disposition on the merits—would have subjected the Court to considerable criticism. The conflict *Gordon* had created among the lower courts on the constitutional issue was clear and needed the Court's attention. Also, the case had become notorious, at least in Kentucky, where it had helped rekindle long-simmering efforts to eliminate nonlawyer judges. A refusal to note jurisdiction would have seemed to indicate judicial blindness to the injustice North had received at the hands of Judge Russell.

Arguments before the Supreme Court

The Kentucky Bar Association, which had helped finance North's case, filed an amicus brief on his behalf, as did the American Judicature Society, the American Civil Liberties Union, the National Legal Aid and Defender Association, and several smaller groups. Only the New York Association of Magistrates, a lay-dominated organization of New York town and village judges, sided with the Kentucky attorney general. The two sides, nevertheless, were well-matched adversaries. Goss and the amici supporting him articulated the obvious legal and policy arguments for declaring nonlawyer judges unconstitutional, and their opponents answered them all.

Appellant's arguments all rested on the premise that nonlawyers cannot fully comprehend legal issues or argument. From that premise flowed several propositions, the primary one of which was the argument that had prevailed in *Gordon*, that nonlawyer judges deny criminal defendants the effective assistance of counsel guaranteed in *Argersinger*:

> Unless the accused's right to counsel is complemented by a competent judge, familiar with the legal process relating to criminal trials, the lawyers mandated by *Argersinger* might just as well advance their arguments to an empty room and save their eloquence for a higher court.[55]

Appellant suggested in addition that nonlawyer judges rely inappropriately on prosecutors, police, and community opinion, that they cause the public to become disaffected with the lower courts, and that they are inefficient and create an excess number of appeals for the higher courts.

Neither appellant nor any of his amici offered any direct evidence on either comparative competence or any of the other contentions. As in *Gordon*, the argument for abolition drew primarily on professional opinion highly critical of nonlawyer judges. This argument stressed the trend among the states toward abolishing justices of the peace and other lay courts.[56] The briefs also included examples of nonlawyer judge incompetence, particularly Judge Russell's. The judge demonstrated his ignorance of constitutional rights in his answers to Goss's questions in a deposition as well as in his handling of North's case:

> Q: Are you familiar with the Fourteenth Amendment to the Constitution of the United States, as to what it provides?
> A: Yes, sir.
> Q: What does that provide?
> A: Right off hand I don't ... something about judicial. I think one of them is judicial procedure or something or another. I'm not for sure. ...
> Q: Are you familiar with the term "due process of law" or "equal protection of the law"?
> A: Yes, sir.
> Q: In legal meaning?
> A: No, that's beyond me.[57]

Nonlawyer judges like Lynch's C. B. Russell, appellant sought to show, have no place in a modern court system, where evolving due process standards have made them obsolete. Appellant quoted from Justice Felix Frankfurter's opinion in *Wolf v. Colorado* to support the argument that due process must grow with the times:

> Due process of law ... is the compendious expression for all those rights which the courts must enforce because they are basic to our free society. But basic rights do not become petrified as of any one time, even though, as a matter of human experience, some may not too rhetorically be called eternal verities. It is of the very nature of a free society to advance its standards of what is deemed reasonable and right.[58]

The Court's responsibility, in other words, was to acknowledge that "the right to have a judge who is trained in the law is recognized as basic to our free society," and to declare Kentucky's reliance on nonlawyer judges in misdemeanor cases unconstitutional.[59]

This argument for judicial activism took account of the possibility that the Supreme Court might acknowledge the inferiority of nonlawyer judges in the abstract but justify retaining them on the grounds that safeguards existed to protect defendants from their incompetence. The existence of judicial training programs and de novo review, in particular, could be used to justify the continued existence of nonlawyer judges. Appellant, therefore, took care to point out the superficiality of existing on-the-job training for nonlawyer judges and to argue for the right of defendants to fair adjudication "in the first instance."[60] Goss believed the Court had already committed itself to the principle that de novo review was not sufficient to cure serious defects in trial-level adjudication.

The Kentucky attorney general's office and the New York State Association of Magistrates had an easier argument to make. Their's was the argument for judicial restraint, for leaving the issue of nonlawyer judges in state hands, and limiting the power of judicial review to cases where constitutional rights were more clearly infringed. Their principal point, of course, was that the incompetence of nonlawyer judges as a class—or even their characteristic inferiority in limited jurisdiction courts—had not been established. Isolated incidents proved nothing, for no one could reasonably contend that lawyer judges in the same posts would act flawlessly either:

> The allegation that a non-lawyer judge cannot be fair and impartial and preside over a fundamentally fair trial is simply that—an allegation. The mere statement that *a* non-lawyer is not a competent judge does not make *all* non-lawyer judges incompetent.[61]

Nor, according to the appellees, was error alone the issue. The constitutional question is whether defendants who come before nonlawyer judges are significantly and systematically prejudiced. The test is whether the forum was fair and impartial and the decision maker neutral and detached.[62]

In suggesting this test, appellees were encouraging the Court to approach the nonlawyer judge issue pragmatically, in light of the legal tasks these courts actually perform. Appellant, the magistrates' association charged, had not been realistic:

> It is fair to say that the awesome standards envisioned by the appellant and his supporters are based upon an unrealistic assessment of the actual practice and procedure required in those lower courts.[63]

Training programs and trial de novo, appellee and the magistrates' association argued, were efficient and economical means of guaranteeing fundamental fairness.

The Court Compromises

A six-man majority of the Supreme Court agreed with appellee that nonlawyer judges are constitutional even when defendants face imprisonment.[64] In coming to this conclusion, the majority relied heavily on the right to trial de novo Kentucky provided for anyone convicted in police courts:

> We conclude that the Kentucky two-tier trial court system with lay judicial officers in the first tier in smaller cities and an appeal of right with a *de novo* trial before a traditionally law-trained judge in the second does not violate either the due process or equal protection guarantees of the Constitution of the United States.[65]

The Court cited and quoted its 1972 decision in *Colton v. Kentucky* to suggest that the legal issues in limited-jurisdiction courts are not usually very complex anyway.[66]

> It must be recognized that there is a wide gap between the functions of a judge of a court of general jurisdiction, dealing with complex litigation, and the function of a local police court judge trying a typical "drunk" driver case or other traffic violations.[67]

The majority's view seemed to be that lay judges *are* inferior but are nevertheless adequate at this level, as

long as full review by lawyer judges is available. Where
nonlawyers were involved in adjudication, the majority
concluded, as appellees had hoped it would, that concern
should be "directed at the need for independent, neutral
and detached judgment, not at legal training."[68]

Justice Stewart, joined by Justice Marshall, dissented,
calling North's conviction "constitutionally intolera-
ble."[69] The dissent relied on the right-to-counsel argument the California Supreme Court had found persuasive
in *Gordon*. Nonlawyer judges, Stewart opined, tend to be
ignorant people, Judge Russell being a case in point.[70]
Their ignorance makes them deaf to legal argument and,
therefore, denies criminal defendants their constitutional
right to counsel:

> A lawyer for the defendant will be able to do little or
> nothing to prevent an unjust conviction. In a trial
> before such a judge, the constitutional right to coun-
> sel thus becomes a hollow mockery—"a teasing illu-
> sion like a munificent bequest in a pauper's will."[71]

No nonlawyer judge, the dissent concluded, should have
the power to send a defendant to jail.[72]

The dissenters were also dismayed at the majority's
willingness to use the availability of trial de novo before
a lawyer judge to cure deficiencies in the initial trial
before a nonlawyer judge:

> The Court seems to say that these constitutional
> deficiencies can all be swept under the rug and
> forgotten because the convicted defendant may have
> a trial de novo before a qualified judge.[73]

The Court's own precedents, the dissent argued, condemned trial de novo as a remedy for defects in the
original proceeding.

North v. Russell and the Lower Courts

The majority's conditional acceptance of nonlawyer
judges produced disappointment in the law reviews and
confusion in the state courts. The case got less attention
from legal commentators than *Gordon* had, and none of it

was complimentary. Allan Ashman and David Lee's comprehensive review of the relevant cases, for example, complained that the Court had abdicated its responsibilities in *North v. Russell* and drawn "not a map, but a maze."[74] Another connected the issue to the Chief Justice's campaign against incompetent trial attorneys noting that "the Supreme Court boss is outraged by know-nothing lawyers. But his attitude toward dimwitted or untrained judges is something else again."[75]

Only one state, Vermont, has applied *North* to limit the authority of its nonlawyer judges. In Vermont, each county's general jurisdiction court is composed of two lay persons, or side judges, and a lawyer. The lawyer is the presiding judge. These courts hear many types of civil and criminal cases, including murder and other serious felonies.

The practice of combining two lay judges and one lawyer judge arose early in the state's history and survived substantially unchanged until 1976, when the Vermont Supreme Court held that *North* disqualified the nonlawyer judges from voting on issues of law, since their judgment was not subject to de novo review.[76] Vermont's side judges, the court held in *State v. Dunkerley*, may participate only in resolving factual disputes and in sentencing. The state supreme court has maintained the fact/law distinction in subsequent cases challenging lay judge powers in civil and criminal cases. It has, for example, affirmed the power of the side judges to outvote the presiding lawyer judge in accepting or rejecting a plea bargain because this is a matter of discretion, not law. In civil cases, however, the lawyer judge must decide all questions involving a mix of law and fact, including the question of whether an issue falls into that category. Other cases are still pending before the Vermont Supreme Court, which is sharply divided on the subject of lay judicial competence.[77]

The only other state which has limited lay judicial authority since *North* has done so in spite of—rather than because of—the U.S. Supreme Court's decision. The Tennessee Supreme Court reduced the authority of the state's nonlawyer juvenile court judges on the grounds that their power to confine juveniles violated state constitutional guarantees. By resting the decision on state grounds, the court was able to distinguish *North*. A biting dissent claimed, however, that the majority should have followed *North* and in its failure to do so had engaged in "improper judicial legislation."[78]

Other courts considering the issue have interpreted *North* to permit them to retain nonlawyer judges. Washington and New Hampshire, for example, relied on their de novo review provisions,[79] while New York, Arizona, Idaho, and Florida had to stretch *North* to fit their states' procedures. The New York Court of Appeals held that statutes permitting removal to a lawyer judge for cause were adequate to protect defendant rights.[80] Arizona found review of lay judge trial transcripts on appeal sufficiently similar to trial de novo to pass constitutional muster.[81] Idaho and Florida even declared mandatory educational programs enough to satisfy the due process standard set forth in *North v. Russell*.[82] This was too much for Ashman and Lee, who suggested that courts willing to equate judicial training programs with review by a lawyer judge "will have to decide whether the Wizard of Oz was correct in asserting that a diploma was almost as good as a brain."[83]

The process of applying *North* to state court systems that bear little resemblance to the one approved in that case can be frustrating, particularly when a state supreme court papers over significant structural differences to save adjudication by nonlawyers. Litigants and inferior appellate courts may not be as ready to ignore local variations from the review structure approved in *North*. New York's experience is illustrative.

In *People v. Skrynski*, New York's highest appellate court, the Court of Appeals interpreted *North* to permit nonlawyer judges, even without provision for de novo review of their decisions.[84] The brief per curiam opinion was unclear, however, on whether defendants may have trial before a lawyer judge on demand, contrary to the history and wording of the state criminal procedure law, which seems to make removal a matter for the superior-court judge to decide.[85] *Skrynski*'s ambiguity and the apparent reluctance of the Court of Appeals to take the matter up again left the rest of the state court system with little guidance for six years, during which time the state's intermediate courts responded in contradictory ways.[86] The court of appeals finally laid the matter to rest in December 1983, holding that "a defendant has no absolute due-process right under New York or federal law to trial before a law-trained judge."[87] The case provoked a sharply worded dissent, and a sarcastic editorial in the *New York Times*, which suggested that "their Honors have matters upside down."[88]

Conclusion

Litigation, it seems, will not eliminate nonlawyer judges in one fell swoop. The lengthy record of lawsuits outlined in this chapter demonstrates judicial reluctance to move dramatically toward wholesale structural reform on constitutional grounds, the only grounds typically available to disturb legislative tolerance for nonlawyer judges and their fee-supported courts. Yet litigation, while not a cutting edge in court reform, has had some impact. A number of courts have vetoed financial arrangements that directly threaten judicial impartiality, and the U.S. Supreme Court has conditioned its approval of nonlawyer judges on the availability of full lawyer-judge review.

In shunning a more active role in lower court reform via constitutional interpretation, the courts have not hesitated to note the significance of practical considerations, such as the paucity of lawyers in rural areas, or the cost of replacing nonlawyer judges with lawyers. Legal and jurisprudential concerns also figure in judicial opinions on nonlawyer-judge courts, of course. At the federal level, the most familiar theme is federalism, and in the state courts it is separation of powers. The rhetoric of judicial restraint is everywhere. How courts actually balance pragmatism and restraint is difficult to determine because both considerations tend in the same direction: toward maintaining traditional nonlawyer-judge courts.

It is clear, however, that nonlawyer judges do not owe their survival to the respect they enjoy among appellate judges. The cases suggest that the prevailing attitude is lukewarm at best. Even courts that deride the absence of evidence against nonlawyer judges may think poorly of their ability to adjudicate. The Kentucky Court of Appeals, for example, found no evidence to condemn nonlawyer judges in *Ditty v. Hampton* but revealed its actual opinion of nonlawyer capacities in *North v. Russell:* "We fully appreciate the absurdity of having a lawsuit— any lawsuit—presided over in this day and age by a person without legal training or experience."[89] Appellate courts, in short, seem less impressed with nonlawyer judges than with their own lack of resources for reorganizing adjudication in limited-jurisdiction courts.

The paucity of reliable information about the impact of legal education on adjudication at this level may nevertheless deter some courts from interpreting individual rights to guarantee adjudication before a lawyer judge. Chief Justice Burger, for example, complained about the absence of empirical information about nonlawyer judges during deliberations in *North v. Russell*.[90] The Court faces an analogous evidentiary void in constitutional litigation over the powers of juries or over the desire of defendants to represent themselves in serious criminal cases.[91]

Constitutional challenges like these also raise difficult questions about the demands the institutional environment places on nonlawyer participants. Those who pursue litigation to eliminate nonlawyer judges emphasize the responsibility to decide questions of law and to supervise jury trials. Yet reviewing courts can hardly fail to be aware that limited jurisdiction courts rarely have jury trials or hotly contested legal issues. Caseloads are too high and stakes too low for many highly adversarial, complex legal contests. One could easily conclude that skill in negotiation, ability to manage limited resources, and common sense are more significant to judicial effectiveness at this level.

4 THE IMPACT OF LEGAL EDUCATION ON JUDICIAL ATTITUDES AND BEHAVIOR

The movement to eliminate lay judges from limited-jurisdiction courts, earlier chapters suggested, has proceeded without much reliable evidence. "It is widely believed that lawyer-judges are preferable, for administrative and substantive reasons," two social scientists observed in 1977, "but there is no significant empirical foundation for this belief. . . . Systematic comparisons of the backgrounds, experiences, attitudes, and behaviors of lawyer and non-lawyer judges do not exist."[1] A few comparisons of lay and lawyer judges have been undertaken since 1977, but all have been quite limited in scope and methodology.

This chapter and the one that follows draw on a more comprehensive investigation of lay justice than any undertaken before, a study combining a mail survey, interviews, and court observation to determine the impact of legal education on judicial judgment. The first section of this chapter describes the study and examines writing on legal education and "thinking like a lawyer" to establish the groundwork for hypotheses about lay/lawyer differences. The remainder of the chapter reports findings. One set of findings concerns the claim that lay judges ignore due-process guarantees to the detriment of criminal defendants; the other set focuses on discretionary decisions. Here the issue is not how well judges protect defendant rights but how they choose among lawful alternatives in sentencing and other matters.

The Study: Problems, Procedures, and Hypotheses

We lack systematic evidence, not just about differences between lay and lawyer judges but also about the organization of decision making in nonmetropolitan limited-jurisdiction courts. Research on judicial process and behavior, a relatively young specialty in social science, centered at first on the U.S. Supreme Court. Only within the past two decades have researchers moved down the hierarchy of courts to the trial level. Even at this level, interest gravitated first toward the federal district courts and full-time, urban felony courts, where caseloads are large, observation and measurement are relatively easy, and penalties are severe. Misdemeanor and other limited-jurisdiction courts, despite their numbers and significance to ordinary citizens, received disproportionately little attention in the recent shift of interest toward trial-court processes. Information remains scarce concerning rural and suburban courts, the settings in which most nonlawyer judges preside.[2] As J. Willard Hurst observed in his survey of the literature on American courts:

> As of 1980, published studies dealt with only small parts of this sprawling country—with a handful of metropolitan-area trial courts, a few federal trial and intermediate appellate courts, almost no courts in rural or small-town settings.[3]

The information we do have about limited-jurisdiction courts outside the major cities indicates tremendous diversity among the states. A 1973 survey prepared by the Department of Justice, for example, found "few similarities among States with regard to the organization of limited jurisdiction courts," and noted significant variation from state to state in the size of geographical areas served, subject-matter jurisdiction, and financial support.[4] Nor do all of these differences disappear when a single state is the focus for analysis. Large differences from court to court in caseload, facilities, and even judicial salaries exist within many states. Attempts to standardize dispute processing at this level have made only limited headway in state legislatures.[5] The financial burden more uniform standards would impose on state treasuries and pressure from local governments—which seek to retain traditional prerogatives over "their" courts—help maintain diversity in limited jurisdiction courts, even as centralization and rationalization occur higher in the judicial hierarchy.

The environment in which nonlawyer judges work would thus be difficult to characterize, even if more scholarship had been devoted to limited jurisdiction courts. This chapter and the one that follows deal with the problem of diversity by limiting investigation to a single state: New York. New York is a logical choice for in-depth analysis because, as stated earlier, it has over 1,600 nonlawyer judges, more than any other state except Georgia.[6] These judges sit in town and village courts throughout the state, where they serve as the bench of first resort in localities of less than 10,000 in population. Most of them are judges only in their spare time; typically they hold court one or two evenings a week or on weekends. They disposed of nearly 3 million cases in 1983.[7]

Town and village justices exercise broad powers in a rather wide range of cases, including misdemeanors, motor vehicle offenses, small claims, and other civil matters. In most courts, traffic cases dominate the rest. These courts are the rural and suburban analogues of the state's city courts. Like city judges, who must be lawyers, the predominantly nonlawyer town and village justices have the power to issue search and arrest warrants, conduct arraignments, and set bail in every type of criminal case, from disorderly conduct to first degree murder.[8] For felonies, their authority ends when the case goes to the grand jury for indictment, but all other crimes and vio-

Table 4.1   Distribution of Nonlawyer Judges across U.S.
Number of Nonlawyer Judges Sitting, 1979

None	Less than 100	100–500	Over 500
None authorized:	Alaska	Alabama	Georgia
Kentucky	Arkansas	Arizona	Louisiana
Hawaii	Connecticut	Colorado	New York
Maine	Delaware	Iowa	North Carolina
Massachusetts	Florida	Kansas	Ohio
District of	Idaho	Michigan	Pennsylvania
Columbia	Indiana	Mississippi	South Carolina
Authorized, none	Maryland	Missouri	Texas
sitting:	Minnesota	New Mexico	
Rhode Island	Montana	North Dakota	
None authorized	Nebraska	Oklahoma	
except by	Nevada	Oregon	
grandfather-	New Hampshire	Tennessee	
ing:	New Jersey	Utah	
California	South Dakota	Virginia	
Illinois	Vermont	West Virginia	
	Washington	Wisconsin	
	Wyoming		

Note: Compiled from Silberman et al., pp. 253–60.

lations can be prosecuted to conclusion. They have civil jurisdiction to hear small claims and to resolve certain other claims up to $3,000.[9] Appeals from town, village, and city courts and the felony cases that survive preliminary proceedings go to the all-lawyer county courts, which operate full-time in each county seat.

New York does not distinguish between its lay and lawyer local justices in legal authority, except to impose some training prerequisites on the nonlawyers.[10] The nonlawyers must pass a five-day basic course before taking office, and they must renew that training with a two-day advanced course during the first and every subsequent year. The purpose of these courses is to acquaint justices with their legal and administrative duties. The introductory course also helps socialize justices to their new role; most are visibly startled, for example, to be addressed as "judge" by their instructors. After each course, the lay justice must take and pass a test on the material covered. Lawyers must attend an advanced course yearly, but they need not take any tests to be certified.[11]

The Study Population

To learn how lay and lawyer judges might differ in carrying out their judicial responsibilities, I began with a mail survey of the town, village, and city judges throughout the state, excluding only judges sitting in New York City and district judges in Nassau and Suffolk Counties, downstate benches whose caseloads and responsibilities differ somewhat from those of their colleagues upstate. I included other city judges, despite their larger caseloads and jurisdictions, primarily to boost the number of lawyers in the survey population. The survey, which I administered in the fall of 1980, included 1,647 nonlawyers and 575 lawyers, 137 of whom were city judges. Seventy-four percent of the nonlawyers and 55 percent of the lawyers responded.[12] The questionnaire was enormously helpful, not just for data on judicial attitudes and practices but for information on caseload and case mix. Centralized records on these matters are too limited to be very useful to social scientists. The state seeks a correct accounting of moneys received and accurate records on individuals convicted of crimes and vehicle offenses, but little more. New York keeps no records at all on numbers of jury trials, plea bargaining, or sentencing patterns in the local courts. Nor is it possible to use central records or the docket books individual justices are required to keep to match litigant characteristics to dispositions. No one gathers detailed information on the criminal defendants and civil litigants that pass through these courts, except in the small minority of criminal cases considered serious enough to merit pretrial or presentence investigation.

During the winter of 1980–81, I began visiting local courts to interview judges and others involved in the judicial process and to observe courts at work. In the course of the year I visited twenty-six judges in five upstate counties in the southern tier. Thirteen were nonlawyer town and village justices; of the thirteen lawyers, seven were city judges. I observed arraignments, plea bargaining, and sentencing in nearly all of these courts, and I witnessed bail setting and motions to dismiss in many. I sat through several trials, including three jury trials. Trials, especially jury trials, are rare in most local courts because caseloads are small and much court business is transacted by mail. I had to return to many courts more than once, sometimes three or four times, to observe the full range of typical court activities.

The courts I visited varied drastically in their caseloads, their facilities, and the size of their surrounding population, variation I sought in my effort to enrich the information I had already gleaned from the more geographically comprehensive survey. Observation and interviews, in other words, helped me to understand and develop the picture of lay/lawyer differences emerging from analysis of the survey data. The courts visited were too few and too unrepresentative of the state as a whole to qualify as a reliable independent source of data on differences between lay and lawyer judges.

In designing the survey and enlisting the cooperation of the judges I visited, my own experience as a town justice and lawyer proved most helpful. I served a term, from 1978 until 1982, as one of the two justices in the rural town of Virgil, New York. My fellow justice was a dairy farmer, a lifetime resident of the town in which we sat; he had been a judge for six years when I took office. This background made me aware of the practical sticking points in the work routines of a part-time, limited-jurisdiction court, and helped me to develop survey and interview questions around the issues judges actually face. My position also encouraged trust, for as a town justice I worked within the same institutional constraints my subjects did.

Lawyers, Legal Education, and "the Lay Mind"

Experience as a town justice helped me craft specific research questions from the broad arguments reformers use to oppose lay judges, arguments that rest on even broader assumptions about what it means to "think like a lawyer." The literature that addresses itself to this question is extensive and complex, but observers, both within and without the profession, do display some agreement about what makes lawyers a breed apart.

The view from outside the legal profession, expressed in forms as varied as fiction, social commentary, music, and humor, tends to be highly uncomplimentary. A tradition of debunking lawyers, in fact, seems to be as old as Western civilization. Plato, for example, described lawyers as "keen and shrewd ... stunted and warped," with "no soundness in them."[13] The shrewdness and coldness to which Plato referred remain favorite criticisms of the legal profession, perhaps because these are the very qualities we demand in our lawyers. We want them to recognize potential adversaries and plan for the worst. The result is that lawyers seem to know too much and feel too little. "A hearse horse snickers," Carl Sandburg wrote, "hauling a lawyer's bones."[14] We also expect that a lawyer will represent a client's interest without regard to community sentiment or the intrinsic value of the endeavor, a standard that causes some to view the legal profession as a social menace, an undesirable fixture in a sound social system: "First thing let's do, let's kill all the lawyers." The sentiment Shakespeare put in Dick's mouth in *Henry VI* persists despite, or perhaps because of, the extent to which modern Americans rely on lawyers.[15]

The very emphasis on rationality that is at the basis of most derogatory comment about lawyers in our popular culture tends to be celebrated in legal circles. Lawyers, Roscoe Pound argued, see law from a broader perspective than lay persons, who search for justice in individual cases. Lawyers understand "that law acts in gross, with rules made for the average case."[16] It must be technical and impersonal if law is to be certain and stable. Professional detachment, accordingly, is a virtue in a lawyer and a necessity in a judge.

Most assessments of lawyers, whether positive or negative, are alike in assuming that legal education and the experience of law practice have a clear impact on an individual. Socialization into the profession of law, Stuart Scheingold suggests, changes one's outlook on life:

> Neither legal education nor professional experience are likely to alter the politics of lawyers in the more obvious ways. Party preferences will not change, nor will radicals be changed into conservatives. The influence is more subtle. It is the influence of ideology on behavior.[17]

Many credit law school, especially the demanding first year, with creating distinctively legal modes of thought, values, and perspectives. John J. Bonsignore, for example, claims that law school has "encompassing tendencies," which tend to crowd out the competing values and approaches new students bring with them.[18] The first few months of classes, Bonsignore argues, "make the student into a fool whose past academic life and ways of thought are not only unhelpful in doing law, but are positively in the way."[19] Later the law student begins to assimilate the new value system:

> As the mortification process runs its course, the privilege system of the law school is slowly introduced and some students are restored to a state of partial grace. Law school questions and ways of answering them, though alien at first, become slowly intelligible.[20]

The approach law school promotes centers around respect for the value of rules in organizing social life and solving public problems, the view that "for each dispute there is either a rule or else a rule can be derived."[21] With heightened sensitivity toward rules comes a tendency to search for critical facts upon which to apply rules. The law student learns to read slowly and carefully for such facts and to dismiss information that is irrelevant under the premises of legal analysis. "Law," Turow observes in his book on his own first year of law school, "is at war with ambiguity."[22] The education process, he argues, has become infected with an impulse toward arbitrary certainty:

We are taught that there is always a reason, always a rationale, always an argument. And too much of that amounts to a tacit tutoring of students in strategies for avoiding, for ignoring, for somehow subverting the unquantifiable, the inexact, the emotionally charged, those things that still pass in my mind under the label "human."[23]

Legal education, perhaps even more than other professional programs, gives students a sense of mastery over their environment that extends well beyond technical problems.[24] Already aware of the disproportionate influence lawyers enjoy in positions of public trust, the law student begins to believe in the general utility and analytic power of legal skills. The broad subject matter of law school courses, which covers an immense range of social endeavor, and the value of legal analysis in clarifying and simplifying complex problems help convince the student of the power of the approach. Abraham Goldstein speaks of the myth of the "lawyer-generalist," which he defines as:

a conceit which converts the accidental fact that the lawyer is an available social handyman, ready to take on a wide variety of complex assignments, into a basis for supposing he has a competence to deal with ever more complex phenomena.[25]

The profession's favorable impression of its own capacities for sound judgment has been evident in its campaign to eliminate nonlawyer judges, as previous chapters have demonstrated. The enthusiasm with which law students have contributed to this campaign suggests that legal education promotes confidence in professional training, even as it temporarily undermines the self-concept of individual students. The key question in our analysis, of course, is whether lawyers are correct in believing that law school education makes a crucial difference in the quality of our lower-court judges.

If those who oppose nonlawyer judges are correct, differences between lay persons and lawyers could be anticipated both in the nondiscretionary phases of a judge's work, where the defendant's right to due process is at stake, and in the exercise of legitimate judicial discretion. One would expect lawyers to be significantly more responsive to mandated procedural guarantees, the value of which is clear only to someone who takes a long view of the criminal process. Decisions the system leaves to judicial discretion could be expected to exhibit a similar pattern, with lawyers more likely than nonlawyers to standardize criteria for judgment and search for consistency across cases. The lay judge would tend to work from intuition, to "treat each case as a unique proposition":

> He has no category or class into which he may place it, no analogies from which to draw to solve the new problem before him. . . . Wholly unlike the judge who is trained in the law, he has no precedents to guide him.[26]

The questionnaire probed both discretionary and nondiscretionary decision making, using a variety of specific questions geared to day-to-day proceedings in local courts. A copy of this instrument appears in the Technical Appendix. The interviews and site visits provided additional data on these issues. The next two sections consider all of this evidence, taking each issue in turn.

Lay Judges and the Defendant's Right to Due Process

If significant differences in judicial sensitivity to rights could be traced to whether the judge has a law degree, this would constitute a powerful reason for restricting the judiciary to lawyers, despite added costs and the drastic depletion it would impose on the pool of available candidates. Americans demand rights-consciousness in a judge, particularly in the early stages of a criminal prosecution when a defendant's guilt or innocence has yet to be established. The argument for a lawyer's expertise in criminal adjudication seems especially telling in light of

the considerable energies the U.S. Supreme Court has
devoted during the last two decades to elaborating due-
process guarantees. The lay judges as guarantor of constitutional rights was suspect, however, even before the
1960s. The Wickersham Commission complained in 1931
that nonlawyer judges could not guarantee fairness to
defendants. The justice of the peace, who might in earlier
times have been able to dispose of cases "offhand with the
assurance of one who knew," could not adjust to the
anonymity of modern adjudication, where orderly fact-
finding might be necessary:

> The methods of the rural magistrate are out of place
> without the personal knowledge on the part of the
> court and the community which they presuppose.
> Without this check, there are opportunities for ques-
> tionable influences in the case of real offenders, and
> there is danger of irreparable injury to the occa-
> sional offender who is not able to command such
> influences.[27]

Contemporary commentators are more likely to stress
the technical difficulties criminal adjudication presents,
with its much-litigated due-process guarantees.[28] Nonlawyer judges allegedly avoid as many of these complex-
ities as possible by encouraging guilty pleas and avoiding
trials, especially jury trials. Defense counsel seek to
exploit the nonlawyer judge's ignorance of proper procedures, some argue, while prosecutors are forced to offer
unreasonably generous plea bargains to gain a conviction:

> The evidence suggests that some lay justices lack a
> sufficient understanding of criminal law, procedure,
> and evidence. Their mistakes may readily be ex-
> ploited by defense attorneys. Thus, the chances of
> successful prosecution are low, if an appeal is likely.
> Therefore, few full trials occur. The expense of ap-
> peals limits their frequency. These facts belie the
> argument that lay justices assertedly can deal effec-
> tively with pretrial proceedings. Although they may
> possess the knowledge and experience to perform
> routine judicial business, their inability to conduct a

trial drastically limits their impact. If defendants knew that justice would be fair, swift and sure at trial, they might be more likely to want to plead guilty or bargain a plea.[29]

This argument presumes, in short, that the lay judge's technical incompetence gives unwarranted advantages to defendants willing to pursue trial and appeal, while exposing more passive defendants to uncorrected procedural irregularities.

Evidence from the New York Study

I looked for differences in lay and lawyer sensitivities to due process in bail setting, motions to dismiss charges, plea-bargaining, and sentencing—all common occasions in the town and village courts in which circumstances sometimes militate against solicitude for defendant rights. I also probed judicial attitudes toward the protection of rights generally and attitudes toward persons associated with law enforcement.

Lawyer and nonlawyer justices, it should be noted at the outset, differ in the kinds and numbers of cases they receive. Differences in numbers are taken into account when appropriate in the discussion that follows. Differences in the mix of cases lay and lawyer judges resolve are not nearly as significant. Criminal work tends to be more plentiful in lawyer-judge courts, where it averages 15 percent of the total caseload compared to 10 percent for nonlawyers. Conservation-law violations, on the other hand, are most frequent in rural areas, where nonlawyers predominate. Nowhere, though, are they a significant part of the caseload. Civil and small claims cases also constitute a small proportion of most dockets. Almost everywhere, traffic citations constitute the bulk of the local court's business.[30]

Eighteen questions in the survey touched upon due-process issues. Most yielded some differences between lay and lawyer judges, but these are generally small and not all are in the direction critics of adjudication by nonlawyers would predict. The three questions concerning plea bargaining elicited the greatest differences between the two groups. One asked judges to estimate how often the prosecutors in their courts suggested reductions in cases triable by jury, a question inspired by the claim that prosecutors are overgenerous with plea bargains in lay courts in order to avoid jury trials. Lawyer judges, presumably better able to cope with the demands of a jury trial, should have fewer reductions.[31] The survey, however, indicates that just the opposite is true. The median is 75 percent reductions in lawyer-judge courts compared to 50 percent for nonlawyers.[32]

Nor do statistics on the frequency with which jury trials are held or the time necessary to prepare for them support the charge that prosecutors will go to any length to avoid jury trials before nonlawyer justices. The incidence of jury trials is low in limited-jurisdiction courts throughout the state, but not proportionately lower in lay courts, after differences in caseload are taken into account.[33] These justices also seem no less capable of preparing for jury trials; in fact, the average time between a demand for a jury trial and its occurrence is 25 percent less in lay courts.[34]

Prosecutors, in short, do not avoid jury trials before lay judges at any cost; they actually appear to avoid them more often in lawyer-judge courts. My fieldwork supports this conclusion. No one I interviewed liked jury trials: they require more time, trouble, and stress than any other means of disposing of cases. The time problem can be acute if the part-time judge has a law practice or other full-time occupation because the proceedings can easily consume a whole evening or most of a weekend. Yet judges do not want defense counsel to think they are unwilling or afraid to conduct a jury trial, so they hold them when a plea bargain seems inappropriate, despite the inconvenience. Over half of the nonlawyer justices I interviewed, including the one in my own jurisdiction, had held one or more jury trials.

Fortunately, the choice between a jury and a plea bargain does not come up too often in the courts at this level because most defendants are not entitled to jury trials. The legal dividing line is the misdemeanor. In cases classified as less serious than misdemeanors—a category that includes most traffic offenses—the defendant is entitled only to a bench trial, so named because the judge conducts it alone. Bench trials are much easier for everyone involved. The legal issues are fewer, and the time demands are much less. Several nonlawyer justices I interviewed even indicated that they enjoy this type of trial, though another described them as "a waste of everyone's time." (This justice encouraged pleas in traffic cases by threatening to hold trials "on the best skiing day of the season.")

A judge's willingness, or even enthusiasm, for holding trials does not necessarily eliminate plea bargaining from a courtroom. Judges have only limited power to prevent plea bargaining in their courts. Nevertheless, most I surveyed do not oppose the process in principle. Asked whether "justice is served by plea bargaining," the great majority responded, "yes." Lawyers, with 94 percent agreeing, were clearly more enthusiastic than the nonlawyers, with 77 percent. The two groups also differed in their comments about why plea bargaining occurs, the lawyers more often mentioning practical constraints, like time pressure. Nonlawyers tended to be more negative, citing the tendency for prosecutors to reduce charges too often at the expense of the public interest in fair dispositions.[35] Both groups were alike, however, in noting justice to the defendant as the primary justification for the practice.

Lawyers may be more enthusiastic about plea bargaining because it occurs with greater frequency in their courts and because they are trained to accept it. Although I do not have any direct evidence that plea bargaining tends to be more frequent in the courts in which lawyers preside, it seems reasonable to conclude that this is the case because these tend to be the most populous jurisdictions, where prosecutors and defense counsel appear most frequently.[36] Bargaining is more frequent, other research has established, where counsel appear most often.[37]

Some nonlawyers oppose plea bargaining because they

regard as disingenuous or dishonest the first step in plea bargaining, a "not guilty" plea from a defendant who clearly is guilty. A lawyer who practices before one of the nonlawyer justices I visited described the mixture of anger and surprise he elicited when he pleaded a client not guilty to the charge of having an unregistered vehicle, when all concerned knew there was no real question of his guilt. A few of the nonlawyer justices I interviewed also resented the propensity of the local assistant district attorney to "reduce everything." Most, however, accept the fact that plea bargaining is likely when a defendant is represented by counsel; they consider it the means by which lawyers justify their fees. One even described hiring a local attorney when his son got a speeding ticket in order to "get it reduced."

The only other clear-cut difference between lay and lawyer perspectives on due-process issues that the survey revealed concerns the trend during the past two decades toward greater constitutional protections for criminal defendants. The nonlawyer justices tended to be less sanguine about the evolution of procedural safeguards, as their critics would predict. Sixty-two percent of the nonlawyers, as opposed to 45 percent of the lawyers, thought the trend had gone "somewhat" or "much too far"; nonlawyers were also less likely to say that the protection of rights had not gone far enough.[38] What this difference in attitudes toward rights means in terms of judicial behavior is unclear. Neither group showed much enthusiasm for the development of a constitutional law of criminal procedure; only 6 percent of the lawyers and 3 percent of the nonlawyers would extend rights any further. Nor did belief that these developments had gone "much too far" bear any relationship to individual differences in the rights-related behaviors discussed below.[39]

There were some differences between lawyer and nonlawyer judges on behavioral indicators in the survey, though none are as large as the attitudinal differences just discussed. The most significant are perhaps in the propensity to dismiss cases. Such dismissals are rare in New York's limited-jurisdiction courts at any stage in proceedings, but especially before trial. The median justice in both groups dismisses only 1 percent of arraignments. Differences are greater as cases proceed: the median lawyer judge dismisses more cases during preliminary hearings (lawyer median = 1 percent, nonlawyer = 0), and at trial (lawyer median = 5 percent, nonlawyer = 0).[40] These differences, small as they are, are in the direction critics of nonlawyer judges would predict because they suggest that lawyers are more likely to see weaknesses in the state's case than nonlawyers. Whether this is a function of the greater frequency with which counsel appear in lawyer-judge courts is unclear.[41]

In my fieldwork, I looked in vain for evidence that lay justices were more willing to overlook procedural irregularities and continue cases to achieve convictions. Instead, I found pride among lawyer and nonlawyer judges alike in recognizing and acting upon legal errors, such as defective informations or improper transfers from one jurisdiction to another. All read with care the papers offered for their signatures, and most kept a desk book, code books, and other material at hand for consultation. A few took special pride in their legal acumen. One, a nonlawyer, even teaches evidence at a nearby fireman's academy. This justice also had published opinions and had persuaded a leading form company to correct an error in its seal order form. He works from his car-repair shop, a grimy establishment strewn with old motors, spare parts, filthy rags, and empty oil cans, but equipped with a two-room suite full of law books, including a complete set of all published New York cases.

The lay justices differed from the lawyers only in that nearly all of them especially enjoyed criticizing and correcting counsel when they made technical errors. They resented the air of superiority some practitioners displayed before them, and some went to considerable lengths to avoid ignorance in the face of any legal question. One justice, for example, kept three lawyers and a local judge "on call." His goal was to be as responsive and knowledgeable as the county judge about procedures affecting his court.

The nonlawyer justices seemed to understand as well as the lawyers that procedural safeguards apply to protect against conviction, even when a defendant who deserves punishment will go free in the process. One described a preliminary hearing in which spousal immunity eliminated the key witness to a burglary; the justice knew this defendant was guilty, but he acted matter-of-fact about "the rules of the game," which required him to dismiss the prosecutor's case for insufficiency. Another criticized judges who are eager enough for a quick conviction to accept a guilty plea from a drunken defendant at arraignment. I learned of only one incident in which a judge I visited violated the defendant's fundamental procedural rights in order to gain a conviction, and this incident involved a lawyer judge. The prosecutor and the defense attorney cooperated to get the case transferred to another jurisdiction when the judge refused to rule on a motion to dismiss for insufficiency of the information.

My fieldwork suggests that nonlawyers not only understand the procedural rights defendants enjoy but that they are at least as effective as lawyer judges in communicating these rights at arraignment. Arraignment is the stage in proceedings when defendants learn of the charges against them, their right to representation, trial, and other provisions that depend on the charge. Defendants can also plead guilty as charged at this time, an opportunity many defendants use to "get it over with." Reciting warnings and protections and accepting pleas soon becomes routine for a judge, a ritual repeated much more often than any other because it begins and ends so many cases. Even a casual courtroom observer witnesses many arraignments.

Nearly all the town and village justices I visited made eye contact with the defendants they arraigned and described rights and procedures in ordinary language. Most of the city judges and one lawyer town justice, on the other hand, kept much more emotional distance from defendants by going through the arraignment process rapidly and speaking in the flat tones of one thoroughly bored. These judges were also less careful to use terms defendants could be expected to understand. When asked by a defendant what a supporting deposition was, one reacted angrily and would offer no definition in terms a lay person could understand.

Bail decisions provide another opportunity to probe for characteristic lay/lawyer differences. If lay justices are insensitive to defendant rights, as alleged, one can expect them to impose bail more frequently than lawyers and to turn more often to arresting officers for bail-setting advice. Nonlawyers, the survey revealed, do impose bail more often, but the differences are not impressive: nonlawyers set bail once for every 11.2 criminal cases on the average, and lawyers do so once for every 12.5 cases. In their propensity to turn to the arresting officer for bail advice, lay and lawyer judges are indistinguishable. Most claim that they never do, or that they reject the officer's advice if offered. The minority of judges who do take the officer's advice into account consist of proportionately more lawyers than nonlawyers, contrary to what lay-judge critics anticipate.[42]

My fieldwork suggests, however, that the decision of whether or not to set bail is sometimes more complex than the survey would indicate. Judges must decide whether they will adhere strictly to the legal justification for bail: to achieve the defendant's return to court—or whether bail will be imposed for additional reasons. Some judges, I found, will set bail to sober up a drunken driver, or to protect a wife from an angry husband, or to clear a recreational area from noisy out-of-town revelers. In such cases, the judge may go to jail the next morning to reduce or revoke the bail. Bail may even be imposed for educational purposes. One lay justice described an incident in which he had asked a local defendant charged with drunken driving how much money he was carrying; on finding he had less than a dollar, the judge set bail at a dollar. This decision sent the defendant to jail, as the judge expected it would, because family and friends refused to get him out. A night in jail on one dollar bail, the justice reasoned, would give the defendant time to sober up and to consider just how disgusted his family was with his drinking.

The threat of high bail can also be used to encourage a guilty plea or to maintain order in the courtroom. I observed both of these abuses in one nonlawyer justice's court. Departures from legitimate practices, however, were not restricted to nonlawyers. One city judge I visited, tired of weekend arraignments, had delegated the power to set bail to the police by signing a pile of commitment forms to be used in his absence. He discontinued the practice only when a defendant the police had jailed under this system hung himself and the state corrections bureau intervened.

The survey and fieldwork probed two other due-process matters on which lay and lawyer judges might be expected to differ: the use of sentencing discretion to punish defendants who demand a trial, and bias in favor of law enforcement personnel. Lay judges, allegedly less willing or able to hold trials than lawyers, should be more inclined to sentence harshly after a trial, in order to discourage trials and encourage pleas. With their diminished sense of defendant rights, nonlawyer judges should also act more favorably toward police and prosecutors than lawyers.

The survey revealed some difference between lay and lawyer judges in the tendency to take account of a prior not-guilty plea in sentencing, though the overwhelming majority of both groups answered the same way: 87 percent of the nonlawyers and 90 percent of the lawyers said they take no account of pleas in sentencing, a difference not statistically significant.[43] Within the small minority that does take this factor into account, nonlawyers are decidedly more likely to sentence more severely: 88 percent of the nonlawyers and 60 percent of the lawyers claim to be more severe in sentencing the defendant who originally pleaded not guilty.[44] This difference, though restricted to a subset of less than one-eighth of the responding judges, is in the direction that critics of lay judges would anticipate.

Differences between lay and lawyer judges on attitudes toward police and prosecutors are in the same direction, but here the pattern is more complex. The survey approached the bias question indirectly, asking judges to

rate the sentencing opinions of prosecutors, defense attorneys, probation officers, and police as "too lenient,"
"about right," "too harsh," or "no usual pattern." The
nonlawyer judges proved much more favorable toward
police and somewhat more favorable toward prosecutor
recommendations than the lawyers, but they were also
more favorable to defense recommendations. Nonlawyers, in short, were less critical of all of these courtroom
regulars than lawyers. Only the probation department
received roughly the same level of support among lay and
lawyer judges, as table 4.2 indicates.

Fieldwork and my own experience as a justice suggest
that this survey question on sentencing really did tap
broader judicial attitudes toward police officers, as it was
intended to do. Police officers, in my experience, do tend to
be held in higher regard by lay than lawyer judges. The
difference is at least partially attributable to geography.
In the rural areas and small villages where nonlawyer
justices are concentrated, law-enforcement officers are
exotics, outsiders who bring gossip and stories about
crime and punishment. They are important to rural
judges in other ways, too. Their readiness to cooperate
with the court, appearing as requested and treating the
judge with respect, helps lend dignity to courts that lack
other indicia of state authority. The support of sheriffs
and state troopers is even an important factor in the size
of a judge's caseload in many courts. These matters will be
discussed in more detail in the next chapter. The busiest
town and village courts, which are usually staffed by
lawyers, and the city courts, which are lawyer-judge
courts by statute, do not have to contend with this
problem.

The justices I visited revealed their attitude toward
police officers in various ways. Some occasionally rode
with police on their rounds, or had done so earlier in their
judicial careers. Once one had even persuaded two police
officers to handcuff him and take him before another
justice as a practical joke. This same justice, however,
kept at bay officers whom he considered overbearing. I
observed him give a conditional discharge in a serious bad

Table 4.2   Judicial Opinions on Sentencing Recommendations

Sentencing Opinions	Lawyers (N = 179)	Nonlawyers (N = 828)
Police officers:		
Too lenient	6	6
About right	41	62
Too harsh	53	32
	100	100
$\chi^2 = 27.887, p = .0001$		
	(N = 206)	(N = 956)
Prosecutor:		
Too lenient	10	15
About right	72	81
Too harsh	18	5
	100	100
$\chi^2 = 46.598, p = .0001$		
	(N = 239)	(N = 967)
Defense Attorneys:		
Too lenient	64	52
About right	32	42
Too harsh	4	7
	100	101
$\chi^2 = 12.889, p = .0016$		
	(N = 226)	(N = 1005)
Probation dept.:		
Too lenient	24	23
About right	72	75
Too harsh	4	2
	100	100
$\chi^2 = 1.890, p = .3886$		

Note: Answers omitted where judges answered "no usual pattern" in response to the question.

check case when he had intended to impose a fine, simply because an officer standing nearby had said, "Make him pay a stiff fine."

Bias in favor of the prosecution seemed to be more evenly distributed. The frequency with which the local prosecutor appears in court, the high percentage of "dead bang" cases, where there is never any real question of defendant's guilt, and the judge's dependence on this official to keep cases moving—all encourage a proenforcement perspective. The trait is so common that the law clerk to one of the city judges I interviewed had labeled it the "anything you say, Mr. D.A." syndrome.

Differences in measures of judicial attitudes and behaviors like the ones discussed in this section are difficult to evaluate. One general conclusion does seem appropriate, though: this study does not support those who argue that we must have lawyer judges if we are to protect the rights of criminal defendants. The lay and lawyer judges surveyed here are virtually indistinguishable from each other on many questions, and the lay respondants are not drastically inferior to the lawyers on any of the measures where they do differ. On some indicators, in fact, the differences favor the nonlawyers. The legal issues at this level are apparently not too complex for a lay person schooled in the basics of criminal adjudication to comprehend and apply. My fieldwork and my experience as a town justice support this conclusion. Violations of procedural standards and bias seemed to be a function, not of lack of legal expertise but of judicial characteristics unrelated to training and expertise as a lawyer, including self-confidence and personal sensitivity. Reasons why this should be so will be explored in the following chapter.

Other Empirical Work That Addresses the Due-Process Issue

Five studies, all of them published within the past decade, examine whether lay and lawyer judges differ in their sensitivity to the rights of criminal defendants. Each of these was designed independently of the others, and each explores slightly different questions related to the protection of defendant rights. The results in every case are consistent with my findings.

One of these studies, conducted by the Appellate Term of the ninth and tenth Judicial District in New York, took a straightforward and simple approach to the question of lay competence to exercise judicial authority. Faced with a challenge to the constitutionality of nonlawyer judges, this court conducted its own inquiry, comparing appeals during 1976 from lawyer and nonlawyer courts within its jurisdiction. The court found that the nonlawyers were actually affirmed on appeal more often than the lawyer justices, and concluded that "there is no denial of any constitutional right in permitting non-lawyer judges to preside in criminal cases."[45]

The authors of two field studies that did not compare lay and lawyer judges directly came to a similar conclusion. In one of these, law students from the University of Oregon observed rural justices of the peace throughout the state. They found that lay justices were capable of managing procedural issues successfully:

> In general, J.P.s handle procedural issues relatively well. In observing the courts in action, the researchers concluded that most of the problems with procedure stemmed from lack of supervision and guidance, rather than from inherent complexities in the procedural system or neglect on the part of J.P.s.[46]

The other research team observed lawyer adjudicators in administrative bureaus charged with resolving traffic cases. Legal education, these researchers concluded after evaluating the case disposition process in several states, is not necessary in a traffic judge:

> There are organizations which insist that traffic offense adjudicators must receive minimum training as lawyers and have some legal experience [e.g., the American Bar Association Committee on the Traffic Court Program]. However, we do not believe that ability as an adjudicator is necessarily related to formal legal training.[47]

A 1979 study designed specifically to compare lawyer and nonlawyer judges reported results consistent with this conclusion. Sponsored by the Institute of Judicial Administration and the National Commission on State Courts, researchers visited courts in seven states but failed to observe any characteristic differences between lawyer and nonlawyer judges:

> In general, the lay judges' in-court method and appearance differed little from that of an attorney judge hearing similar cases of limited jurisdiction ... Differences between attorney and non-attorney judges in these courts were largely "stylistic"; attorney judges were more likely to use legal terminology in referring to matters in the case. In some cases, the "decorum" in the non-attorney courts was more "judicial" than in the courts with attorney judges. Our impression was that the "professionalism" and "decorum" in the court was dependent largely upon the conduct and personality of the individual judge and not upon attorney or lay status.[48]

Nor did these researchers find excessive reliance on prosecutors or problems in plea bargaining among nonlawyer judges, possibilities they were particularly interested in exploring.[49]

The authors of the study concluded, nevertheless, that "the criminal jurisdiction of lay judges should be narrowly defined to ensure that legal rights of defendants are within the control of attorney judges whenever possible."[50] They also recommended limitations on the authority of nonlawyer judges in civil cases and an end to their power to conduct jury trials.[51] These recommendations flowed, not from any particular mistakes observed in the courtroom visits but from concern that legal issues that *might* arise might be too difficult for nonlawyers:

> We did not observe litigation involving complex legal issues, but our impressions from both the proceedings we did witness and our various interviews were that there are many legal issues which can arise in these proceedings which would pose difficulties for lay judges.[52]

The only other relevant research findings published to date were based on a mail survey comparing forty-nine lawyer and thirty-seven lay judges in large towns and villages and small cities in New York. The authors, political scientist John Ryan and his student, James Guterman, found little direct evidence of differences relevant to adjudication, but concluded nevertheless that:

> non-lawyer judges tend to tilt—slightly—the delicate standard of due process away from individual defendants. Equally, the knowledge that the non-lawyer will be presiding in the lower court may subtly influence police and prosecutors away from responsible investigative and evidentiary procedures.[53]

The authors based their conclusion on three sets of questions, the first measuring judicial attitudes toward police and prosecutors. They asked judges to rank these courtroom regulars on preparation, fairness, honesty, etc. They found differences between lay and lawyer respondents of half a unit or less on a seven-point scale for eleven of eighteen items reported, and differences of approximately a full unit on another six.[54] On only one question, on how well prepared the prosecutor tended to be, did the two groups differ by as much as a unit and a half. Most of the differences on this series of questions indicated the lay judges were more impressed with police and prosecutors than with defense lawyers, but it is impossible to determine from the data presented whether these differences are statistically significant.[55] The authors probed attitudes toward litigants by asking respondants to react to statements like "women can't be good politicians because politics is a man's game."[56] They found a statistically significant difference on only one of fourteen such items.[57]

Only one question attempted to tap actual judicial behavior. The authors asked whom, for various types of cases, the judge usually spoke with before and after trial. Analysis of responses revealed no differences in the frequency of pretrial discussions but indicated that lay judges were somewhat more likely to discuss pending cases with the prosecutor without defense counsel present.[58] The importance of this difference, which is statistically significant, is not clear, and may depend on the tendency of the lawyer judges to sit in busier, more central courts that meet by day, courts where defense attorneys are more often present.[59]

Studies like this one suggest the hazards of drawing conclusions from survey data about the relative competence of nonlawyer judges. It is difficult to frame questions that measure judicial sensitivity to defendant rights and to decide how significant small differences are. Nevertheless, it seems fair to conclude that none of the research discussed here lends significant support to the broad due-process arguments so characteristic of reform rhetoric and constitutional litigation hostile to lay judges.

Nonlawyer Judges and the Exercise of Discretion

Reformers also claim that lay judges are incapable of exercising judicial power evenhandedly and dispassionately, that they are ad hoc when they should be more uniform in discretionary decisions. Such a failing in a lay judge would not necessarily work to the disadvantage of criminal defendants, as inattention to procedural safeguards always does. A sympathetic nonlawyer judge might well be more lenient with most defendants than a judge with legal training, who would tend to emphasize consistency in decision making.

This line of reasoning has been applied to help explain why juries tend to be more lenient than the lawyer judges who sit with them and hear the same evidence.[60] Juries acquit when a (lawyer) judge would convict, the authors of *The American Jury* speculate, partly because the jury is "non-rule minded" and "gives recognition to values which fall outside the official rules."[61] Whether such lay willingness to forsake rules in favor of ad hoc justice should be institutionalized in juries remains a lively source of debate in Anglo-American jurisprudence.[62]

When the lay person involved in the judicial process is

not a member of the jury but a judge, the tendency to be "non-rule minded" is more dangerous, for neither collegiality or the guidance of an authoritative lawyer are available to check the lay judge's power. Lacking the lawyer's sensitivity to rules applicable across the board, the lay judge may well fall prey to all-too-human weaknesses: bias in favor of locals, racial prejudice, hostility to litigants who fail to show sufficient deference, and inappropriate reliance on one's own personal likes and dislikes in making judgments. Nonlawyer judges, as Chapter 2 indicated, have been subject to all of these criticisms.

Evidence from the New York Study

If lay and lawyer judges tend to differ in how they understand discretionary decision making, this tendency should be manifest in many areas, civil as well as criminal. In the survey, I probed small claims procedures and sentencing philosophies. In the field, I restricted myself primarily to sentencing decisions, an occurrence much more frequent than small claims cases, indeed, almost as frequent as arraignments.

Small claims, though relatively rare in the local courts I visited, nevertheless provided an appropriate area for inquiry in the survey. The applicable statutory standard in New York, "substantial justice according to the rules of substantive law," is intentionally broad.[63] This standard leaves much to the trial judge's discretion and discourages appeals, a tendency appellate courts have done nothing to change in interpreting the relevant statutes. Small claims cases thus present trial judges with an ambiguous mandate: informality and simplicity in procedures are statutorily prescribed goals in these cases, but decisions are no less binding on the parties than decisions in other cases.

Lay judges, presumably less informed than lawyers about the legal rules that may be applicable or dispositive in the small claims cases before them, and unconstrained by the lawyer's desire to formulate clear standards where choice is inevitable, can be expected to take a more personal, folksy approach to these cases. The process of decision should tend to be more informal, with litigants more free to air the mixture of legally relevant and irrelevant concerns typical of disputes between individuals. Final decisions should reflect this flexibility, nonlawyer judges giving more compromise awards than lawyers, who would be more likely to use legal rules to arrive at all-or-nothing decisions. One might, in short, expect lay judges to be more likely to respond, as one interviewee claimed to have done, when a widow and her deceased husband's children by a former marriage could not agree on how to divide the household furniture. He ordered each side to come to the house with a truck one Sunday afternoon; he came too, and divied up the goods item by item, teasing the parties into compromise when they threatened to argue.

Although I witnessed too few small claims cases from which to generalize, I did ask three questions about these cases on the survey: (a) the formality typical of proceedings, (b) the frequency with which judges "split the difference" to resolve these cases, and (c) the frequency with which counsel represented at least one party to the dispute. The answers to these questions suggest that lay and lawyer judges handle small claims quite similarly. Nonlawyers describe proceedings as "very" informal somewhat more often than lawyers, but neither group characterized these proceedings as "somewhat formal" or "formal" very often.[64] The two groups are virtually indistinguishable in the frequency with which they report resolving small claims cases by "splitting the difference" in dispute between the two parties. Although 34 percent of the lawyers and 30 percent of the nonlawyers report that they never do this, most of the remainder range between 10 percent and 50 percent in the frequency with which they split the amount in question.[65] The median for both groups is 10 percent, even though representation by counsel is over twice as prevalent in lawyer-judge courts, where an average of 21 percent of small claims cases involve appearances by counsel.[66]

Sentencing leaves even more discretion in the hands of

judges than small claims adjudication. In sentencing, no statute mandates the applicable criteria for decision, and appellate review or guidance of any kind is virtually absent; plea bargains and the habits and expectations of the courtroom work group are the only practical constraints. Judges must, therefore, develop their own criteria for sentencing offenders.

I asked five questions about sentencing in the survey, all concerned with what judges consider in making these judgments. The two groups differ on each of these questions, though most of these differences are quite small. There is also one consistent overall pattern that distinguishes lay and lawyer judges: lawyers typically consider more factors relevant to a sentencing decision than nonlawyers do.

When asked whose opinion they take into account in a sentencing decision, for example, the lawyers were more likely to consider the opinions of counsel (78 percent v. 54 percent), the victim (72 percent v. 68 percent), the arresting officer (61 percent v. 56 percent), and the family and friends of defendant (50 percent v. 37 percent).[67] Lawyers were also more likely to use the offense itself as a basis for designing a punishment to fit, though only 16 percent of the lawyers and 11 percent of the nonlawyers reported that they custom tailor a punishment "fairly often"; 38 percent of the lawyers and 46 percent of the nonlawyers said they never do this.[68]

The same pattern obtains in routine traffic cases, where uniform traffic tickets provide judges with a wide variety of factors to use in sentencing offenders.[69] Lawyers and nonlawyers tend to cite the same considerations as relevant, but where there are differences, it is the lawyers that tend to take more variables into account. Table 4.3 illustrates the pattern in speeding cases.[70] The pattern is similar when the question concerns considerations relevant to reductions in drunk-driving cases. The two groups were indistinguishable in their tendency to cite defendant's record, marital status, and employment status, but the lawyers were more likely to pay attention to age (50 percent v. 36 percent), demeanor (62 percent v. 53 percent),

Table 4.3   Considerations in Speeding Cases:
Lawyers versus Nonlawyers

Consideration	Lawyers (%) (N = 305)	Nonlawyers (%) (N = 1215)	χ^2	p
Miles/hour over limit	96	96	.000	.9892
Defendant's prior record	92	88	3.166	.0752
Location of the offense	62	53	8.205	.0042
Age of defendant	24	21	1.056	.3042
Whether defendant has appeared personally	8	13	5.010	.0252
Year and make of car	4	4	.061	.8042

and other factors not specified in the question (33 percent
v. 21 percent).

The tendency for lawyers to take more considerations
into account in sentencing decisions does not necessarily
mean that they are more reform oriented than nonlawyers. I asked judges to rank the importance of the traditional criteria for jailing offenders: individual reform,
general deterrence, punishment, and isolation. The responses of the two groups are virtually indistinguishable.[71] For both groups, when an offense is serious enough
to make incarceration a realistic possibility, the primary
consideration is punishment. Reform takes second place,
getting slightly more attention from nonlawyers than
lawyers.[72]

Overall, responses to the survey questions on small
claims and sentencing suggest no drastic differences in
the way lay and lawyer judges exercise their authority.
The survey evidence clearly does not support the charge
that lay judges typically exercise discretion with less
consistency and evenhandedness than lawyers. To the
extent that the two groups differ, in fact, it is the lawyers
who seem less rule-bound. Their responses to the sentencing questions suggest that they tend to be more wide-

ranging in their search for information about defendants and more free-wheeling in applying that information. This pattern does not necessarily mean that lawyers are more likely to go beyond the range of appropriate considerations in sentencing, however. The survey format offered no obvious way to probe actual bias in sentencing decisions.

Fieldwork put me in a good position to assess these findings and to search for other characteristic differences in judicial sentencing behavior, including bias. The site visits supported the primary conclusion drawn from the survey, that, on the average, the two groups are not very different in how they exercise sentencing authority. All the judges I visited stayed within the bounds of traditional sentencing purposes and practices most of the time; the lawyers did not distinguish themselves in this respect. Observation and interviews, however, did reveal several interesting aspects of sentencing behavior that the survey failed to tap.

I learned that some judges were willing, on occasion, to go well beyond the usual sentencing techniques of fines, brief lectures from the bench, or a jail term in particularly serious cases. Three laymen and one lawyer, all town justices, fell into this category. Each of these men was willing to exploit his sentencing authority to the fullest in order to make a strong impression on litigants, and each demonstrated considerable resourcefulness in using the powers available to him. A case one justice described, for example, involved two young Canadians the police had picked up on the interstate highway for hitchhiking. The young men were chilled from an unexpected spring cold spell, penniless, and friendless. The justice took them to his own home for hot chocolate and cookies and then sentenced them to a night in jail in order to provide them with free lodging and breakfast. Another case I learned of involved two defendants charged with assault whom the justice believed were incompetent to stand trial. The justice ordered a competency exam, which the defendants passed. Still convinced that it would be unfair to try them, he bought them bus tickets out of town. In telling me of this incident, which happened some years ago, the justice said that he would not go so far today; defendants, he explained, have become more conscious of their rights over the years. Yet this justice and one of the lawyers, both interested in counseling young criminal defendants, were not adverse to using repeated continuances to keep cases open for a year or more, thereby ensuring that the young people would return to court to talk things over.

These justices were also willing to spend off-the-bench time on some defendants. One of the nonlawyers had visited defendants in jail who wrote him to complain of their sentences, and another went so far as to try to feed one jailed defendant's livestock. When he failed because the man's dogs attacked him, he hired the defendant's nearest relative, a convicted arsonist, to take care of the animals. The same justice described an incident in which a father, anticipating arrest, claimed to have tied up his children in the woods. The justice and several police officers spent the day searching for the children. Failing to find them, they let the man go so that he could retrieve the children.

Incidents like these, none of which I actually observed, are difficult to interpret. Even if exaggerated in the telling, they indicate an understanding of the judicial role and a capacity for involvement quite beyond the ordinary. Is lack of legal education somehow responsible for such behavior? One lawyer justice told me, for example, that she "would shiver" at some of the things the lay justices in her county did. The preponderance of nonlawyers in this group of judicial activists suggests that a judge's education is at least relevant. It should be noted, however, that only four subjects are involved here, and that the environments in which my lay and lawyer interviewees worked tended to be dissimilar. Seven of the thirteen lawyer judges served in cities, while most of the nonlawyers I interviewed held office in rural or suburban settings, where judges have more time for individual litigants. In the absence of environmental controls and a larger number of subjects, it remains unclear whether educational background is related to an activist conception of the judicial role.

The vast majority of the judges I observed, both lay and lawyer, were unwilling to become personally involved in the problems of defendants. This does not mean, of course, that they did not have strong opinions about defendants and their offenses. My fieldwork suggests that judicial attitudes about "just deserts" are complicated, and that they are more variable than the single survey question on the purposes of punishment indicated. Judges vary, for example, in the weight they give to the explanations defendants offer for their misbehavior. Only two judges, a layman and a lawyer, said that they give almost no weight to excuses; they assume most defendants are lying most of the time. Both men, not surprisingly, were harsh sentencers.

The question of how much punishment is enough is an even more fertile source of disagreement among judges. Some believe that for many defendants, particularly first-time offenders, the process of appearing in court is in itself a significant punishment. The typical defendant, one explained, is "tied up in knots just being there at all." Judges also varied in how they assessed the seriousness of some offenses. For some, personal experience with the offense determined certain fines. I found a city judge, for example, who never gave a fine for out-of-date vehicle inspections because he himself had once been caught with an expired sticker. A judge's personal frame of reference also helps determine the dollar amount of fines, because a dollar is worth more to some than others. Some judges counted the fee defendants pay their lawyers or restitution paid the complainant in calculating penalties, and some tried to take account of the economic circumstances of the defendants that came before them. I could see no characteristic lay/lawyer split on any of these issues, though it did seem that several of the nonlawyer justices set lower fines than any of the lawyers.

Observation and interviews yielded no support for the argument that lay judges are more likely than lawyers to be biased in favor of local residents, racially prejudiced, or oversensitive to defendants who do not show proper deference. I was privy to racist comments from two judges, one city judge and a lay town justice, but could discern no differences in the sentences these judges levied on white and minority defendants. I also saw both lay and lawyer judges get angry at a defendant occasionally, but their anger was seldom reflected in the sentence imposed. The only exception I witnessed was when a drunken defendant spit on the justice's dining-room rug at a home arraignment; the justice, usually a light sentencer, gave that defendant the maximum $50 fine for disorderly conduct.

The question of bias in favor of local residents is more difficult to assess. What is a judge to make of personal knowledge of the background and character of some defendants but not others? The judges I interviewed, both lay and lawyer, claimed to bend over backward not to favor local defendants. One even contended that he was harder on his acquaintances because "they should know better." Yet I could see that many of the locals who came before these judges expected some form of personal recognition. The situation is delicate because these defendants are neighbors and voters, and many would not hesitate to tell others in the community about their courtroom experience if they found "their" judge to be aloof or high-handed. The judges I observed solved this dilemma by acknowledging the relationship to defendant with body language and a friendly greeting, and then shifting to a rather formal mien. The shift to more formal language and manner effectively signaled acquaintances that they should not expect favored treatment and that a fine was not to be taken personally. I saw both lay and lawyer judges adopt this solution to the familiarity problem, though it is lay judges who face acquaintances most often, because they tend to serve in smaller communities.

Without a careful sentencing study, it is impossible to go further and assert that lay and lawyer judges are alike in their handling of local defendants. Fieldwork is not designed to reveal subtle biases in fine setting or in other aspects of case disposition. Limited as it is concerning questions of sentencing inequality, however, the evidence presented here does suggest that neither lay nor lawyer judges routinely exhibit gross forms of bias toward locals or other types of defendants and that both lay and lawyer judges are well aware of the problem of favoritism.

Education and Judicial Judgment: Other Studies

Research comparing the exercise of discretion by lawyer and nonlawyer judges has taken a variety of forms. Three of the relevant studies focus on European courts, where lawyers and nonlawyers sit together in criminal cases in varying combinations as "mixed benches." The remainder consider lawyer and nonlawyer judges sitting alone in courts in Chile, Canada, and the United States. All of these studies are suggestive, though none furnish very precise guidance on fundamental differences between lawyer and nonlawyer judges in American limited-jurisdiction courts.

The mixed-bench evidence reveals that lawyer and nonlawyer judges usually agree on dispositions and sentencing; when they do disagree, most often in sentencing, the nonlawyers tend to be more lenient. Zeisel and Casper, whose analysis of lay judges in German criminal courts is the most extensive and best known of the three mixed-bench studies, found that lawyers and nonlawyers disagreed about guilt in only 6.5 percent of the 1,245 cases they examined; they disagreed initially on sentencing in 20.1 percent of 1,093 cases.[73] Nonlawyers either abandoned their positions or were outvoted in most of these cases; their presence actually affected only 1.4 percent of the verdicts and 6.2 percent of the sentences. In these cases the votes of nonlawyers resulted in acquittals or reductions nearly twice as often as convictions, and in lighter sentences nearly three times as often. Stanislaw Pomorski's report on lay judges in Polish criminal courts is similar, though he noted higher rates of initial disagreement and more lay impact on outcomes.[74] Direct observation of deliberations by apprentice judges, according to Pomorski, indicated that nonlawyer judges had an impact on discussion, usually in favor of the defendant, in about 40 percent of the 257 cases examined.[75] Zeisel and Casper's estimate of lay influence may be more modest because

they relied solely on the presiding (lawyer) judge's interpretation of the deliberations for information.[76] The only
other data on lay influence in mixed-bench proceedings
also comes from a presiding lawyer judge. F. Lucas, in a
1944 tabulation of disagreement between the three lawyers and the three nonlawyers in his Danish appellate
court, reported unanimity in 85 percent of the 123 cases he
examined, with at least one lay judge favoring acquittal in
most of the remainder.[77]

None of these studies analyzed lay/lawyer differences in
detail; their primary objective was to determine what
impact nonlawyers had on criminal case processing and in
what direction.[78] The studies are nevertheless intriguing
because their patterns of lay/lawyer disagreement are
consistent with each other, and with evidence from studies comparing (lay) jury verdicts with (lawyer) judicial
decisions. In all of this research, agreement between lay
and lawyer participants is the norm, but where disagreement occurs, the lay decision makers tend to favor the
defendant. The question remains, of course, whether the
same pattern obtains in single-judge courts.

In assessing the applicability of this research to single-
judge courts, it is important to bear in mind that lawyer
and nonlawyer judges do not play identical roles on a
mixed bench. Their relationship is in some respects more
like that of judge and jury.[79] The nonlawyer judges, like
jurors, can usually outvote the lawyers, but in other
respects they are subordinate. A lawyer always presides,
enjoying the power to summarize evidence and write the
court's opinion.[80] Even more important, perhaps, are
differences in tenure. The lawyers are professional, full-
time judges, while the nonlawyers, like jurors, are essentially amateurs. In Germany, for example, nonlawyer
judges are supposed to serve only one day per month over
a four-year term.[81] The nonlawyer judges are to be ordinary citizens, free from the day-to-day responsibilities of
judicial office; as such, they presumably add legitimacy
and independent judgment to criminal adjudication.[82]

Nonlawyer judges who serve alone, on the other hand,
are equal to and independent of lawyer judges at the same

level. Findings from mixed-bench studies, like those from jury research, must, therefore, be viewed with caution in the single-judge context. The studies that do examine the impact of legal education on sentencing and other discretionary activity in single-judge courts have reached contradictory conclusions. Only one supports the lay-leniency hypothesis and that evidence is weak, the authors having failed to isolate the lay/lawyer variable in assessing major structural changes in Iowa's limited-jurisdiction courts.[83] Two other research reports point in the opposite direction. They suggest that, under some circumstances at least, nonlawyers are likely to be less flexible than lawyers and harsher in sentencing offenders.

The more wide-ranging of the two is a 1971 study of the sentencing policies of Ontario trial judges by John Hogarth.[84] Although his principal research interest was in understanding the considerations involved in sentencing decisions, Hogarth did use questionnaire responses to probe attitudinal differences between the fifty-seven lawyer and fifteen nonlawyer judges in his study. Nonlawyer judges, Hogarth concluded, tend to be more legalistic than lawyer judges:

> It appears that lay magistrates adhere strictly to the formal requirements of the law. In contrast, legally trained magistrates are likely to interpret the law more flexibly, responding more to what they believe to be its true meaning and spirit.[85]

Hogarth apparently based this conclusion on questionnaire items indicating that the lawyers took more factors into account in sentencing, were more willing to follow the advice of prosecutors and probation officers, and had a more positive attitude toward parole.[86] Hogarth also found the lawyers to be more confident, though on this point his evidence is more tenuous. Here relevant differences included the lawyers' greater sensitivity to political limits on judicial authority, their greater willingness to take public opinion into account in sentencing, and their greater tendency to discuss sentencing with friends.[87]

Evidence from the New York survey supports the

implication from Hogarth's research that lay judges are less defendant oriented than lawyers. The survey, sponsored by Cornell University's Department of Natural Resources, concerned sentencing practices in conservation cases involving deer.[88] The researchers asked lay and lawyer town and village justices what sentences they would give under various circumstances. The fines nonlawyers suggested in response to the questionnaire were over twice as large, and their sentences to imprisonment up to six times longer, depending on the specific violation.[89] The authors constructed a severity index to take account of sentencing propensities for all deer-related violations, and concluded that the nonlawyer justices were over three times more severe than the lawyers.[90]

Two other studies, these based on interviews and observational data, reported no evidence of characteristic differences in the exercise of authority attributable to legal education per se. One of these is the 1979 Institute of Judicial Administration/National Center for State Courts study discussed in the previous section.[91] The other is an analysis by Jack Spence of dispute processing in two different types of Chilean courts.[92] Spence compared nonlawyer neighborhood courts with state-run lawyer courts and found, to his surprise, that educational distinctions were much less significant than controversy in Chile over nonlawyer judges would lead one to expect:

> Focusing on what initially seemed a critical variable—the distinction between the lay judge and the professional judge—seems inadequate. This might seem odd, because I have strongly emphasized the importance of this variable within the national political arena when considering the political issue of neighborhood courts. The idea of working-class judges made the notion of neighborhood courts a threat to upper-class conservative opponents. . . . Also, the literature analyzing the procedures and outcomes of courts has stressed the importance of the character and background of judges, among other factors, as a critical explanatory variable.

Nonetheless, the distinction between the two types of judges provides only a very partial explanation of the different styles of dispute processing found in the two courts.[93]

Spence's study, like the other four just discussed, is not primarily concerned with assessing the impact of legal education on judicial decision making.[94] In all of them other considerations dictated both research design and the amount of analysis devoted to lay/lawyer differences. Still, taken together, these five studies and the mixed bench research do suggest that if there are inherent differences in how lawyers and nonlawyers exercise judgment, they are indeed elusive.

Conclusion

Critics of lay judges will find little support for their position in this chapter. The survey and fieldwork, designed to test familiar arguments for the elimination of nonlawyer judges, failed to expose any major differences between lay and lawyer judges in attitudes or behavior. Other published evidence is consistent. None of it supports the charge that nonlawyers are unable or unwilling to adhere to due-process standards, or less likely to be fair in the exercise of discretion.

The conclusion that there are no important differences between lawyers and nonlawyers as adjudicators will be criticized by some as insufficiently sensitive to subtle, but important, distinctions in judicial demeanor and behavior, distinctions that might not be captured in surveys, interviews, or site visits. Centering as it does on the day-to-day administration of law, the evidence of lay/lawyer similarities presented here will also be criticized for its failure to take account of the exceptional case, where legal education might plausibly be expected to make a difference to litigants.

In coming to a conclusion that conflicts with beliefs so widespread in the legal profession, one must, of course, consider carefully the quality of one's own evidence.

Subtle differences are important if they significantly disadvantage litigants who appear before nonlawyer judges. But it is also possible that the argument for eliminating nonlawyer judges is fundamentally misconceived. Lawyer critics of lay judges may be mistaken in their assessment of lay capacities because of bias and insensitivity to institutional constraints within which most lay judges—but few lawyer judges—must work. If I am right, reform efforts should be directed at the structure of local justice, not at judicial credentials.

5 NONLAWYER JUDGES AND THE IMAGE OF JUSTICE

Nonlawyer judges are the worst paid, worst housed, worst outfitted, and least supervised judges in the nation. Their courts tend to be more vulnerable to forum shopping by police and more dependent on the largesse of local municipal authorities than any others. Local control over court finances, more common than not at this level, endangers the independence of lay courts and helps keep them poor and separate from each other and the rest of the court hierarchy. It is not surprising that nonlawyer judges—regardless of their capacity for fairness—have an image problem with lawyers and other critics. The casual observer, especially one who begins with negative assumptions about lay legal capacities, tends to overlook the extent to which the courts where nonlawyer judges typically preside are sui generis—a separate species in an otherwise more urbanized, centralized, and better-funded judicial system. The isolation and deprivation traditional in lay courts thus help give lay judges a bad name.

The nonlawyer judge's image problem may be inescapable. Were working conditions somehow markedly improved, pressure to replace nonlawyers with lawyers would increase proportionately. They survive, in other words, largely because their positions are not very desirable to most practitioners. Some lawyers do run for these positions, of course; as an exception to the general rule, they provide a useful point for controlled comparison like that undertaken in the last chapter. Their existence, however, should not obscure the fact that lay persons are much more common than lawyers in the stratum of the judiciary where a law degree is not a prerequisite for office.

This chapter considers conditions in that bottom layer of the court system where nonlawyer judges predominate. Analysis proceeds first at the systemwide or macrolevel, and then up close at the level of the individual courtroom. Here, as in the previous chapter, New York is the focus for discussion, and the survey and fieldwork are again prime sources of data. In this chapter, though, I divide the data set somewhat differently. I treat all town and village justices (lay *and* lawyer) together throughout much of the chapter, and I contrast their common problems with those of better-endowed courts closed to nonlawyer judges. It is not satisfactory, however, to treat lay and lawyer town and village justices as if they are similarly situated in every respect because they are not. The lawyer minority on the town and village bench tends to be concentrated in higher-volume, wealthier courts. Where appropriate, therefore, I distinguish the nonlawyer from the lawyer justices. (City judges, included with the lawyer town and village justices in the last chapter, are treated separately here.)

The Structure of Local Justice in New York

The town and village courts in which New York's approximately 1,600 lay and 400 lawyer justices serve still bear a strong resemblance to the justice-of-the-peace courts the state inherited in emerging from the colonial era.[1] Like the old-fashioned justices of the peace, the town and village justices tend to be self-supporting, or nearly so, relatively independent of appellate supervision and administrative control, and sensitive to local politics. Requirements for office are even the same as they were a century ago: local residence, adulthood, and, of course, election.[2] The state dropped the title "justice of the peace" in 1967, but many of the lawyers who practice before the town and village justices still call them "j.p."s. Officially though, the town and village courts are now "justice courts" staffed by "justices," terms which reflect the institutional origins of these courts.[3] This section describes the triangular relationship between local communities, their justice courts, and the state agencies charged with supervising them.

Local Authority over Justice-Court Finances

Town and village justices act in the name of the state, but they must turn to their local communities for financial support. Town and village boards set judicial salaries, fix the level of clerical and other support, and decide what courtroom facilities will be available. State government plays virtually no role in any of these decisions, though the state's Office of Court Administration, the Attorney General, and the Comptroller do occasionally exhort communities to provide adequate salaries and facilities.

Such dependence on local largesse used to be the rule rather than the exception at the trial court level. Trial courts of every kind depended on their localities for financial support until the 1950s in New York, according to Frederick Miller, who dates the policy of decentralized judicial administration from the state's 1846 constitutional convention. The policy of decentralization, Miller observes, proved both durable and inexpensive: "The state's financial obligation to the courts was minimal. By and large, each local court looked to its local government unit for its budget needs, including facility needs."[4] Decentralization and local independence from state authority remains the norm in limited jurisdiction courts across the United States according to Russell Wheeler and James Whitcomb, experts on court administration:

> Limited-jurisdiction courts are almost always creatures of local government agencies, which inhibits their adaption to statewide needs. Indeed, the names

of their judges, and perhaps even the existence of all the courts, are unlikely to be known to central state administrators. They are not part of the state system; their judges are not subject to transfer by the chief justice. . . . They may not report case-load data to any central source, making it difficult to analyze their behavior within the totality of state judicial activity . . . Inadequate funding is a chronic complaint. And to the degree that they rely on local funding, the quality of services local courts provide may well depend on the tax base and spending preferences of their locales.[5]

Since World War II, however, the trend across the United States has been toward central budgeting for trial courts. A 1980 constitutional amendment finally brought New York's city courts fully under centralized financial and administrative control.[6] The town and village courts are now the only ones in the state system still completely dependent on local government authority.

The dependence of the town and village courts on whatever local support is forthcoming has two very important consequences: local financial control produces tremendous diversity from community to community in court spending; it also allows communities to be miserly in their appropriations. Lacking any minimum state standards, some communities spend virtually nothing on their courts. New York, it should be noted, does not even require a local community to provide a courtroom or courthouse for its town or village justice.[7]

The views of the affected justices may or may not be taken into account when local officials make these decisions. As a state senate task force assigned to study justice-court finances reported:

> On budget adoption night, citizens meeting at the town or village hall tend to deny justices what they need. As a result, the local justice court must continue to operate in inappropriate facilities, often in the justice's home, while at the same time, many judges report that their case load and jurisdiction continue to increase. For example, in one town which

budgets $3200 for its court, 20,000 cases are processed annually. The judges cannot retain a stenographer, because the town refuses to finance the cost.[8]

One justice I interviewed had a similar experience. He lost his equipment budget unceremoniously one night when the town board learned that the town road crew had overspent its budget.

The impact of local control over court budgets was evident in the courts I visited. I saw courtrooms of every description, including several in abandoned schoolhouses, one in a municipal recreation hall, one in village police headquarters, and another in a cavernous assembly hall. A few communities had devoted considerable resources to providing functional and dignified facilities. Elsewhere the justices themselves had taken a major role in renovating and furnishing their courtrooms. I watched as one enterprising justice offered the town supervisor $500 for the chairs in his office. Often, though, no one had contributed much money or thought to these facilities. One justice I visited held court in a school building the town board had acquired for one dollar. No one had done anything to remodel the place, which was unrecognizable as a court to most litigants, despite the efforts of the justice's wife to tidy it up on court night. Upon entering litigants would ask, "Is this the court?"[9]

The amount of clerical help justices have also varies considerably. Equally impressive is how little clerical help most justices have. Half of those I surveyed reported that they had none at all. Of the remainder, only 19 percent had one or more full-time clerks or assistants. Busier courts, not surprisingly, tended to have more assistance. Most of the town and village justices I visited had some help with dockets and bookkeeping, usually from a wife who worked for free or for a small sum, or from a town clerk hired part-time to assist the court.[10]

The presence of equipment, such as filing cabinets, desks, and a copier, varied considerably in the courts I visited. Some busy justices worked with little besides docket books and essential reference volumes, while a few much lower-volume courts enjoyed excellent resources. Judicial salaries follow a similar pattern. A handful of respondants reported salaries of over $40,000 a year, but others revealed that they are essentially volunteers, taking a token one dollar a year for their services. On a per hour or per case basis, the range of compensation is even greater. Here again, though, most of the diversity is within a context of relative poverty in the town and village courts.

The median justice earns only $5.20 per hour, or $2,600 per year for a ten-hour-per-week job, a paltry rate in comparison to other New York judges. The upstate city judges I surveyed, who are also rather poorly paid in comparison to other trial judges in the system, make a median $18 per hour and earn a median $18,000 annually for what is for most of them a part-time job. Full-time district judges, whose jurisdiction is roughly equivalent to the city, town, and village judges, earned over $20 per hour (about $40,000 per year in 1980). Full-time trial judges with more authority currently earn an average of $65,163 a year.[11] Table 5.1 summarizes the pattern at the town and village level.

Table 5.1   Judicial Compensation

	Annual Judicial Salary ($)	Salary/ Hour ($)	Salary/ Case ($)
Mean (standard deviation)	3,687.87	7.35	10.46
	(3,958.68)	(7.43)	(27.70)
Lowest five values (av.)	5.80	.03	.02
First quartile	1,500.00	3.28	3.39
Median	2,600.00	5.20	6.00
Third quartile	4,500.00	9.07	11.00
Highest five values (av.)	42,198.00	72.46	338.93

Local Courts from the State's Perspective

The products of a tradition of local control—tremendous variation in judicial compensation, court resources, and operating procedures, relative poverty, and a large number of courts (over 2,000 in 1980)—have frustrated state efforts to supervise the justice courts. The problem is exacerbated by the part-time, avocational character of the office of town or village justice and lack of clerical help, factors that make it difficult for the courts to cooperate very satisfactorily with the burgeoning demands of state bureaucracies for case-related information.[12] The problem, as Max Weber noted a generation ago, is that when an office is largely honorific, as this one is, procedures tend to be "slower, less bound by rules, more amorphous, and hence less exact, . . . less unified, . . . less continuous, . . . and more uneconomical" than in a full-time bureaucratic organization.[13]

Yet to bring the system more fully within the umbrella of the state court system would be to impose huge new costs on the state. The senate task force suggested the financial outlay that would be involved if the state took responsibility for court facilities at this level:

> If the state assumed court costs, municipalities that now provide no special facilities would justifiably bill the state for use of municipal space, as would justices who use their own homes. If this were, as likely, found an unsatisfactory situation, the state would be faced with a monumental construction effort. This would also be the case if a district or regional court system were chosen.[14]

The overall benefits of such an undertaking are uncertain. If the state took over costs and reorganized the justice-court system, the number of justices would almost certainly be drastically reduced. With fewer justices handling more cases per capita, procedures would become more uniform, judge shopping could be eliminated, and information flow would improve. But courts would become less convenient and less familiar for many citizens, making it unclear whether those who interact with the current system at the local level would deem reorganization an improvement.[15] Legislation aimed at centralizing and standardizing the justice court system would also meet sharp opposition from local governments, which are well-organized in New York. Local government associations, which lobby state government on a variety of issues, have always maintained an interest in the justice courts. One of them, the Association of Towns, even provides educational seminars, forms and informational guides, and a monthly newsletter for town justices.[16]

While the present system of dispersed financial and political authority satisfies local government organizations, it creates a tempting target for state bureaucracies that seek to expand their own jurisdiction. The Department of Motor Vehicles, many justices believe, has already embarked on a campaign to aggrandize itself at the expense of the town and village courts. The department first became involved in adjudicating traffic cases in 1969, when it established an Administrative Adjudication Bureau in New York City. Three years later, the program expanded to include the cities of Buffalo and Rochester. Adjudication bureaus, using highly standardized techniques, dispose of many of the vehicle and traffic cases that would otherwise go to the local courts.[17] The department has sought to increase the number of these bureaus, encouraging localities to adopt the system with the promise of generous paybacks from fines. The department has also been eager to have adjudicators deemed "judge," a proposal the Association of Magistrates and Association of Towns have so far defeated, at least on paper.[18] (In the one adjudication bureau I visited, staff and defendants referred to bureau adjudicators as "judge" at all times, and this title even appeared on their stationery.)

The justice courts have been challenged from another direction by proposals to establish a network of district courts statewide. Court-reform groups have long argued for such a system, which would involve an all-lawyer bench financed from state revenues. The towns in Nassau and parts of Suffolk County have had district courts since 1939, but the idea has not caught on anywhere else, voters having consistently rejected the concept in referenda. Even in Nassau and Suffolk Counties, voters have been unwilling to dispense with their presumably superfluous justice courts.[19]

A more successful state-level initiative, one that has affected nearly every town or village court directly or indirectly, is the Commission on Judicial Conduct. This eleven-member disciplinary body has been active since its inception as a temporary agency in 1975. It has authority to investigate and act upon complaints about judges at every level. The commission, whose powers have grown almost yearly, now has authority to instigate its own investigations and to discipline judges even after they resign. Its staff in 1984 included forty-one full-time employees, supplemented by part-time and summer student help. The commission screens out about 80 percent of the complaints it receives each year, but in the course of its nine years of existence it has taken disciplinary action in 371 cases and cautioned an additional 348 judges; 139 judges resigned during investigation.[20] A significant, though not disproportionate, fraction of these enforcement actions have involved misconduct in the town and village courts.

Town and village justices tend to view the Commission with a mixture of approbation and apprehension. The network of informal communication among judges at this level makes them aware of behavior that should be curbed, but it provides no effective means of coping with judicial misconduct locally. Most recognize the necessity for an outside organization with disciplinary power sufficient to protect citizens and the image of the judiciary as a whole. Yet at the same time many justices I interviewed believe that the commission is biased against the justice courts, or at least insensitive to the difficulties they face. Some also suspect the commission of prejudice against nonlawyer judges; such fears seem to be based partly on the fact that nine of the commission's eleven members are lawyers. Not surprisingly, justices also fear the expense and embarrassment of investigation by an Albany-based organization, particularly one which sustains itself by discovering judicial misconduct. One I interviewed had spent several thousand dollars to defend himself, without success, before the commission.[21] Yet there is no concrete evidence that the commission is prejudiced against nonlawyer judges. Chief Administrator Gerald Stern, in fact, has stated that he believes them to be doing "an excellent job."[22]

Whether or not such judicial concerns are justified, it is undeniable that the commission has had some impact on the process of adjudication in the justice courts. The commission's much-publicized campaign against ticket fixing illustrates its power to reshape judicial behavior. The commission defines ticket fixing as "the assertion of influence to affect decisions in traffic cases."[23] The practice by which judges contact other judges to request reductions or dismissals for third parties has been the commission's particular concern.

When the commission first began to investigate the problem in 1976, violations were legion and easy to spot, because judges often saved incriminating letters and even attached them to pages in their docket books. Many apparently thought that suggesting reductions or dismissals for local residents was part of their responsibility to constituents. Some may have been confused about the propriety of these requests for reductions because attorneys routinely write such letters to prosecutors on behalf of their clients, and reductions usually follow as a matter of course.

Within a year the commission had found 250 judges involved in inappropriate requests for reductions in traffic cases, and had concluded that "this abhorrent practice is widespread and only a small fraction of it has been identified."[24] The efforts of the commission and the publicity it fostered, however, have now made the limits of permissible behavior in this area clear to nearly everyone. Complaints of ticket fixing had dropped off sharply by 1979, and in 1982 the commission reported no new cases. Judicial bookkeeping has changed, and so, almost assuredly, have norms concerning communication between judges about pending cases.

The campaign against ticket fixing, however, is not typical of the Commission on Judicial Conduct. To date at least, most of its work has been reactive, the commission taking the initiative against judges case by case upon complaints from litigants and other observers. The commission's capacity to standardize and regularize justice court proceedings is, therefore, limited by its normal modus operandi.

Nor does appellate judicial authority often have a direct impact upon the justice courts. The rate of appeal from decisions in these courts is less than 1 percent.[25] Divestiture to the county court for trial de novo is also uncommon, rights under the applicable statute having been construed narrowly, as Chapter 3 indicated. In their isolation from appellate scrutiny, New York's justice courts are typical. Appeals are rare everywhere, and trial de novo, the traditional means of supervising justices of the peace, has apparently never been attractive to litigants.[26] The justice courts remain more responsive to local conditions and initiatives than to direct state-level authority, whether administrative, disciplinary, or judicial.

Paying for Local Justice

The state does play an important—albeit indirect, unanticipated, and undesirable—role in the operation of the town and village courts. State law encourages localities to tie court spending to the number of cases their courts handle. On the surface, this does not seem undesirable— the size of the caseload gives a municipality a rough idea of how much work a justice does. The relationship between caseloads, local revenues, and financial support for local courts, however, is more compelling and less benign. Many of the town and village courts, unlike any others in the state system, actually depend on their caseloads to pay their expenses.

The money justices collect from litigants in the form of fines and fees pays a little more than half of the operating costs in the average town and village court. Many communities, however, require their courts to be completely self-sufficient, to "pay their own way" with the money their courts collect. The mayor of one village whose court I visited joked about "the ski industry" nearby that provides most of the caseload; he explained to me that the village would simply abolish the court if it ceased to be "profitable."

In their tendency toward self-sufficiency, the town and village courts resemble their much criticized ancestor, the justice of the peace. The financial support litigants provide travels a more circuitous path than it did in an earlier era, though. State and local government now determine the proportion of the sums the town and village justices collect that will be available for the justice courts.

The state's financial role is relatively passive; it acts as conduit and skimmer in relation to the local courts. Justices send the money they collect from litigants directly to the Department of Audit and Control, which checks these payments for accuracy and returns some of them, not to the courts, but to the local communities in which they sit.[27] The remainder of the money becomes part of the state's general revenues.

The amount of money the state returns to the local communities depends on the number and mix of cases a court closes. Fines in local ordinance cases and penalties and bail forfeitures in motor vehicle cases, for example, are returned in full, unless they involve speeding or reckless or drunken driving. Most civil cases, misdemeanors, and most other criminal proceedings and traffic offenses net the community a fixed fee of $5 or less, no matter how much time the case involved, and no matter how it came out.[28] The flat-fee cases make up the bulk of the caseload in most courts.

The state's reimbursement procedures preserve local control over the justice courts, but they also contribute to the state budget at the expense of the local courts and their communities. In 1983, for example, the state retained over $16 million of the $44,633,868 it received from the town and village courts, or 36 percent of the total intake.[29] The state's practice of withholding fine moneys has long been a source of serious irritation to local governments and to the town and village justices. The localities, chronically short of cash for their courts, believe they should be entitled to enough fine money to pay the costs of operating the town and village courts. To the president of the state magistrates association the state's policy indicates that the town and village justices are "overworked, underpaid, and appreciated less."[30] Bills to increase the $5 per case formula—established by the state legislature in 1939 and never revised since then—have been unsuccessful so far, however. The state, in fact, recently increased its share of the take from the town and village courts, creating a schedule of mandatory additional penalties for persons convicted of crimes beyond fines, including $40 for misdemeanors and $15 for violations. This money goes into the state's general revenues.

The practice of paying communities a set amount per case, regardless of the outcome of the case, is designed to discourage judicial bias in adjudication. Giving local government discretion to decide whether or not to use court revenues for court expenses also puts some distance between adjudication and court funding, and provides the only insulation in the types of cases where state payments do depend on decisions adverse to defendants, such as local ordinance violations. Together, these arrangements help protect the system against constitutional challenges based on the principle that judges should be free of a financial interest in the outcome of the litigation before them.

The likelihood that New York's reimbursement system would survive such a constitutional attack grew stronger in 1976, when the state barred justices from membership on town and village boards.[31] With that ruling, the state finally endorsed a purely judicial role for its town and village justices. The newfound independence of the justices from law-making and budget-setting responsibilities came minus the financial independence characteristic of other judges, however. The justice courts became more vulnerable than ever to economy-minded local governing boards.

Even when local authorities take a generous view toward funding their courts, the state's practice of pegging its contribution to the amount of business each court handles inevitably sensitizes everyone to caseload. Nearly all the justices I interviewed knew approximately how much they collected from litigants each year and how much came back from the state. Several noted that this amount was the key to their own annual appropriations. The senate task force found the same tendency to link court revenues to court budgets when its staff interviewed local justices:

> On the surface, it may be true that since 1938, New York State's justice courts have not been fee-dependent courts, since the convoluted fine disposition structure in the current Vehicle and Traffic Law dates to that time. That surface is thin, however, and the conclusion is inescapable that many local courts regard traffic fines as a reliable portion of the general fund of the municipality from which the court budget is drawn. Justices indicated in interviews that town and village boards take into account how much the court generates for the municipality in determining their salaries.[32]

The state's reimbursement formula encourages several types of undesirable behavior at the local level. Villages with their own police forces sometimes take advantage of the distinction the state draws between the flat $5 fee for most state motor vehicle law violations and repayment of the full fine for village ordinance cases. To increase remittances, they simply pass local ordinances covering virtually the same ground as the state motor vehicle law, and then instruct their police officers to prosecute these rather than the comparable state laws. Such behavior violates the spirit, and possibly the letter, of the state's home rule legislation.[33]

Town and village justices may also be tempted to inappropriate efforts to increase their caseloads and thereby increase their salaries, operating budgets, and local prestige. Town justices in neighboring jurisdictions can compete for cases by encouraging police officers to stop speeders and other "continuous" highway offenders within their own jurisdictions. Village justices and the justices in the towns that envelope them can come into conflict over civil cases arising within the villages because civil jurisdiction is concurrent between towns and the villages they contain. Two justices within the same town are also likely to find themselves in competition if they hold court at different times, for law enforcement officers can set appearance dates to put cases before the justice they prefer. I experienced this type of pressure when I took office, and found it disturbing to have to win the support of local law enforcement officers in order to get any cases on "my" night.

The senate task force also noted the problem of overlapping jurisdiction and competition for cases, and suggested that it can create a temptation "for a justice to develop a reputation as 'the judge to go to with a traffic offense' since the municipal boards do, despite the views of the commentaries to the statutes, set different salaries for one and another justice in the same town."[34] Several of the justices I interviewed complained, sometimes bitterly, of fellow justices who "took business away."

In general, the lawyer minority at this level is less susceptible to competition for caseload than the nonlawyer majority. My survey revealed that in jurisdictions with more than one justice (about 80 percent of the total), 48 percent of the nonlawyers, but only 31 percent of the lawyers, complained of forum shopping by police. The lawyers are more likely to be insulated from this problem because they hold a large proportion of village, rather than town, judgeships. (Lawyers constitute about 40 percent of the village bench but only 8 percent of the town bench.)[35] The town/village distinction, irrelevant in most respects, is significant when competition for cases is the issue, because between two village justices in the same jurisdiction the lines of authority are usually much clearer than between two town justices. State law permits the villages to elect one justice and appoint a second as acting justice, to have authority only when the elected justice is unavailable. Between two town justices, however, the law provides for no division of authority.[36]

One can only conclude that the state's method of financing its town and village courts, however inexpensive and responsive to local conditions, is at the same time frought with serious disadvantages. Making the state's contribution depend strictly on the number of cases each court processes, and "taxing" this income heavily before returning it to the local communities, helps keep the town and village courts poor and makes them highly sensitive to caseload. Such sensitivity encourages justices to compete with each other for the support of police officers, who, in a fairer system, would not have the ability to pick and choose among justices. None of the all-lawyer benches in the state system are subject to such financially induced pressures.

Current policies also ensure that some justice courts will be much better provided for than others. Where caseloads are large, courts may generate considerable revenues through rapid case processing and economies of scale. State returns, even though capped at $2 per resident, may be adequate for these courts.[37] Where caseloads are low, however, and fixed costs are high, support for the local court may be problematical. Localities may be unwilling or unable to contribute needed funds. State reimbursement based strictly on caseload, of course, takes no account of actual costs, or of differences in the ability of local governments to contribute to the cost of maintaining their local courts.

Geography and Lay Courts

The burden of fee-dependent, locally controlled court financing does not fall equally on lay and lawyer justices. The state's passive posture toward the town and village courts affects the nonlawyer justices as a group more negatively than the lawyers, primarily because nonlawyers tend to serve in smaller communities. The survey revealed that the median population in the nonlawyer-judge jurisdictions was 2,500, with 19 percent holding court in towns of less than 1,000. Among the lawyers, however, the median population was 9,000, only 4 percent presiding in towns of less than 1,000. Table 5.2 indicates the distribution of nonlawyer and lawyer justices by population.

Table 5.2   Populations Served: Nonlawyers versus Lawyers

Population	Under 1,000 (%)	1,000– 2,499 (%)	2,500– 5,000 (%)	Over 5,000 (%)
Nonlawyers (N = 1223)	19	30	24	27
Lawyers (N = 252)	4	12	12	73

Caseload, not surprisingly, bears a strong relationship to the size of the community in which a justice sits: the correlation between the two was .67. This means, of course, that lawyer justices get more cases on the average. These differences are dramatic, with the median lawyer-justice caseload 1,500 cases per year, over four times the median caseload for nonlawyers (350 cases annually). Thanks in large part to smaller caseloads, nonlawyer justices earn less and have less assistance than their lawyer colleagues. The median lay judicial salary was $2,400 in 1980, compared to $6,150 for lawyers. Fifty-seven percent of the lawyers had at least one full-time assistant, while only 12 percent of nonlawyers had that much help. Fifty-eight percent of the nonlawyer justices had no support staff at all.

The assistance available to lawyer justices helps create an even greater gap in the amount of time they spend per case, the average lawyer justice disposing of five cases for every one a nonlawyer handled. Such efficiency saves municipalities money on a per case basis, while at the same time providing most lawyers much higher hourly pay. Table 5.3 indicates some overall differences in support, compensation, and productivity among lay and lawyer justices.

Population and caseload differences between lawyer and nonlawyer justices, however, do not entirely explain

Table 5.3   Case Processing Differences: Nonlawyers versus Lawyers

	Nonlawyers	Lawyers
Support:		
Annual judicial salary (median)	$2,400	$6,150
Assistance:		
With full-time help	12%	57%
With no help	58%	3%
Compensation:		
Salary/hour (median)	$4.80	$12.31
Productivity:		
Cases considered/hour (median)	.7	3.5
Judicial salary/case (median)	$6.50	$3.38

why the lawyers tend to be better compensated. Regression analysis suggests that, even with caseload and population taken into account, legal education is positively correlated with the amount of assistance the community provides. A justice's legal credentials also seem to have some effect on efficiency, even when differences in clerical assistance are taken into account. In short, lawyer justices appear to be more likely to insist on clerical help and to be more likely to use that help efficiently if they get it. Table 5.4 suggests the relative importance of each variable:

Table 5.4   Stepwise Multiple Regression Analysis of Support and Productivity

Dependent Variable	Independent Variables	Standardized Estimate	Total R^2
Judicial salary	Caseload	.327	
	Population	.491	
	Lawyer or not	.075	.63
Assistance	Caseload	.319	
	Population	.343	
	Lawyer or not	.174	.50
Cases/hour	Caseload	.687	
	Assistance	.233	
	Lawyer or not	.137	.38

Lay justices not only get less pay and assistance than lawyers at this level, they are also more vulnerable to charges of personal bias based upon previous contacts with litigants. The survey showed that lay town and village justices tend to know a much higher proportion of the plaintiffs and defendants that come before them than lawyers do. Among lay justices, the median rate of precourt acquaintance with civil plaintiffs was 50 percent; for lawyers, the median was 10 percent. Nonlawyer justices also claimed to know more defendants in criminal cases. Table 5.5 summarizes some of these differences.

Table 5.5   Acquaintance with Litigants: Nonlawyers versus Lawyers

	Nonlawyers (%) (N = 1,152; 1,190)	Lawyers (%) (N = 196)
Civil plaintiffs (%)		
Knows 0–25	39	79
Knows more than 25	61	21
	100	100
Criminal defendants (%)		
Knows 0–25	54	88
Knows more than 25	46	22
	100	100

One might ask at this point why the town and village justices do not simply disqualify themselves when they recognize a litigant. The justices surveyed here rarely interpret the norm of impartial judgment that strictly, in part because limited administrative resources and independence between jurisdictions make most disqualifications awkward and inconvenient. It is administratively easy to disqualify oneself only in communities that have a second justice who does not know the litigant in question. At least as important, though, I discovered in my fieldwork, is the widespread feeling among justices that knowing one's clientele is a help, not a hindrance, to fair adjudication. "Out-of-court knowledge about defendants," one of them explained, is "an unequivocal advantage in my work." This man, a town justice for twenty years, estimated that he knows at least 50 percent of the defendants he sees. No one seemed to be concerned with the problem of bias, either for or against, litigants they knew. One justice even boasted that he had sentenced his own daughter, the mayor, and several members of the town council in traffic cases.

In their reluctance to transfer cases involving acquaintances, New York's town and village justices are typical, according to Keith Stott et al., authors of *Rural Courts:*

> Urban judges automatically disqualify themselves when a litigant or criminal defendant whom they know appears before them. For rural judges to follow such practice would create significant problems of judicial assignment. One rural judge remembers disqualifying himself only once during his thirteen years on the bench—when the defendant was accused of hitting the judge's car.[38]

The reasons why lay justices tend to know more litigants than lawyers are somewhat obscure. Lawyer justices seem to be more socially isolated, not just from litigants, but from the nonlitigants and would-be litigants who rely on the town and village courts for legal advice. Lawyers, despite their obvious expertise as practitioners of law, play a more limited advising, or ombudsman, role than nonlawyers. Forty-six percent of the nonlawyers reported frequent communication from residents on matters other than pending cases, as opposed to 38 percent of the lawyers.

The tendency for nonlawyers to serve in the smallest, most isolated jurisdictions is obviously relevant to the role they play in the local community. In small jurisdictions, particularly those without an interstate highway, large-scale recreational facility, or nearby city, community life is intimate. Deaths may be recorded on the firehouse door, and the voluntary ambulance crew supplies the details of every mishap to nearly everyone. When a notorious case, such as an assault between feuding neighbors comes to court, friends and associates on both sides will attend and may seek to participate. The local court resolves local problems for a local clientele, much as justices of the peace did before the advent of the automobile.

Yet in the aggregate, population and caseload in a jurisdiction are not strongly correlated with the tendency to know litigants and act as ombudsman, certainly not strongly enough to rely on geography alone to explain lay/lawyer differences.[39] Why then do lay judges tend to know more litigants and to act more often as ombudsmen? Some who would replace elected lay judges with an all-lawyer (preferably appointed) bench have an answer. Those hostile to nonlawyer judges often assume that lay persons win election only because they are politically well-connected and parochial in their outlook— "goodoleboys" in the words of one critic.[40] Lacking any legitimate grounds for their election, they must rely on long-term residence, family connections, political activity, and organizational memberships to win votes. Lawyers, on the other hand, can appeal to voters on qualifications alone; they need not become entrenched in local affairs to garner support for a local judgeship (though no one would deny that such connections could be helpful!).

Judge and Community

My survey suggests that the differences between lay and lawyer justices in how they relate to their communities are not what the reform movement presumes them to be. I found no clear-cut differences in the family ties that bind lay and lawyer justices to their local communities. Members of both groups tended to be long-term residents of the jurisdictions in which their courts were located. Half of the lawyer justices had spent at least half of their lives in the communities they served; for nonlawyers the median is 60 percent. Almost as many of both groups had grown up in the town or village in which they held court. Many came from long-established families in their areas: 25 percent of the nonlawyers and 15 percent of the lawyers reported that their parents had lived in the community fifty years or more. About two-thirds of both groups had other relatives in the community. In other personal respects that might establish community linkages too, the lay and lawyer justices were virtually indistinguishable. Almost all I surveyed were male, married, veterans, and parents, usually of two or three children. The median age among nonlawyer justices was fifty, and the lawyer median was forty-seven. Both groups tended to stay in the post the same length of time, with the median at six years.

When nonlawyers are split into those with high school education or less and those with some college experience, some differences do emerge. Justices who had not gone beyond high school tended to serve in smaller communities, handling fewer cases. They tended to be a few years older, and a higher percentage were retired. They were also more rooted to their communities by their own residence and the residence of parents and other relatives. The college-educated justices were in all of these respects more like the lawyers.[41]

Political ties to the local community were similar for both groups, regardless of the educational level of the nonlawyers. Most justices reported that they were active in only a few organizations; they tended to have been loyal to these organizations for long periods of time. Only a minority of either group had held political office before, and it tended to be lawyers who had the political experience, contrary to the rhetoric of the reform movement. A third of the lawyers, but only one-fourth of the lay persons, had held elective or politically appointed office before becoming a justice.

In their survey responses and in interviews, the lawyer justices also revealed themselves to be more politically ambitious than the nonlawyers. Asked whether their current judgeship might be a stepping-stone to higher judicial office, 70 percent thought this possible or likely. In interviews, several lawyers even used the term "stepping-stone" to describe their town or village judgeship. They explained that the office offers an important advantage to a lawyer interested in moving on to a full-time judgeship because it makes few demands on an active law practice, yet at the same time provides the exposure and experience necessary to move up in the judicial hierarchy. The lay justices I interviewed, on the other hand, did not see their judgeships in instrumental terms, as a point on the way to some other political office. For them, of course, the route to higher judicial office is closed.

Whatever the difference between lay and lawyer justices in political ambitions, it is clear that they are alike in exhibiting unusually strong local roots. The tendency for local judges to be long-term residents of the communities they serve is at least as strong on the all-lawyer city bench. Upstate city judges, the survey revealed, were even more likely than either lay or lawyer town and village justices to have grown up and remained within the jurisdictions they served. Seventy-eight percent hold court in the city in which their parents resided, and 76 percent have other relatives there. Over 60 percent of the city judges reported that their parents had lived in the jurisdiction 50 years or more.[42] One city judge I interviewed, in fact, lived only three doors down from the house where he was born.

Such connections obviously help candidates win elections. Even more important, perhaps, is the possibility that strong local roots nourish interest in taking on a local political office, particularly an unremunerative town or village judgeship.[43] Perhaps, in other words, the individuals with long-term ties are the only ones who would consider becoming justices, shouldering what could be regarded as a thankless job. Most citizens, according to sociologist Elvin Hatch, do not particularly want to become local officials anymore:

> Active involvement in local life has lost much of its importance as a measure of social standing because local affairs have come to seem somewhat petty in relation to the affairs of business. ... By the mid-1960's the man who devoted his time to conducting local affairs instead of to business would have been known, not for his sense of civic responsibility, but for his misplaced sense of importance.[44]

Returning once more to the question of why lay justices tend to know more litigants than lawyers and act as ombudsman more often, it is clear now that the answer does not lie in the differences in length or breadth of their local ties. Both lay and lawyer justices are generally long-established, well-connected local citizens, though few in either group could be called politicos. The one potentially relevant respect in which lawyer and nonlawyer justices do tend to diverge significantly is in socioeconomic status. Class differences between the two groups may thus help explain why lay justices interact more with litigants and would-be litigants: closer than lawyers to the social status of the court's clientele, lay justices are more likely to travel in the same social orbits.

The socioeconomic gulf between lay and lawyer justices is wide. Lawyer justices tend to be better educated, better paid, and occupationally distinct from most of the rural and suburban citizens they serve. The median annual family income among the lawyer justices I surveyed was $48,000, which nearly all of them earned almost entirely through law practice. Half of these justices had practiced law twenty years or more.[45]

The nonlawyer justices, on the other hand, were more ordinary citizens. Fifty-eight percent had no education past high school, and 29 percent had completed or attended college; an additional 13 percent had some graduate education. Family income, too, was much more modest among nonlawyer justices. The median was $23,000, less than half the lawyer-justice median. About a dozen nonlawyer justices reported incomes under $5,000 per year; the least a lawyer justice claimed to have earned, on the other hand, was $14,000. Table 5.6 suggests the difference in socioeconomic status between the two groups.

The nonlawyers also reported a wide variety of full-time occupations. Among those with some college education, over half held professional or other white-collar jobs. Another 15 percent operated small businesses, and the remainder were divided fairly equally between civil service, farming, and blue-collar occupations like truck driv-

Table 5.6   Family Income: Nonlawyers versus Lawyers

	Less than $10,000 (%)	$10,000– $24,999 (%)	$25,000– $49,999 (%)	$50,000 or more (%)
Nonlawyers (N = 1031)	11	44	35	10
Lawyers (N = 179)	0	7	44	49

ing. The justices without college experience were more concentrated in these blue-collar occupations and less often involved in professional work.[46]

In none of these respects are New York's nonlawyer justices unusual. Studies elsewhere reveal a nonlawyer judiciary of modest educational, economic, and occupational attainments.[47] Nor is this a new pattern. Research conducted in the 1930s, discussed at length in Chapter 2, revealed justices of the peace to be poorly educated and low in economic status, a fact critics of that era used in arguing for their abolition. What has disappeared over the years is not the socioeconomic gap between lay and lawyer judges (although that may be closing), but our willingness to use social class as an argument for limiting the bench to lawyers.

Taken together, the available evidence suggests that the nonlawyer justices who dominate the town and village bench are like the lawyer minority in many personal respects, but inferior in income and education, a difference that may help explain why they know more of their clientele. Both groups are also alike in being subject to the perils of local control and case-based state financing. Here again, though, it is the lay justices who tend to be worse off, primarily because they are concentrated in rural areas, where caseloads are small. The vagaries of local control and the state's piecework approach to financing its justice courts thus put New York's nonlawyer judges in a double bind: they are confined to the level in the system that receives least from the state, and, their courts tend to be the smallest and poorest at this level.

The facts of institutional life described here, ironically, fuel arguments for the abolition of nonlawyer judges. Court reformers seem at once oversensitive to the accoutrements lay judges lack, and insensitive to the institutional constraints with which they must contend. Predisposed to see great significance in the presence or absence of a law degree, they conflate the impact of circumstances and credentials, and miss the overriding similarity between lay and lawyer judges in responding to the fundamental demands of fair adjudication.

Judicial Authority in Justice Court

Most town and village justices, the previous section established, hold court in their spare time in courtrooms designed for other purposes, with little or no staff, isolated from other courts and other government agencies but not from friends and acquaintances. The informality of the setting inevitably has an impact on proceedings. Indeed, the town or village justice who tries to resist the surroundings and insist upon inflexible procedures and a large measure of deference from litigants and court personnel appears faintly ridiculous to everyone in the courtroom. I observed one town justice's vain struggle to keep proceedings solemn in a courtroom adapted from an old two-room schoolhouse. He was perched atop a makeshift podium on a stage with worn brown curtains behind him, a nonfunctional clock on a nearby bare wall, and a no-pest strip hanging rakishly over his head; his dour formality accomplished nothing and seemed almost laughingly out of place.

It is important to establish in a systematic way how the constraints peculiar to the town and village courts affect adjudication. The relationships between the justice and courtroom regulars, such as the local prosecutor, are of special concern because they affect the balance of power in adjudication, and this balance influences outcomes in close cases. Generalizations are hazardous, however, when personalities are involved and when courts vary as

much as New York's justice courts do in caseload and
other characteristics.

This section draws upon my fieldwork and my personal
experience as a justice to create a rough sketch of typical
working relationships in justice court. I have relied upon
organizational theory in interpreting my data, an approach that has by now become standard in describing
case processing in criminal trial courts. The largely rural
and suburban justice courts differ in important ways from
the full-time urban courts that have provided the basis for
most previous research on courtroom process, of course,
but the similarities between all trial courts are great
enough to make this familiar perspective congenial.

Social scientists have found organizational theory useful in studying trial courts because the reality at this level
is shared power. The judge in a criminal trial court,
contrary to what one might expect, is not the undisputed
master of the courtroom and the caseload. Prosecutorial
discretion over the decision of whether and when to
pursue cases and the prevalence of plea bargaining limit
the judge's real authority. One city judge I interviewed
made the point directly when he said that "reductions are
the city prosecutor's department." Even when a case goes
to trial, the judge is expected to be relatively passive,
thanks to our adversary tradition, which gives counsel
the dominant role in proceedings.[48]

Others also retain important powers in case disposition;
in urban settings they include bondsmen, bailiffs, and the
court's clerical staff. In a busy criminal court these actors,
whom scholars refer to as "the courtroom work group,"
learn to rely on each other to some extent, for cooperation
and routinization are the keys to moving cases efficiently
through the system. The defendant, in contrast, plays but
a minor role in the courtroom. In one of the city courts I
visited, for example, the judge turned to the defendant's
lawyer, not the defendant, to ascertain the spelling of his
name, and the work group became so engaged in another
discussion that no one noticed when the defendant, whose
fate they were discussing, dissolved into tears.

The courtroom work group develops norms of process

and outcome through working together. These rules of the game may become so important to the group that members may sanction deviations from them. Defendants, ostensibly the subject of the process, are not part of this network, though they too may be punished for departing too far from what is expected of them. "The court," as Maureen Mileski has observed, "has a social integrity which can be disrupted."[49]

In the town and village courts, the work group is smaller and it operates more intermittently in both civil and criminal cases. Police officers, the assistant district attorney assigned to the court, and a handful of defense lawyers are usually the only ones that work with the justice regularly. Even these courtroom regulars attend only some of the time in most courts because the cases are neither numerous enough nor serious enough to demand more of their attention. The typical justice-court caseload is composed primarily of relatively minor traffic matters, with a significant sprinkling of small claims and criminal violations that carry a maximum $50 fine. Criminal charges like these are minor enough that many defendants view them as not worth contesting; these defendants come to court to plead guilty without trying to negotiate a reduction in the charge or requesting the aid of counsel. In traffic cases they often plead and pay by mail. Civil litigants frequently argue their own small claims because too little is involved to make hiring counsel worthwhile. The upshot is that the town or village justice often interacts directly with litigants, disposing of many cases with no assistance from the courtroom work group.

It is not easy to preside in a courtroom full of unrepresented litigants, with no bailiff to command everyone to rise upon the justice's entry and exit and quiet the assembly in between these events. The justice in such a situation also misses the helpful model of behavior that counsel and police officers provide in a courtroom. Their gestures of deference to judicial authority, though often exaggerated and ritualized, nevertheless help create an atmosphere that may impress outsiders. A court clerk, if the justice has one, can provide some instruction to defendants in how to behave. Often a wife or daughter, the clerk tends to be very loyal and exhibit a large measure of deference to her justice. One daughter I observed never missed an opportunity to call her father "your honor" on court night, and she reacted angrily to the slightest show of disrespect from anyone present. She even suggested raising the fine on one rude, gum-chewing defendant, advice her father rejected.

Keeping defendants under control without assistance in the none too awe-inspiring physical surroundings typical of justice court is only one of the problems town and village justices face. Relations with counsel and police officers are also problematical. A justice needs their support to maintain credibility (and even a caseload in some instances), but an effective judge must also be able to act independently. Finesse, therefore, is required when opposing a member of the courtroom work group. Town and village justices feel particularly vulnerable in such circumstances because they know that their courts do not rate very high in the eyes of lawyers and the police, who tend to rank courts by the seriousness of the sanctions they mete out. Nor do courtroom regulars find the justice courts convenient to attend; lawyers, in particular, dislike the evening and weekend sessions far away from the county seat, the very features that make these courts so convenient to litigants. Courtroom regulars constantly remind a justice in subtle ways that they attend court sessions only reluctantly, a message no justice can fail to internalize.

It should not be surprising, then, that the question of how to maintain the control necessary to be effective is salient to town and village justices. I found during my own term as a town justice that when justices talk with each other they often complain of being "jerked around" by others, especially lawyers and defendants. Nearly all the justices I spoke with described situations in which they "almost" held a lawyer or defendant in contempt of court. (Actual contempt orders are extremely rare in justice court, in part because there is seldom anyone present to enforce the order if the subject fails to defer voluntarily.)

This overview suggests that the issue of judicial authority and its cultivation is important in any detailed examination of relations among participants in justice court. Given the structure of the town and village courts, it could hardly be otherwise, for these judges are more vulnerable to recalcitrance from litigants than most, and less easy in their relations with courtroom regulars, who consider justice courts unimportant and inconvenient. The perception that these courts are insignificant, a view that is widely shared outside law-enforcement circles, does carry with it one advantage, however. It frees town and village justices from the scrutiny of news reporters, court watchers, and the bar, giving them room to respond creatively to some of the limitations built into the system. The most successful town and village justices take advantage of this flexibility and learn how to maximize cooperation from those with whom they must interact. The specific subsections that follow describe some of these strategies and the underlying tensions that bring them into play.

Coping with the Lay Clientele

The courtroom is a theater, whether a justice wants it to be or not. Except in the busiest, noisiest town and village courts, all present focus on the bench. A perennial topic of discussion among justices is whether to dress the part and wear robes to lend dignity to proceedings, covering what one referred to as "that unforgiveable affliction . . . fat." As in the entertainment world, a session without many cases is referred to as "a slow night" and is a source of apology when there are visitors. To the justice, those waiting for their cases are the audience; some justices I interviewed even referred to them as such, and a few admitted that they suffered stage fright. Several could not eat before court, and many said that it took time to unwind afterward. One town justice even brought his four-year-old child to Saturday court sessions to help ease the tension.

The typical court session, as noted earlier, may well require the justice to spend the whole time, or most of it, dealing with lay persons, nearly all of whom are defendants in traffic and criminal cases. In the smaller courts, defense counsel are likely to be present only when the prosecutor is, on "d.a.-night," or "prelim day," a bi-monthly or monthly occasion for plea bargaining and trials. Without lawyers present, the clientele tends to be scruffy, blue-jeaned, and rather ill at ease in the courtroom. Justices refer to the most confused and ignorant of this lot as "packrats" or "woodchucks," which one justice defined as "people who don't know to take their hats off in court."

The justice, as lead player in the courtroom, must decide what type of relationship to establish with this clientele. It is in setting the tone for interaction, however, that the justice is most clearly limited by physical circumstances, and, in a significant fraction of cases, previous acquaintance with the litigant. The town or village justice must use indirect means to achieve the cooperation necessary to effectiveness in the courtroom. The best strategy is to turn the unavoidable informality of the situation to advantage, to extract deference from litigants without any obvious show of authority.

Some justices use tone of voice and manner to instruct litigants on proper courtroom behavior. Two I observed addressed defendants at arraignment by their first names and thus established an almost paternal atmosphere. One of these men went even further with elderly women who appeared in his court; he held their hands and would say, "I need a hug," to any that seemed willing to oblige him. Most justices I observed simply rewarded those who cooperated with cordiality, and sanctioned the unpleasant and the unrepentant with uncharacteristic coldness and formality.

A judge can also gain cooperation by exhibiting superior access to information. In a quiet courtroom, this can be done through lengthy discussion with a polite defendant who appears early in the court session. Those waiting learn that cooperative behavior may be rewarded with information about the possible ramifications of a traffic conviction or other matter. Encouraging the clientele to pick up behavior cues by listening to prior cases can be hazardous, however, because defendants may develop expectations about how their own cases should be handled. To obviate this problem, some justices use two rooms on court night, one for proceedings, and the other for waiting. This minimizes the information the court provides the clientele, and thus discourages informed argumentation. This approach also has the advantage of keeping the relationship with defendants one on one.

Sometimes the situation is reversed, and the justice needs information from a litigant. Justices sometimes lack the record of prior traffic offenses that they need in sentencing, for example, because communication from other state agencies is slow and unreliable. (In the administrative adjudication bureaus that are designed to compete with justice courts, in contrast, referees work behind computer terminals that display the defendant's entire driving record.) If town and village justices are to get information about prior offenses, they may have to rely on defendants. Honesty can be encouraged, however, if a justice simply looks knowledgeable. One town justice I observed accomplishes this by appearing to follow the papers before him as defendants speak. When the speaker pauses, he asks, "Is that all?" with a frown and a finger on his papers. Those who appear before this justice never find out that they have been tricked into complete disclosure.

When judicial control threatens to slip away because a litigant is unhappy with a decision, justices tend to take one of two indirect approaches. Some ease resentment with a joke or unflappable good humor, sending a signal that the decision should be accepted in the same spirit. Others make unpalatable decisions seem inevitable, which encourages defendants to externalize the underlying offense and defuses resentment and excuse making. I observed one justice do this by asking his clerk rhetorically, "What is the penalty for . . . now?" He would even remark occasionally that the fine for an offense had "gone up" that year, as if penalties, like inflation, were out of any individual's control.

Another method of avoiding trouble is to schedule sentencings to jail for the beginning of a busy court session. The image of a defendant being handcuffed and led away by the police creates a lasting impression on the whole courtroom. Several of my colleagues urged me to try and arrange such a scene early in my judgeship in order to develop a reputation as a tough judge. A raised voice or angry words can also help control troublesome defendants, but I only witnessed one clear case of this type of sanctioning, which occurred when a defendant insisted that the outcome of his case was a foregone conclusion.

Experience helps a justice develop techniques for dealing with defendants and gives a justice an air of knowledgeability and authority in routine cases. Time in office and a reasonable flow of cases also provide valuable coping skills when events take an unexpected turn, an eventuality which occurs less often the longer a justice sits. Experience alone, however, does not ensure that one will exercise authority with subtlety and finesse.

To be effective, a justice must also display a sense of conviction about minimum standards of behavior to be observed both in and out of court, and a justice must acquire a good sense of how far a person can be pushed. Some justices I interviewed seemed to enjoy the process of discovering these limits. I watched one veteran justice, for example, order three ill-mannered young men to leave a crowded courtroom and "start again like gentlemen," an approach to dealing with their misbehavior that I would have been afraid to try for fear that they would have walked out and failed to come back. A wise justice also knows when to give up a case gracefully, transferring it on some plausible pretext, if possible, or continuing it rather than issuing a bench warrant, or even offering a "flyer" (speeding defendant) a "gift" (light sentence) when there is reason to suspect the police officer who serves as complaining witness will not come to a trial.

Controlling Police Excesses

The town or village justice must also exercise sensitivity in relations with state troopers and members of the county sheriff's office, for they can have a considerable influence on proceedings in justice court. Their discretion to decide which justice within a jurisdiction gets cases has already been noted. This power to send or withhold cases looms important, not just because judicial incomes depend on how often troopers and sheriffs "write" them but because a justice's prestige and sense of personal success depends to a significant extent on caseload. Justices are pleased and flattered at being selected over someone else, an attitude they reveal indirectly, with their intense curiosity about the size of other justices' caseloads, and their pride in citing the size of their own. None of the high-caseload justices I interviewed felt comfortable speculating about why they got so many cases, but all of them acted as if the police were exercising good judgment in selecting them.

Police officers can also affect proceedings directly by failing to appear at trials and hearings, failing to file required supporting papers on time, and, of course, failing to charge properly. Police officers can sometimes even shape the course of a trial because they prosecute some of their own cases in over half of the state's justice courts, a practice that has nearly disappeared at other levels in the judicial hierarchy. A police officer's assessment of a justice can thus have a real impact on judicial effectiveness, especially since individual officers tend to share their opinions with each other and other court personnel quite freely.

Justices are usually aware of roughly how they stand in the estimation of law-enforcement officers, but officers may even take direct action to let their feelings be known. One justice described a case involving an abusive out-of-state truck driver charged with several vehicle and traffic law violations, including driving while intoxicated. The driver had been violent with two troopers, who had to use mace twice to subdue him. They brought the man in for an immediate arraignment, anticipating that bail would be high enough to jail him for the night. The justice set bail at $500, assuming the trucker couldn't pay that much on the spot. To everyone's surprise, the trucker paid the $500 from a large roll of bills, which angered the police officers so much that they walked out of court, leaving the justice alone to protect his bail and deal with the defendant. These troopers, the justice commented wryly, "must have thought I'm a hell of a fighter." Such behavior is rare. Usually officers simply let their feelings be known by boycotting the justice for a time. When this happens, justices say that an officer is "mad" at them.

Police pressure can take other forms, too. Obvious attempts at influencing the court, like an unsolicited suggestion about the proper disposition of a case, often bring a response, especially among the more experienced justices accustomed to protecting their own interests. Police department policies can also be intrusive from a justice's perspective, but an experienced justice can sometimes take action to contain them. One justice I observed, for example, started imposing minimal $1 fines for snow ordinance violations, penalties she nicknamed "January specials," because she felt the police had overloaded the docket with too many of these unpopular cases.

Their vulnerability to judge shopping, police gossip, and other unpleasantness, however, encourages justices to cooperate with law-enforcement personnel when they can. Police officers who come to court without essential papers, I observed, often escape without a word of reproof from the justice who has been inconvenienced. Some justices even act affirmatively to accommodate the law-enforcement perspective on adjudication. One interviewee, for example, responded to police hostility toward plea-bargaining sessions (which they call "dollar days") by including officers in the bargaining sessions.

Town and village justices cooperate with the state police and sheriff's department not only because they must but also because they enjoy their association with law enforcement. A few of the justices are former police officers, or have friends or relatives who are. But even

those who have no personal acquaintance with police
work tend to be favorably predisposed. Police officers, as
Chapter 4 noted, bring gossip and privileged information
to a town or village court, and their presence in a courtroom enhances a justice's sense of importance and power.

Keeping Counsel in Line

The prosecutor who "services" a court and the handful of
local lawyers who appear there regularly can have a
significant impact on case disposition. These actors become important, however, only when a litigant seeks the
aid of counsel, which, as noted earlier, is relatively infrequent in justice court. Only middle-class litigants, a rarity
in the rural upstate courts where I did my fieldwork, insist
on trials or negotiations in the typical minor or "garbage"
cases. These defendants usually hire private counsel,
though they occasionally deal with the prosecutor on
their own, even conducting their own defense at trial.

In the few criminal cases serious enough that a jail
sentence is a realistic possibility, however, representation
by counsel is the rule rather than the exception for
moneyed and unmoneyed defendants alike. Poor defendants are eligible for, and usually take advantage of,
assigned counsel or a public defender, depending on the
system the county has adopted. Defendants with means
hire their own lawyers. When defense counsel becomes
involved in a criminal case, the local prosecutor assigned
to the court does too, and the justice must cope with their
combined power to influence the pace and outcome of
proceedings.

For the most part, these lawyers desire to minimize the
time and effort they must spend on the ill-paying, insignificant cases they handle in justice court, but defense
lawyers also want to get the best deal that they can for
their clients. Defense counsel's desire to reduce charges
as much as possible and the desire on both sides to keep
court commitments to a minimum often makes a justice's
work more difficult. The system provides justices with few
weapons to deal with self-serving behavior by counsel, but

the most creative and determined find ways to counter some of it.

The failure of defense counsel to show up for court dates is one of the most persistent problems the practicing bar presents for the local justice. "No shows" embarrass the justice, slow adjudication, and make the court process seem less important to those who do attend. Justices handle this problem in several ways. One interviewee had his clerk telephone offending attorneys while their clients waited in court; another made failures to appear costly for lawyers and their hapless clients by giving only one opportunity for plea bargaining per case; other justices refuse to be easily accommodated when the attorney finally does get in touch to dispose of the case. Or the justice may sanction persistent offenders with a warrant for the client's arrest; the unlucky client can usually be depended upon to make the attorney more responsive to appearance dates. Most justices, however, accept the minor insult of an unexcused absence and simply adjourn the case to the next regular court session. The fact that the justice has been "stood up" is thereby disguised from the public.

Another problem for justices is that defense attorneys find it convenient to plea bargain in court or in chambers between cases or just before court begins. They thereby save the trouble of contacting the assistant district attorney ahead of court time. Many justices dislike the bazaar-like atmosphere open plea bargaining produces, and some take steps to avoid it. One solution is to isolate plea bargaining from public view by confining it to a special "pretrial" day. These sessions allow for judicial involvement in the process, an advantage justices lose when they solve the problem of in-court bargaining by banning it from the courtroom.

Problems for the justice can also arise when defense counsel tries to use defendant's right to a jury trial to get a more favorable plea bargain from the assistant district attorney. When the stratagem fails and the jury is waiting for the case, counsel sometimes advises the defendant to plead guilty. Lawyers like to offer such last-minute pleas quietly, at the bar, leaving the justice the unpleasant task of explaining to the jury why their services are unnecessary. One justice avoids this problem by requiring counsel to announce the guilty plea to the jury, along with the reasons for the delay in entering it and an apology. Only at that point would the justice accept the plea and dismiss the jury.

The assistant district attorney assigned to the justice court usually avoids such conflicts and maintains a cordial working relationship with the justice. In one court I visited, the prosecutor, a young man who raised chickens, even collected the justice's egg cartons each week before court. There are built-in tensions in the relationship between prosecutor and justice, however, most of which are traceable to the prosecutor's broad discretion in plea negotiations. Prosecutors in New York's town and village courts, like their counterparts in many other jurisdictions, enjoy the power to reduce cases or to refuse to prosecute them at all. The prosecutor's power almost forces justices to ratify proposed plea bargains, even if they think the prosecutor's offer unduly lenient.[50] Justices must give vent to their own view of some cases in sentencing, or not at all. Only occasionally can the courtroom work group settle upon some way to plea bargain enough to satisfy defense counsel but not "give away" much. In one county I visited, for example, officers "double-charged" drunk drivers with two separate, but overlapping driving offenses, and prosecutors dropped one of them in plea bargaining. Defendants seemed not to have caught on to the fact that they gained nothing in this bargain because they could not have been convicted under both sections for the same offense anyway.

The predominance of plea bargaining as a means of resolving contested cases not only reduces judicial power over ultimate dispositions, it gives the assistant district attorney more authority over the pace of proceedings than many justices consider appropriate. Usually, the reality of prosecutorial power is obscured by habits of feigned deference to judicial authority. Occasionally, though, a prosecutor slips and adjourns a case without asking the justice for permission, or commits some other breach of courtroom etiquette. Such lapses invariably provoked anger from the justices I observed, perhaps because they were so revealing.

Town and village justices might resent the prosecutor's power less if it were exercised by an experienced and prominent veteran attorney. The prosecutors who appear in justice courts, however, tend to be just the opposite. The district attorney for the county, an important elected official, never comes to these courts and seldom spends much time supervising proceedings there. The prosecutors who are assigned to justice court tend to be the youngest, most inexperienced attorneys in the office. Often just out of law school, they may be twenty-five years the justice's junior.

Whatever their differences with these young assistant district attorneys, justices usually value their role in managing the state's case during a trial. The alternative, police prosecution, is unattractive to most justices. My own county magistrates association, for example, objected strenuously when the district attorney proposed that sheriffs begin prosecuting certain traffic cases, a proposal the justices found demeaning and problematical. Prosecution by a sheriff or trooper puts extra burdens on a judge, not only because officers lack litigation skills but because they tend to make proceedings more emotionally charged than they would be otherwise. Defendants who insist on trials are often still irked about their arrests, and prosecution by the arresting officer can provoke an angry courtroom confrontation. When a member of the district attorney's office is prosecuting, on the other hand, the trial tends to be insulated from the original incident. Despite these considerations, police prosecution of some cases occurs in over half of the justice courts in New York, an indication of the significance district attorneys, who set such policies, attach to proceedings there.

Given the difficulties associated with police prosecution, plea bargaining, and defense-delaying tactics, it should not be surprising that town and village justices sometimes try to encourage guilty pleas at arraignment. A guilty plea at this stage short-circuits involvement from other members of the courtroom work group and allows cases to be closed quickly.

The justices I observed who encouraged guilty pleas at arraignment used various techniques, all too mild to violate the rights of defendants but effective enough to encourage pleas of guilty as charged. One joked with defendants who seemed uncertain about pleading not guilty and retaining counsel, suggesting that the only way to "pay a fine twice" was to hire an attorney. Another was fond of pointing out the corollary proposition that the only way an innocent person could still pay a fine was to hire a lawyer. Others were more subtle, using their personal warmth to gain the trust of defendants reluctant to plead guilty as charged. One even encouraged defendants to talk about the offense, responding to self-serving versions of events, not with anger but with a much more effective show of sympathy. He would say, "Well, if that's the way it happened, I wouldn't plead guilty either." Defendants, having voiced their resentment and met unexpected sympathy, often pleaded guilty "to get it over with."

Lay Justices versus Lawyers in Court

Conflicts of interest ensure that relations with counsel will be somewhat strained for any town or village justice, as the previous subsection indicated, but the tensions between these actors are likely to be greater if the justice is a lay person. Obvious class and educational differences analogous to those between lay and lawyer justices noted earlier complicate the relationship. But it is not simply socioeconomic differences that separate lay justices from the lawyers who come before them. Lay justices, I found in my research, have mixed feelings about lawyers and the ethics of law practice.

Many of the lay justices I interviewed were repelled by the willingness of lawyers to represent anyone, guilty or not, for a fee. Some also resented the way counsel for the prosecution and defense use plea bargaining to save time and trouble, even when the defendant is clearly guilty as charged. Lay justices were particularly irritated by the high fees many defense lawyers charge for "reducing" a case. Justices told me almost increduously about counsel fees as high as $1,000 for reductions earned simply by a couple of telephone calls or informal negotiation face-to-face with the prosecutor.

The prevalent attitude among lay justices—that lawyers are grasping and will do anything for money—comes through in this poem one gave me. He wrote it about a prosecutor who had gone on to become a public defender:

> There was a lawyer in our state and xxx was his name.
> He prosecuted criminals—he knew they were to blame.
> When criminals were brought to him they didn't stand a chance.
> With evidence on every side they were sure to lose their pants.
> But when the dust was settled and criminals out on bail,
> The money tree had shed its leaves and xxx did set sail. . . .
> Then down to yyy City, a visit to bestow,
> A pot of gold was seen to rest beneath that old rainbow.
> I will defend the guilty crook, tho guilty he may be,
> For now I see there are green leaves upon that money tree.[51]

My lay interviewees were troubled, not only by the ethics of law practice, but by professional hostility to nonlawyer judges. All were aware of the position bar associations have taken on nonlawyer judges, and many sensed an attitude of superiority, even in the lawyers they worked with regularly. These justices, not surprisingly, relished opportunities to put lawyers in their place. Nearly every one of them told and appreciated jokes about lawyers, and many recounted instances where they had set one straight on a legal issue.

Yet at the same time, nonlawyer judges often gave signs that they admired lawyers, or at least legal education. Many said they wished they had gone to law school; these judges valued their judgeships for what the work taught them about law. A few demonstrated the importance they attached to degrees by hanging the certificates they received for completing training courses on the walls of their judicial offices.

Evidence of mixed feelings about professional education also emerged in the local-court survey. When questioned about significant differences between lawyer and nonlawyer judges, the nonlawyers, not surprisingly, were less likely to acknowledge any, but when asked to explain their answers, they proved less confident than the lawyers about their own assets. A fifth gave reasons favoring, not themselves, but lawyers, and over a third cited advantages of both groups. Lawyers on the other hand, responded to the same questions in terms more favorable to themselves, as table 5.7 indicates.

Table 5.7   Judges on Lawyer/Nonlawyer-Judge Differences

Significant Differences?	Lawyers (%)	Nonlawyers (%)
	(N = 290)	(N = 1,136)
No	18	39
Yes	82	61
	100	100
If yes:	(N = 187)	(N = 701)
Pro-nonlawyer (citing fairness, closeness to public, etc.)	4	46
Pro-lawyer (citing legal knowledge, authoritativeness, etc.)	75	20
Cites advantages of both	21	34
	100	100

Nonlawyer judges, the survey and interview data suggest, are people in the middle: they work with lawyers enough to know some of their weaknesses, and many of these judges sense that they are victims of professional prejudices. Yet they do not necessarily reject the lawyer's version of adjudication out-of-hand: most believe that legal education does make a difference in adjudication, and nearly half of those think lawyers enjoy some or all of the advantages. Nonlawyers who serve as judges are thus caught between the lawyer's imagery about courts and law and their own experience with professional prejudice.

Conclusion

New York's lay justices, this chapter has shown, are in no position to disabuse lawyers of their prejudice against adjudication by nonlawyers. Confined to the bottom of the court system, and even at that level, concentrated in the courts with fewer cases and less impressive facilities, the lay judiciary contends with problems no other judges in New York face. The imaginative overcome some of the structural limitations associated with the justice-court system, but other limitations are unavoidable. Many justices, for example, do not have enough cases to become very expert or efficient adjudicators. The strains of running a dignified court from a facility like the town barn and keeping up with the law without deciding many cases show in the average tenure in office: only five years.

The small fraction of judges at this level who are lawyers also suffer deprivations, of course. New York's archaic approach toward the organization and administration of its town and village courts affects everyone. But the image of lawyers as adjudicators does not depend on their performance in courts like these. The same cannot be said for the nonlawyers.

The problems discussed in this chapter are typical of lay courts in other states. Local control—to a degree that sets lay courts apart from the rest of the court system—is important in many states. Twenty-six, like New York, allow local governments to set and pay the salaries of their nonlawyer judges.[52] Thirty-three states besides New York elect their nonlawyer judges from among the local citizenry, usually for short terms.[53] These arrangements obviously contribute to the sense in which lay courts really are, as they are often touted to be, "the courts closest to the people."

Concentration in rural areas, a pattern that has a decided impact on court funding in New York, is also the rule elsewhere for nonlawyer judges. Rural courts, researchers have found, tend to have certain things in common, including "part-time personnel, small, often inadequately trained staffs, shortage of court-related services, ... informality of procedures, ... inadequate court facilities, and more personal familiarity among criminal justice personnel and with litigants before the court."[54] Though lawyer judges in rural areas share these characteristics, the tendency, nevertheless, is to identify them with adjudication by lay persons.

To emphasize, as this chapter has, the extent to which lay courts deviate from a lawyer-influenced ideal of how courts should be organized, is not to accept that ideal without qualification. Informality in the setting and process of case disposition and familiarity between judge and litigant have their advantages, particularly when disputes are minor enough that most litigants do not seek counsel. The election of lay judges from among ordinary citizens to serve the local community also brings a democratic element to the process of adjudication; what one interviewee said of the justice courts may be true more often of lay courts than others: "a town gets the judge it deserves." Given the extent to which the questions at this level require judgment, not technical expertise, informality and democratic influences are probably desirable in most cases. These are matters beyond the scope of the argument here, which is that the working conditions characteristic of lay courts tend to obscure the extent to which lay judges succeed at protecting the fundamental rights of those who come before them.

6 JUDICIAL CREDENTIALS, PROFESSIONALISM, AND THE RULE OF LAW

Empirical evidence that lay persons are no less competent than lawyers as lower-court judges will not extinguish arguments for their abolition. Those who labor to eliminate lay judges are not particularly concerned with evidence. Lawyers and their allies, after all, have opposed lay judges for nearly a century, with but scant attention to empirical research on limited-jurisdiction courts. Reform arguments flow, as they always have, from broad, unverifiable presuppositions about how litigation works and what the impact of legal education is. In this respect they resemble other progressive-era proposals for professionalizing our courts, which tend to favor abstract propositions over careful observation of working judicial institutions.[1] The effort to abolish election of judges and inaugurate Missouri-plan appointment throughout the states, for example, also has drawn heavily upon broad assumptions about differences in appointive and elective processes; empirical research has proven both proponents and opponents of the plan equally wrong concerning its impact on judicial recruitment and behavior.[2] "Most writing about court reform," Henry Glick concludes after analyzing a number of reform proposals,

166

is more like a sales pitch or boosterism than a cool evaluation of the impact of changes on court operations. Reformers assert that justice will be improved by making changes in the courts while defenders of the status quo praise the sanctity of tradition and local control, but neither side provides any dispassionate research or other evidence to support its political position.[3]

The campaign to eliminate nonlawyer judges, despite its meager empirical foundations, has been moderately successful. The contemporary movement to consolidate courts, reduce excess judges, and increase judicial accountability all work against lay judges. The long-term trend is toward their elimination. The upsurge of interest during the past two decades in access to dispute-resolution facilities and in reducing the financial and emotional costs of litigation does not appear to indicate a significant countertrend. Support for neighborhood justice centers and analogous experiments with informal dispute resolution comes from some of the very elements most opposed to nonlawyer judges. Nonlawyer mediators are tolerable while nonlawyer judges are not because, theoretically at least, mediators derive their authority from the consent of the parties and they offer judgment in the name of reconciliation. Where rights and social sanctions are at issue, on the other hand, the argument for legal expertise has grown stronger with time.

The campaign to eliminate lay judges has been slowed, however, by "political" opposition from associations of nonlawyer judges, local governments seeking to preserve local prerogatives, state legislators sensitive to costs and votes, and appellate judges reluctant to disturb existing arrangements for staffing limited-jurisdiction courts. Financial considerations loom large in the calculus favoring the status quo; were cost problems to disappear, so would nonlawyer judges. Support for nonlawyer judges, in short, rests to a considerable extent on practical considerations, not ideological ones. No one proselytizes for greater lay involvement in adjudication.

The lay public has never become aroused to the political implications of the bar's long-standing efforts to monopolize all judicial offices. Instead, the popular assumption seems to be that their training and experience qualify lawyers to assume primary responsibility for suggesting the proper organization of our courts. The public has therefore consigned to lawyers all the leading roles in the effort to improve our limited-jurisdiction courts. The upshot, of course, is that our frame of reference for understanding judicial-policy issues is essentially the lawyer's perspective. Discussion, in newspaper features as in the law reviews, centers on whether nonlawyers sufficiently understand the concept of due process and whether they can be even-handed, issues that reflect the bar's traditional concern with individual rights. Whether preserving nonlawyer judgeships increases socioeconomic diversity on the lower-court bench or makes the local courts more available to litigants gets much less attention because these issues are of little direct concern to lawyers.

This chapter considers the legal profession's campaign to eliminate nonlawyer judges in social and political context. This perspective suggests at least three questions: *(a)* Just how "principled" is the legal profession's long-standing antagonism toward nonlawyer judges? *(b)* Why do arguments against lay judges—which so clearly favor lawyers and so often patronize nonlawyers—appeal to the lay citizenry? *(c)* How common are the social and political issues raised here and in the preceding chapters in other nations that rely on lay adjudicators? The three sections of this chapter consider each of these issues in turn.

Lawyers versus Nonlawyer Judges

On the surface, at least, the bar's campaign to eliminate nonlawyer judges is highly principled. It draws on broad arguments about social justice and public welfare that seem to speak to the interests of the laity in fair, efficient adjudication. But the very generality of these reference points, the failure to include clear, unambiguous criteria for evaluating the judicial process, helps keep lawyers at the center of the dialogue about judicial credentials. The problem, as one observer sees it, is that the relevant qualities desirable in a judge "are either unobserved by those outside the legal process or simply inaccessible to objective assessment. The effect is mystifying, reinforcing the symbolic image of the 'cult of the robe.' . . . "[4]

Lawyers also can rightfully be accused of professional conceit in their arguments for restricting judgeships to themselves. Previous chapters have detailed the extravagant claims lawyers and lawyers-to-be make for legal education and practice. When subjected to empirical analysis, clear evidence for lawyer-judge superiority proves difficult to find, as Chapter 4 revealed. The rhetoric for reform thus emerges as overblown and self-serving.

To label reform rhetoric self-serving may seem unfair. Those who have fought to eliminate nonlawyer judges have not sought these judgeships for themselves; most reformers have been elite, urban lawyers and law professors with no practical interest in judging in, or practicing before, limited-jurisdiction courts. Nor do ordinary practitioners stand to gain in obvious ways from the elimination of nonlawyer judges. One criticism of these judges, after all, has been that they are too easily swayed by the lawyers that appear before them. Many lawyers, not surprisingly, consider efforts to restrict the bar to lawyers to be a public service in the highest tradition of the profession.

Efforts to eliminate nonlawyers from judgeships do, nevertheless, serve the interests of lawyers as an occupational class. The relationship is obvious upon close analysis of the reasons lawyers cite most often for opposing nonlawyer judges. This section discusses three of these broad themes that recur in the professional literature and in discussions with practitioners:

1. Nonlawyers do not have the legal knowledge necessary to be judges.

2. Their courts lack dignity.

3. While most nonlawyer judges are well-meaning, too many lack the intelligence and moral sensitivity to be judges.

Lay Ignorance of Legal Rules

Among lawyers, the most common argument against nonlawyer judges is that they do not know enough about law to be judges. This contention rests on an idealized view of adjudication, one in which the guilt or innocence of criminal defendants is often at issue. If defendants are without counsel, the judge must struggle to protect their rights. If a defendant has counsel, the judge's function is to preside over a verbal contest between committed advocates in which it is necessary to call upon one's technical knowledge often to rule on motions, to give instructions, and to issue the appropriate orders to the parties. The focus, in short, is on the process of adjudication in fully litigated cases. The expertise legal education and practice provide, in consequence, seem highly significant in a judge.

This conception of adjudication in limited-jurisdiction courts is almost impervious to mounting evidence that guilty pleas prevail at this level and that even when defendants plead not guilty at first, plea bargaining, rather than trial, is likely to follow. Confronted with the reality of negotiation and shared information about law and defendants, lawyers are likely to contend that it is still important for judges, like counsel, to be prepared to go all the way in litigating any case. Few acknowledge the possibility that a nonlawyer judge could gain the requisite expertise through on-the-job experience or that judges might not need the same educational background that counsel require. Such reluctance to concede the insignificance of credentials to decision making, sociologists of the professions have pointed out, is characteristic: "Professionals tend to turn every problem of decision-making into a question of expertise."[5] Professionals are able to do this because, within the realm of their acknowledged expertise at least, they have established some independence

from the standards of ordinary citizens; such independence, it seems, is self-reinforcing: "Professional autonomy allows the experts to select almost at will the inputs
they will receive from the laity."[6]

Their ability to define reality in terms favorable to
themselves, to "live within ideologies of their own creation,"[7] helps make lawyers more sanguine about the
court system (or at least lawyer-judge courts) than those
without the insulation professional socialization provides.
Survey research reveals, for example, that lawyers are
much more favorably disposed toward courts in general
than the laity, especially those members of the public with
direct experience in the judicial system.[8]

The Informality of Lay Courts

Lawyers also reflect and reinforce their own professional
interests in criticizing the informality characteristic of
nonlawyer-judge courts. Nonlawyer judges, lawyers have
always complained, conduct court in surroundings unsuit-
ed to serious proceedings. The report of the state senate
task force assigned to study New York's largely
nonlawyer town and village courts suggests how much
significance lawyers attach to courtroom facilities:

> While many attorneys, including prosecutors, ad-
> vanced what they believed to be positive aspects of
> town and village courts, almost all conceded that
> justice court proceedings could not generally be
> characterized as dignified. Stories of the time attor-
> neys tried cases before a justice in the kitchen, while
> in the barn, or when a television set in the back-
> ground appeared to command most of the justice's
> attention, abounded.[9]

Lawyers are poorly served by such surroundings because they inspire no awe in clients or the public. The
homespun atmosphere helps put defendants at their ease,
which in turn makes counsel seem less necessary and less
important. Counsel's role shrinks from legal specialist to
sentence broker. Many defendants believe they can do

without counsel entirely in the unpretentious courts in which nonlawyers preside.

Awe-inspiring formality, of course, is not characteristic in any criminal court, well-furnished or not. The clientele and its problems keep these courts noisy and disorganized, "on the outer limits of respectability," in Austin Sarat's words.[10] Such informality threatens respect for law, and with it, respect for lawyers. The problem is most obvious in misdemeanor and traffic courts where cases move quickly and the lawyer's role tends to be circumscribed. Not surprisingly, these are also the courts most criticized by lawyers, especially elite lawyers well aware of the profession's prerogatives. Consider, for example, Justice Charles Whittaker's comments about traffic courts:

> With notable but all too rare exceptions [they] are so poorly housed, staffed and equipped, the proceedings in them are so lacking in deference, dignity and decorum and their judgments are so stereotyped and perfunctory, that they not only miserably fail to create respect, but in the defendants brought before them—a greater number than appear in all other courts combined—they actually create disrespect, if not, indeed, contempt, not just for the traffic laws and traffic courts, but for all laws and courts.[11]

In his sensitivity to decorum and respect, Justice Whittaker displays a concern typical of professionals in every field. Professional authority, after all, depends to a certain extent on appearances. Deference from subordinates, dignified surroundings, and emotional distance between clients and professionals are all important because the product the professional has to offer, expert judgment, is intangible.[12] High-status professions and high-status professionals are able to maintain working environments that show their expertise to good effect.[13] Lawyers who represent poor persons charged with crimes inevitably lack status, but the homey trappings typical of nonlawyer-judge courts make it even harder to look the part of the expert.

Lay Insensitivity to the Judicial Role

Professionalism also helps explain why lawyers often complain that nonlawyer judges lack analytical ability and moral sensitivity. Lawyers complain of arbitrary, even bizarre decisions by nonlawyer judges, favoritism to local residents, the police and plaintiffs who bring business to the court, and other politically motivated behavior. Critics imply that nonlawyers are prone to such behavior because they lack a firm conception of the judicial role, an understanding of one's responsibilities apparently only legal education can provide.

The attitude that nonlawyers, however well-meaning, cannot really grasp judicial responsibilities is reinforced every time a report circulates about error or unfairness in a nonlawyer judge. Such behavior tends to be attributed to the judge's lack of legal education. When a lawyer judge errs, on the other hand, criticism focuses on the individual, not on lawyer judges as a class. Had lay judges done some of the things lawyer judges in New York have been charged with in the past year or so—throwing dice to determine a sentence, taking a defendant home for the night, taking a poll of spectators to vote on a case, or inviting a defendant to share the bench—undoubtedly the behavior would be attributed to the educational status of the judge. It should also be noted that lawyers, as experts on the legal system, determine what is and what is not a mistake. Nonlawyers, by definition amateurs in the judicial system, risk condemnation whenever they deviate from what lawyers expect in a judge.

The kinds of judgeships nonlawyers hold exacerbate the problem of negative stereotyping. Small caseloads managed part-time over relatively short terms with poor support facilities make it difficult for any judge to keep current with the law and manage the work efficiently. Yet lawyers seldom take these mechanical obstacles into account in evaluating adjudication by nonlawyers. The pattern instead has been, as Chapter 5 noted, to lump environmental constraints with lack of judicial education in the call for reorganized, lawyer-judge courts.

Were nonlawyer judges typically business associates of lawyers or simply their social equals, prejudice borne of professionalism might be less rampant; out-of-court contacts might mitigate the tendency to blame everything open to criticism in a lay court on lack of legal credentials. Yet, everywhere, nonlawyer judges tend to be socially inferior to lawyers. Many are poorly educated, and their full-time occupations are often poorly paid. Outside of court, lay judges are farmers, truck drivers, blue-collar workers, storekeepers, insurance agents, and, more recently, civil servants and white-collar employees. Lawyers seldom interact with such persons socially or professionally. Social distance and unfamiliarity thus make nonlawyer judges an alien and unpredictable element in the life of a practicing lawyer.

Relationships between judge and counsel on lawyer-judge courts, on the other hand, tend to be easier, or at least more predictable. Bar association meetings, and, among part-time lawyer judges, the relationships that develop through practice, help make lawyer judges at every level known quantities to the bar. Purely social interaction is also common, lawyers and lawyer judges regarding themselves as social and intellectual equals. Off-the-bench relationships, professional collegiality, and a common educational background thus promote tolerance between lawyer judges and the practicing bar.

The impact on-going relationships and shared understandings have on lawyer attitudes was evident to me in the field when I compared the interaction between bench and bar in lay and lawyer-judge courts. Where lawyer judges were relaxed, joining with counsel in conversation and joking between cases, most of the nonlawyers were reserved. In lawyer-judge courts I often sensed comaraderie under the veneer of deference required when counsel addresses the bench; such undercurrents were usually absent in the lay courts I visited. The lawyer judges even dressed more like practitioners than the nonlawyers did, wearing the same three-piece, expensive suits that mark lawyers unmistakably in a courtroom.

Lawyers, this discussion suggests, evaluate lay judges

through the prism of their own professional values and experience. Professionalism not only fails to provide lawyers with a neutral framework for evaluating the qualities desirable in a judge but actually makes such evaluation impossible. Lawyers reveal in the arguments they cite most often against nonlawyer judges that the professional's concern with status, authority, and colleagiality is inconsistent with adjudication by nonlawyer judges.

Professionalism and Reform from the Lay Judge's Perspective

Nonlawyer judges are highly sensitive to the arguments lawyers use against them, but much less sensitive to the ideological roots from which they spring. Nonlawyers respond to calls for their elimination, not with broadsides against professional hegemony but with points and programs designed to neutralize the specific complaints lawyers have about them. Organizations of nonlawyer judges campaign hard for more judicial training and welcome incremental improvements in law and regulations that make their courts more efficient and effective. The judges also seek to turn some of the arguments lawyers use against them in their favor. They respond to complaints about informality in nonlawyer judge courts, for example, with the suggestion that unpretentious surroundings and relaxed proceedings benefit litigants. Nonlawyer judges also cite the advantages they offer over lawyer judges, such as virtually twenty-four-hour availability for arraignments, bail decisions, and other emergency proceedings, service to the local community as ombudsmen, and "closeness" to the people they serve.[14]

Broad-gauged proposals to revamp local court systems, however, put lay judges in an awkward position. Many proposals, of course, envision the elimination of nonlawyer judges. But even those that do not explicitly ban nonlawyer judges are designed to reduce their numbers drastically. Typically, they propose consolidating low-volume courts, raising judicial pay, and mandating increased local spending on courtrooms—all changes lay judges would welcome were they not afraid that lawyers would then take over the new positions. Reformers do not disguise the fact that their object is to replace nonlawyer judges with lawyers—rather, they use this as a selling point.[15]

It should not be surprising, then, that nonlawyer judges tend to be quite skeptical about efforts to overhaul their courts. Researchers examining the impact of Iowa legislation replacing justices of the peace with a salaried, appointive bench came to appreciate this skepticism when they surveyed the nonlawyer judges displaced by the change.[16] The justices, they concluded, were "remarkably cynical about the reform."[17] Over half believed that the legislation had been designed to satisfy professional interests of the bar, not the public interest. The fact that nearly half of the new magistrates were lawyers, nearly half of whom had practiced two years or less, only confirmed their suspicions that the bar's primary interest in pushing reform had been part-time employment for struggling young attorneys and a more congenial courtroom environment for counsel.[18]

Prevailing Opinion on Lay Judges and the Rule of Law

Few except the affected judges are disturbed when a state does move to curb or eliminate its nonlawyer judges; most people, to the extent that they think about the issue at all, apparently regard such legislation as progressive. Replacing nonlawyer judges with lawyers seems to acknowledge the importance of individual rights in adjudication and the necessity of regularizing procedures and improving accountability in the lower courts. To eliminate nonlawyer judges thus counts as a step toward greater respect for litigants, particularly defendants accused of criminal violations. The enthusiasm of the American Civil Liberties Union and reform-minded legal-aid groups for the abolitionist effort only reinforces the view that nonlawyer judges stand in the way of a more responsible, rights-conscious judicial system.

This litigant-minded view of the credentials issue rests, of course, on the incorrect assumption that lay judges cannot really understand law and legal rights, that they instead refer to their own attitudes or those of the community in reaching their decisions. While lawyers adhere to the rules we enact through legislative proceedings, nonlawyer judges presumably represent public opinion in a more local, informal, and immediate sense. So stated, the choice is obvious for most Americans. We are suspicious of direct democracy in the courtroom because it runs against our constitutional tradition and our individualistic ethos. The concept of individual liberties, so important in popular attitudes about law, is necessarily countermajoritarian.

To reject direct democracy in judicial decision making is not to assert that public opinion should be irrelevant in court. The jury is a venerated American institution, and most accept its power to assert lay values to frustrate the application of legal rules under some circumstances. We are comfortable, too, with the idea that judges sometimes take public opinion into account. Many judges freely acknowledge a role for public opinion in decision making, particularly in sentencing.[19] We encourage such sensitivity to community sentiment in elective and even appointive methods for choosing our judges and in the way we shape judicial districts to follow local political boundaries in both the state and federal systems.[20] Our concept of justice in the disposition of law thus involves a balance between law and local opinion, but one which can be achieved only if judges are lawyers and, therefore, well-versed in law and its traditions.

The belief that only lawyers should be judges has grown stronger as the constitutional law of criminal procedure has become ever more extensive and as localism in criminal adjudication has become less acceptable. The informal checks a community can impose on its local judiciary no longer seem adequate to assure judicial accountability, particularly when more and more litigants are out-of-towners. As community authority has declined, we have turned increasingly to professionalism and more exacting standards of procedure to protect us against judicial excesses. To appreciate the change that has occurred, one need only recall that in 1927 the Supreme Court felt compelled to remind Ohio that its mayors' courts were part of the state judicial system, not simply agencies of local government enforcing local regulations.[21] The municipal court, the Court warned, "is not to be treated as a mere village tribunal for village peccadilloes."[22] Such a statement in a modern case is virtually inconceivable. We now routinely impose minimum standards of due process on every court that has the power to incarcerate, and, by the same token, even the lowliest judges in these courts are aware that they have the power of judicial review.

The growing tendency to supplement or supplant community controls with professional standards is evident in other areas as well. States are forsaking popular election of judges and moving toward Missouri-plan appointment systems in which practitioners and lawyer judges dominate the initial screening.[23] Bar associations also seek to influence selection itself by evaluating and ranking candidates.[24] Disciplinary bodies, a significant means of imposing accountability on judges only in recent years, have been dominated by lawyers from their inception. New York's Commission on Judicial Conduct, for example, has only two lay members on a panel of eleven.[25] Confidence in the profession's wisdom does have limits, of course. Missouri-plan selection systems include some lay persons on screening panels, and on disciplinary panels, too, a few places are usually reserved for nonlawyers. Yet it seems clear that the tension between legal and democratic control built into our judicial system increasingly favors legal, or at least professional, control.

The widespread belief that lawyers should control the delivery of justice coexists, ironically, with considerable popular hostility to lawyers as an occupational group. Antilawyer rhetoric has always been common in America, but antilawyer activism seems to be increasing. Lay persons are growing more sophisticated about challenging the monopoly lawyers enjoy on legal advising and are winning some of these battles in court. The membership of the one national lobbying group dedicated to curbing the excesses of the profession, HALT (Help Abolish Legal Tyranny), has grown to 160,000 in just over five years. Derek Bok, president of Harvard University, former president Jimmy Carter, and other influentials, have sharply criticized the legal profession. America's love/hate relationship with lawyers, however, seems to have little impact on popular attitudes toward nonlawyer judges. Cyril Sagan, an early presidential candidate in the 1984 election, did vow to ban lawyers from becoming judges, but he was taken no more seriously than a fellow candidate who would ban miscegenation.

The mass media has done nothing to enhance the image of nonlawyer judges. Journalists, in fact, are often as hostile to lay judges as lawyers are. Typically, newspaper articles on lay courts either patronize lay judges as quaint but anachronistic, or treat them as a menace, adopting the lawyer's technique of relying on specific instances of inappropriate behavior to condemn lay judges as a class.[26] Idaho governor Cecil Andrus discovered just how enthusiastically some journalists embrace the lawyer's perspective when, in 1976, he nominated a layman for a position on the state supreme court. The *Idaho Statesman,* a Boise newspaper, labeled the move "puzzling" and "strange," and other newspapers throughout the state were equally critical; bar association officials, the newspapers noted, were "shocked." The state attorney general warned, and the press seemed to agree, that "historical, legal, and practical considerations effectively preclude the nomination or appointment of a lay person as justice of the Idaho Supreme Court." Andrus at that point withdrew the nomination.[27]

Why has the legal profession been so successful in convincing the press and the laity that its interests are well-served by professionalism in adjudication? "The lay public by and large adopts the professional perspective," suggests Murray Edelman, because "its major concern is to believe that others can be trusted to handle problems

which are potentially threatening to them."[28] Historian
Burton Bledstein traces the tendency to trust professional judgment over so-called common sense to the rise
of the university in the nineteenth century, a development that brought with it increasing self-doubt among
the laity:

> The development of higher education in America
> made possible a social faith in merit, competence,
> discipline, and control that was basic to accepted
> conceptions of achievement and success. ... But
> regard for professional expertise compelled people to
> believe the voices of authority unquestioningly,
> thereby undermining self-confidence and discourag-
> ing independent evaluation. Historically speaking,
> the culture of professionalism in America has been
> enormously satisfying to the human ego, while it has
> taken an inestimable toll on the integrity of individ-
> uals.[29]

The culture of professionalism to which Bledstein refers
has had an ironic impact on policy debate over nonlawyer
judges. The professional perspective insists that all
judges have appropriate credentials and, presumably, a
professional outlook, but beyond that it offers the public
only sketchy guidance concerning limited-jurisdiction
courts and competence in a judge. Law school education
and legal tradition do not supply any answers. They
emphasize the issues that concern appellate courts. Problems that judges face in trial courts—particularly those
which handle large numbers of routine offenses—are
quite different, and legal learning, for the most part,
ignores them.

The result is that we move toward consensus that legal
credentials are necessary to adequate judicial performance in the lower courts without drawing nearer to
consensus on what these judges should be doing. Americans remain profoundly ambivalent about what they
expect from the lower courts. Our expectations and criticisms, Susan Silbey claims, tend to be contradictory:

> The lower courts are a paradox. The limited juris-
> diction courts are described as invisible, neglected by

the bar, scholars and the citizenry, and at the same time as the only judicial experience for most who enter the court system. It is repeatedly suggested that they be done away with, but at the same time it is suggested that they perform vital functions at the juncture of several official hierarchies and systems. They are applauded for being flexible and informal, and chided for failing to fulfill the forms and techniques of due process. They are recognized to be responsive to local community situations and needs and criticized for their variability. They are second class citizens in the eyes of the bar and the judiciary but constitute the majority of our trial courts and hear ninety percent of the nation's criminal cases.[30]

Mandating law school education for all lower-court judges cannot eliminate the contradictions to which Silbey refers, of course; most judges in urban areas and those with the largest caseloads are already lawyers, anyway. Requiring the remainder to be lawyers nevertheless remains appealing, even without consensus on how the lower courts should function. Clearly, ours is a credentials-oriented society. The difficulties the courts have had in determining what to do when educational requirements have a disproportionate impact on minorities, and the prevalence of pay scales pegged to degrees rather than to job performance, attest to the significance of credentials in our economic and social arrangements.[31]

The Credentials Issue Elsewhere

Credentials-consciousness and deference to professional authority are not peculiarly American phenomena, of course. Nor is political conflict over adjudication by lay persons. Practical considerations dictate the survival of nonlawyer judges in the face of professional hostility and lay indifference in many nations. This section considers lay adjudication cross-culturally: the forms it takes, the criticisms it evokes, and the political dynamic that sustains it.

Lay Adjudication: Justifications and Organization

The debate over lay participation in adjudication has displayed a remarkable consistency over time and space. The reasons Alexis de Tocqueville cited in 1835 to defend trial by jury, for example, are still cited, not just to support the jury system but to defend all types of lay participation in adjudication.[32] The arguments, political scientist John Richert discovered in an exhaustive survey of the foreign and domestic literature, are not just old, they are also rather impervious to major ideological cleavages:

> Present day advocates and critics often rely on arguments which have not changed significantly over the years and which do not differ from one country to another. More surprisingly, perhaps, is the fact that many of the arguments advanced cut across legal traditions and political ideologies. For example, the justifications for involving the public in the courts of socialist states and those of western democracies are similar.[33]

Richert discovered four common justifications for lay participation in adjudication:

1. It promises independence from executive authority because the lay decision-makers are generally not employees of the state with career aspirations in the judicial hierarchy.
2. It educates participating citizens about civic affairs and helps prepare them for self-government.
3. It helps legitimate court decisions because decision-makers represent the local community and can communicate in terms the local citizenry understands.
4. It reduces the isolation of the law from prevailing moral standards and at the same time helps prevent the routinization and cynicism which sometimes infects decision-making by full-time, law-trained judges.[34]

Nations vary, of course, in the degree to which they deem these justifications persuasive and in the extent to which they use lay participation to assist in the delivery of legal services. The forms such participation takes also vary: lay persons serve with lawyers on mixed benches, as jurors, and as judges who sit alone or together with other nonlawyers. Mixed benches are common throughout much of Europe, though responsibilities and other terms of office vary considerably from country to country. Juries as a vehicle for lay participation are much less common, only the United States remains committed to jury trial for a broad range of civil and criminal disputes. The United States is less unusual in relying on nonlawyer judges, although here, too, arrangements differ significantly from country to country. In some, nonlawyer judges serve alone, without day-to-day supervision or assistance from lawyers, as they do in the United States. In other systems, part-time or full-time professionals, usually lawyers, assist nonlawyer judges, who often sit in groups of three or more.

Systems vary too in the extent to which they use lay participation to encourage the expression of local community sentiment in case disposition and sentencing. Juries, for example, can reject law and impose their own sense of just deserts, a controversial power that has been increasingly circumscribed by judicial authority.[35] Where nonlawyers serve as judges, opportunities for the infusion of community sentiment are more varied. Audience participation may or may not be encouraged;[36] substantive law and procedural standards may or may not be clear, specific, and detailed;[37] appeal may be difficult or easy.[38] The role professionals play in the process also has an impact on the degree to which local influences will be felt. The issue is most clear-cut in Africa, where lay judges apply local customary law, while lawyers educated outside the community, and sometimes even outside the country, are much more sensitive to the applicability of state law and the desirability of creating uniform national standards.[39] Modernization, some believe, requires professionally educated judges at every level to counter divisive local and tribal influences on the administration of justice.[40]

Such differences should not obscure important similarities in the role most nonlawyer adjudicators play within their court systems. When nonlawyers serve alone as judges or on lay panels, they tend to serve on the front lines of the court structure, handling disputes between neighbors, co-workers, and family members, and sometimes awarding custody and licenses. As in the United States, petty crimes and traffic infractions often make up a substantial portion of the docket.[41] Lay authority seldom extends to civil disputes involving large amounts of money or to major crimes, unless the lay persons serve on juries or on mixed benches under the supervision of a lawyer judge.

Nor do the disputes nonlawyer judges hear alone often involve contested issues of law. Litigants at this level usually appear without counsel, and, when disputes over liability or responsibility occur, they generally involve issues of fact. Much of the time, as in the United States, the only significant decisions nonlawyer judges make involve sentencing.

Working conditions reflect the fact that the cases lay judges decide are widely regarded as routine and insignificant. Courtrooms and materials tend to be inadequate. A frequent complaint in East Germany, for example, is lack of space, secretarial help, books, and working materials.[42] The deficiencies are particularly noticeable in relation to the rest of the court system; lay courts are, in the words of one Canadian observer, "the forgotten child in our system of criminal justice."[43] Often, as in Britain and Canada, they must depend on local support for all resources. The amateur status of lay judges and their part-time service reinforces the sense of isolation from the rest of the judicial system. Typically unpaid or poorly paid, these judges serve, sometimes intermittently, for short terms. The result, of course, is that lay courts everywhere tend to be less imposing, less efficient, and less authoritative than those with full-time personnel and more adequate budgets. The situation is allowed to continue, according to one British Columbian magistrate, because the governments that lay judges serve have never taken them seriously:

> In spite of the long service of the lay judges and magistrates, I do not believe for one moment that the principle has been given a fair trial. Lay judges have been carelessly selected and given no opportunity for training. They have been grossly, in fact contemptuously, underpaid. They have had little or no access to law libraries, and have had to work in totally inadequate courtrooms, often without clerical assistance. Far too often they have had to sit without the benefit of lawyers either for the defense or for the prosecution. They have been expected to understand criminal, family and juvenile, and sometimes small claims work equally well.[44]

Nonlawyers in these positions operate under some of the same constraints teachers, welfare workers, police officers, and health workers do. They exercise broad discretion that is difficult to supervise or control administratively, yet they lack strong financial support and high status. Michael Lipsky has labeled such public officials "street-level bureaucrats," and he notes that they "chronically lack the resources to do their jobs as they are generally articulated."[45]

Criticisms of Lay Adjudication

The unimposing surroundings in which lay judges in other countries typically work and their association with large numbers of unrepresented defendants who do not contest their guilt provoke the kinds of criticism that have always been directed against lay judges in America. Lay judges are often regarded as propolice or insufficiently sensitive to defendant rights. Middle-class defendants, who usually consider themselves law-abiding citizens, are particularly likely to take this view.[46]

In nations that have responded to criticism of nonlawyer judges by requiring them to share power with lawyers, the usual result is that the lawyers dominate the judicial process, or at least exercise a disproportionate

influence over it. Sometimes, as in the mixed-bench jurisdictions discussed in Chapter 4, statutes give the lawyer
judges more power than their nonlawyer colleagues. But
lawyers exercise considerable influence even when they
ostensibly assist the lay bench. The role of the justice's
clerk in Britain, for example, has been the subject of
criticism for years. Justices' clerks, who must be lawyers,
and their assistants, who are not necessarily, manage
court routines and offer legal advice to magistrates—but
critics charge that they actually run the court.[47] Harold
Laski cited this as a problem in British lay courts nearly
half a century ago: "In any case which involves more than
common sense, they tend to be at the mercy of the clerk of
the court who acts as their technical advisor."[48]

Observations like this about the lay judge's dependence
on professional authority belie a deep sense of doubt
about the competence of nonlawyers to adjudicate. Laski,
for example, believed that "the place for the lay mind is
emphatically in the jury and not on the bench."[49] Many
British observers apparently share Laski's negative impression; the lay magistrate has fared badly in English
literature for centuries.[50] Modern-day efforts to increase
the representativeness of the bench and improve its
performance have not eliminated negative comments.
Progress in making the lay bench more representative, in
fact, has helped sharpen criticism from those concerned
about the difficult technical issues that might arise in
proceedings before nonlawyers. As one British appellate
judge complained:

> A question which the Divisional Court or Court of
> Criminal Appeal, assisted by experienced counsel,
> would have difficulty answering has to be answered
> by the retired farmer, the checkweighman and the
> school-caretaker.[51]

Lawyers everywhere, it seems, have doubts about the
competence of lay persons to adjudicate. The institutional
form that lay participation takes hardly matters. Even
the American jury, with its rather constricted role for lay
participation, provokes regular charges of incompetence

from practitioners, lawyer judges, and other observers.[52] Criticisms of nonlawyer judges on mixed tribunals are similar. Some lawyer judges complain that their nonlawyer colleagues are too emotional and are easily swayed by the histrionics of a skilled attorney; others claim that the nonlawyers are simply irrelevant in the search for intelligent decisions.[53] Where nonlawyer judges sit alone, lawyers allege that they are arbitrary and dangerously ignorant of the law.

Curiously, the lay judges who are the butt of these criticisms are usually but dimly aware of the low regard lawyers have for their contribution. Stanislaw Pomorski, for example, reports that the overwhelming majority of lay criminal-court judges in Poland

> believe that they exert substantial and beneficial influence on the verdicts by bringing them into harmony with public opinion at large. The legal profession is, on the other hand, less enthusiastic. Although the majority of legal professionals polled support the *idea* of lay participation in the administration of criminal justice, they are extremely critical of the actual implementation of the idea.[54]

Nico Roos found a similar pattern in his study of lay and professional judges on Dutch social security tribunals.[55] Like American lay judges, the Dutch judges who were not law-trained were more positive about their contributions than the lawyers who work with them.[56]

The Future of Lay Adjudication

Among those favorable to the continued participation of nonlawyers in adjudication, the call nearly everywhere is for more education. The nonlawyer adjudicators themselves seem as anxious as anyone for more training. Education for personnel ostensibly chosen because they are *not* lawyers, however, raises difficult questions. The temptation is to try to make the nonlawyers more like lawyers; indeed, criticism of lay capacities and performance is usually couched in terms of their deviation from professional standards. Yet lay persons who internalize

professional criteria for judgment lose some of the very
characteristics that rationalize their presence in the
system. Lay participants become more like experts in the
institution. A legal system, it seems clear, cannot simul-
taneously satisfy desires to represent citizen opinion on
tribunals and at the same time satisfy professional standards for performance.[57]

Accommodating lay decision makers to judicial systems
managed by lawyers is further complicated by the pressure developing in most countries to increase efficiency in
adjudication. Problems arise because training, experience in office, and full-time participation enhance efficiency in any endeavor, but they also change one's orientation to tasks. Improving lay efficiency by increasing
training periods or expanding the time commitment involved thus promises to change the character of lay
participation. Such changes also would increase the practical costs of participation for individuals, and representativeness among lay participants, already an elusive
goal, would be even harder to achieve. "The problem of
participation," as Zenon Bankowksi and Geoff Mungham
have observed "is one of managing the contradiction
between efficiency and democracy.[58]

Lawyers are not usually sensitive to these problems in
the institutionalization of lay participation. Lawyers,
foreign and domestic, emphasize rules and rule following
in adjudication, not representation, which acknowledges
limitations in the significance of law to decision making.
The legal profession's major concern with lay participation centers on its divergence from professional standards. This is a self-centered view of the issue, warns
Elizabeth Burney, who has written on lay adjudication in
England:

> It is noticeable that nearly all the demands for the
> replacement of lay by professional magistrates come
> from lawyers. What they really mean is that they
> would like magistrates to be more like them, which is
> what the rest of us on the whole wish to avoid. At
> present, we risk getting the worst of both worlds. The
> bench, already seen as an exclusive, unrepresenta-

tive set of people, is in grave danger of seeming to be cut off from the mainstream of public opinion when decisions appear to be made in terms dictated by the court professionals.[59]

Nonlawyer judges, such comments suggest, do not coexist easily in any legal system dominated by lawyers. It should not be surprising, then, that the trend nearly everywhere appears to be toward professionalization of adjudication: some nations have abolished nonlawyer judges, and most others would if they could afford to; the mixed bench survives, according to Richert, "more from sentimental and strategic reasons than from a belief that citizens contribute to a better administration of justice";[60] the jury is more available than availed of in the countries where it survives. Nor has the worldwide search for more accessible, inexpensive facilities to resolve disputes brought with it a surge of enthusiasm for adjudication by nonlawyers, though mediation by nonlawyers has found favor.[61] Adjudication by nonlawyers, on the other hand, runs counter to deepseated beliefs about courts and law in industrialized and industrializing nations.

Conclusion

In the United States, the nonlawyer remains an anachronism, a reminder of an era of highly localized administration of justice patterned on a familiar English example. Nonlawyer judges survive in the lowest reaches of the judiciary for practical and political reasons, but not because they enjoy widespread popular support. We are too committed to a view of adjudication the legal profession has helped create to be comfortable with judicial authority in one not trained as a lawyer. The tendency to assume lawyers are better equipped to be judges even infects nonlawyer judges, who are well-acquainted with limitations in the profession's vision of the judicial process.

One might conclude from the lack of enthusiasm nonlawyer judges arouse in the popular imagination that they should be abolished, even without clear evidence of their actual inferiority as decision makers. The perceived legitimacy of the judicial system is, after all, an important concern, and if litigants are convinced that only lawyers know enough law to be judges, litigants will not be satisfied with a nonlawyer judge, no matter how competent. Institutional arrangements in a democracy, it might be argued, should reflect public wants.

To eliminate nonlawyer judges, however, is to institutionalize the very self-doubts that rob the laity of political power, for the elimination of nonlawyer judges suggests the incapacity of lay persons to comprehend the rules they must live by. One could reasonably argue, as Roderick Haig-Brown has, that the law should not be so complex, that the intelligent lay mind should be able to administer the law that binds ordinary citizens, and that the abolition of lay judges represents a surrender to "the triangle of lawyer judge, lawyer prosecutor, and lawyer defense counsel" which can only make the law more incomprehensible.[62]

My evidence suggests that Haig-Brown is probably wrong in implying that nonlawyer judges tend to arrest tendencies toward complexity and remoteness in law. In America, the ultimate irony in the debate over lay judges is that lay and lawyer judges in comparable courts are not so very different. Nonlawyer judges, like other Americans, are steeped in the lawyer's version of the judicial process. Yet the broad dissemination of the profession's vision of disputes and dispute resolution—which helps explain why lay judges are so similar to their lawyer counterparts—also prevents us from appreciating their similarities.

TECHNICAL APPENDIX

Local Justice in New York State
(A Survey of Town, Village, and City-Court Judges)

*Thank you for participating in this study of the town, village, city, and district courts of New York State. Your participation is an essential step for increasing knowledge and public understanding about the workload and personnel of these important courts. Of course, **none of your answers will ever be reported or released to anyone as individual data, and your name will never be associated with the information you supply.** Thank you for your help in this study. Your participation is essential to its success.*

Your Community and Caseload

1. Approximately how many people live in your jurisdiction?
   _____ people

2. Are you the only judge in your jurisdiction?
   _____ yes
   _____ no. If no, do the decisions of law enforcement officers partly determine which judge gets which cases?
   _____ yes   _____ no

3. Approximately what is your annual caseload?
   _____ cases/year

4. Please estimate what percentage of your caseload falls into each category:
   a. motor vehicle ...._____%

191

b. civil & small claims ...._____%
c. criminal ...._____%
d. conservation ...._____%
e. other: _____%
TOTAL   100%

5. About how many hours a week do you work as a judge?
   _____ hours/week

6. Roughly how many weddings do you perform a year?
   _____ weddings/year

7. Do you have assistance, such as a court clerk, for routine
   court work?
   _____ no support staff
   _____ one part-time assistant
   _____ one full-time assistant or the equivalent in part-time
         help
   _____ more than one full-time assistant

8. Please rate the following aspects of your community:

	Very Good	Adequate	Not Quite Adequate	Seriously Deficient
a. financial support for your court	_____	_____	_____	_____
b. understanding of your role as judge	_____	_____	_____	_____
c. court-related social services	_____	_____	_____	_____

9. Do police officers prosecute any cases in your court?
   _____ no
   _____ yes. If yes, what type of cases? _____

10a. Roughly how many jury trials do you conduct a year?
    _____ jury trials/year

10b. How much time usually passes between a request for a jury
     trial and the trial?
     _____ days

11a. Roughly how often do you set bail?
     _____ times/year

11b. Does the arresting officer sometimes recommend bail?
     _____ no
     _____ yes. If yes, how often do you follow his advice?
           about _____% of the time

Adjudication and Sentencing

12. Roughly how often do you dismiss a case
    a. at arraignment? ...._____% of arraignments

b. at preliminary hearing? ...... _____% of preliminary
hearings
c. during trial? .... _____% of tried cases

13. For those offenses triable by jury, roughly how often does the prosecutor suggest a reduction after a not guilty plea?
_____% of cases triable by jury

14. What characteristics of the defendant do you consider when asked by the prosecutor to reduce a DWI charge to DWAI? (Check all that apply.)
_____ prior record of alcohol-related offenses
_____ marital status
_____ age
_____ employment status
_____ demeanor of defendant
_____ other: _____

15. In general, do you believe justice is served by plea-bargaining?
_____ yes, _____ no. Please explain: _____
_____
_____

16. In the past twenty years courts have interpreted the Constitution to require increasing attention to procedural safeguards in criminal cases. Do you think this trend has gone:
_____ much too far
_____ somewhat too far
_____ about far enough
_____ not quite far enough
_____ not nearly far enough

17. What do you usually consider in setting a speeding fine? (Check all that apply.)
_____ number of miles/hour above the legal limit
_____ defendant's age
_____ defendant's prior record (if known)
_____ whether defendant has appeared personally
_____ year and make of the car
_____ location of the offense
_____ other: _____

18. When you are deciding on a sentence in a criminal case, would you take into account the opinions of the following: (Check all that apply.)
_____ the probation report
_____ counsel in the case
_____ the arresting officer
_____ the victim

_____ family or friends of defendant
_____ other(s): _____

19. In general, how would you rate the opinions on sentencing of
     the following persons who appear in your court?

	Too Lenient	About Right	Too Harsh	No Usual Pattern
a. prosecutors	_____	_____	_____	_____
b. defense attorneys	_____	_____	_____	_____
c. probation department	_____	_____	_____	_____
d. police officers	_____	_____	_____	_____

20. Do you ever sentence a defendant to an unusual punishment
     designed especially to fit the offender or the offense, such as
     ordering a litterer to clean up a roadside?
     _____ I never have
     _____ I have a few times
     _____ I do this fairly often

21. When a defendant pleads not guilty and is later found guilty
     after a trial, do you take this into account in sentencing?
     _____ no
     _____ yes. If yes, how? _____
     _____

22. In deciding whether to jail a defendant, how important are the
     following considerations?

	Very Important	Quite Important	Of Some Importance	Of Little Importance	Not Important
a. reforming defendant	_____	_____	_____	_____	_____
b. deterring others	_____	_____	_____	_____	_____
c. punishing defendant in proportion to his crime	_____	_____	_____	_____	_____
d. keeping defendant "out of circulation"	_____	_____	_____	_____	_____

23. How often does an attorney represent at least one side in a
     small claims case?
     about _____% of small claims cases

23b. How would you describe most small claims proceedings in your
     court?
     _____ very informal

_____ somewhat informal
_____ somewhat formal
_____ quite formal

23c. In small claims, how often do you "split the difference"
between the parties?
about _____% of small claims cases

Background Information

23a. How much of your life (apart from time away for military
service and/or schooling) have you spent in the community you
serve?
_____% of my life

24b. Did your parents ever reside in this community?
_____ no
_____ yes. If yes, for how long? _____ years

24c. Do you have other relatives in this community?
_____ no
_____ yes. If yes, how many? _____ relatives here.

25. Are you active in local charitable, social, or business
organizations?
_____ no
_____ yes. If yes, in what organizations are you an active
participant?

Organization	Years Involved

26. Did you ever hold public office before becoming a judge?
_____ no
_____ yes. If yes, what office(s)? _____

27a. How often are you acquainted with the criminal defendants
that appear before you?
about _____% of criminal defendants

27b. How often are you acquainted with the civil plaintiffs that sue
in your court?
about _____% of civil plaintiffs

28. How often do members of your community try to consult you
informally about legal matters other than pending cases?
_____ very often
_____ quite often
_____ occasionally
_____ rarely

29. How many years have you been a judge?
_____ years

30. Do you have another occupation(s) in addition to being a judge?
_____ no. If no, your occupation before becoming a judge? (If retired, your occupation before retirement.)

_____

_____ yes. If yes, your occupation? _____

31a. What is your annual judicial salary? $_____/year

31b. Roughly what percentage of your total family income comes from your judicial salary?
_____% of total family income

32. Are you
a. _____ married   _____ unmarried
b. _____ a veteran   _____ non-veteran
c. _____ male   _____ female

33. Your age? _____ years

34. How many children do you have? _____ children

35. How many years of education do you have? _____ years (High school graduate = 12 years)

36. In New York, some judges at this level in the judicial system are attorneys. Do you believe there are significant differences between attorney and nonattorney judges?
_____ yes   _____ no. Please explain: _____

_____

_____

37. Finally, do you enjoy being a judge?
_____ on the whole, yes   _____ no. Please explain: _____

_____

_____

**THANK YOU VERY MUCH FOR YOUR COOPERATION
IN COMPLETING THIS QUESTIONNAIRE**

Additional questions for lawyer-respondants to the local-court survey:
(Item no. 35 on nonlawyer questionnaire [years of education] omitted.)

35. How long have you practiced law?
    _____ years

36. Have you previously held another position(s) in the court system?
    _____ no
    _____ yes. If yes, what position(s)? _____

37. Could a judgeship like yours be an important stepping stone in an attorney's career?
    _____ definitely no
    _____ probably no
    _____ perhaps
    _____ probably yes
    _____ definitely yes

**Nonlawyer Interviewees Compared to
Nonlawyer Survey Respondents**

Selected Characteristics	Mean	(N)[a]	Standard Deviation	Probability
Population in district:				
Interviewee	11,538	13	15,688	.1224
Survey	4,304	1,142	5,575	
Annual caseload:				
Interviewee	1,965	13	1,414	.0075
Survey	706	1,143	1,054	
% criminal cases:				
Interviewee	14.54	13	9.72	.9746
Survey	14.45	1,188	11.50	
Work hours per week:				
Interviewee	23.23	13	12.80	.0117
Survey	12.68	1,193	9.24	
Assistance:				
Interviewee	2.15	13	1.07	.0667
Survey	1.55	1,203	.77	
% judge's life in community:				
Interviewee	76.15	13	30.63	.1858
Survey	64.18	1,181	31.20	
% defendants acquainted with:				
Interviewee	29.31	13	25.88	.6573
Survey	32.59	1,177	27.83	

[a]All thirteen interviewees responded to the survey, compared to 74 percent of nonlawyer justices overall.

Lawyer Interviewees Compared to Lawyer Survey Respondants

Selected Characteristics	Mean	(N)[a]	Standard Deviation	Probability
Population in district:				
Interviewee	33,500	6	13,111	.0367
Survey	18,393	305	16,650	
Annual caseload:				
Interviewee	2,917	6	1,563	.8072
Survey	3,087	264	3,243	
% criminal cases:				
Interviewee	16.43	7	18.19	.4791
Survey	21.67	295	19.62	
Work hours per week:				
Interviewee	26.43	7	14.35	.0577
Survey	13.71	292	11.56	
Assistance:				
Interviewee	3.29	7	.95	.5013
Survey	3.03	308	1.01	
% judge's life in community:				
Interviewee	74.29	7	30.06	.2746
Survey	60.51	305	32.99	
% defendants acquainted with:				
Interviewee	19.67	6	34.96	.6652
Survey	13.10	280	16.83	

[a]Seven of thirteen lawyer interviewees responded to the survey, the source of all information in this table. The proportion among lawyers overall was about the same, 58 percent.

NOTES

Introduction

1. Everett C. Hughes, "Professions," in Kenneth Lynn, ed., *The Professions in America* (Boston: Houghton Mifflin, 1965), pp. 1–14, esp. p. 3.

Chapter 1

1. Richard B. Morris, "Legalism versus Revolutionary Doctrine in New England," *New England Quarterly* (April 1931): 196.

2. George Lee Haskins, "The Sorts and Conditions of Men," in *Law and Authority in Early Massachusetts* (New York: Macmillan, 1960), chap. 7; Anton-Hermann Chroust, *The Rise of the Legal Profession in America* (Norman: University of Oklahoma Press, 1965), 1:22–23; Erwin C. Surrency, "The Courts in the American Colonies," *American Journal of Legal History* 11 (1967): 258–59.

3. Surrency, pp. 260–61; Corinne Gilb, *Hidden Hierarchies: The Professions and Government* (New York: Harper & Row, 1966), pp. 9–10; Mark de Wolfe Howe and Louis F. Eaton, Jr., "The Supreme Judicial Power in the Colony of Massachusetts Bay," *New England Quarterly* (September 1947): 291–316.

4. Stephen Botein, "The Legal Profession in Colonial North America," in Wilfred Prest, ed., *Lawyers in Early Modern Europe and America* (New York: Holmes & Meier, 1981), p. 131; Lawrence Friedman, *A History of American Law* (New York: Simon & Schuster, 1973), p. 36. On the similarities of court systems throughout the colonies, see Friedman,

p. 40. See also William E. Nelson, *Dispute and Conflict Resolution in Plymouth County, Massachusetts, 1725–1825* (Chapel Hill: University of North Carolina Press, 1981), pp. 22–25.

5. To the same effect, see Michael G. Kammen, "Colonial Court Records and the Study of Early American History: A Bibliographical Review," *American Historical Review* 70 (1965): 739; and see generally, Russell K. Osgood, "John Clark, Esq., Justice of the Peace" (Ithaca, N.Y., 1981, Mimeographed); and Nelson.

6. Joseph H. Smith, ed., *Colonial Justice in Western Massachusetts (1639–1702): The Pynchon Court Record* (Cambridge, Mass.: Harvard University Press, 1961), pp. 197–98.

7. Francis R. Aumann, *The Changing American Legal System* (Columbus: Ohio State University Press, 1940), p. 36; for a similar observation from a contemporary scholar see Friedman, pp. 50–51.

8. Haskins, pp. 114–15; and Joseph H. Smith, "Administrative Control of the Courts of the American Plantations," in David A. Flaherty, ed., *Essays in the History of Early American Law* (Chapel Hill: University of North Carolina Press, 1969), pp. 284–85.

9. Larry M. Boyer, "The Justice of the Peace in England and America from 1506 to 1776," *Quarterly Journal of the Library of Congress* (October 1977): 323–25; and Aumann, pp. 36–37.

10. Quoted in Daniel Boorstin, *The Americans: The Colonial Experience* (New York: Random House, 1958), p. 189. William Byrd lived from 1674–1744.

11. John M. Murrin, "The Legal Transformation: The Bench and Bar of Eighteenth-Century Massachusetts," in Stanley N. Katz, ed., *Colonial America* (Boston: Little, Brown, 1971), pp. 417–19; Haskins, pp. 186–87; Friedman, pp. 81–83.

12. Gerard W. Gawalt, *The Promise of Power: The Emergence of the Legal Profession in Massachusetts, 1760–1840* (Westport, Conn.: Westport, 1979), p. 16; and Charles Warren, *A History of the American Bar* (Boston: Little, Brown, 1911), pp. 4–8, 128–29.

13. Gabriel Thomas (1698) quoted in Milton Klein, "New York Lawyers and the Coming of the American Revolution," in Leo Hershkowitz and Milton Klein, eds., *Courts and Law in Early New York* (Port Washington, N.Y.: Kennikat, 1974), p. 94.

14. F. W. Grinnell, "The Bench and Bar in Colony and Province (1630–1776)," in Albert B. Hart, ed., *Commonwealth History of Massachusetts* (New York: Russell & Russell, 1966), 2:161–62; David T. Konig, *Law and Society in Puritan Massachusetts* (Chapel Hill: University of North Carolina Press, 1979), p. 140; Murrin, pp. 420–21; George E. Woodbine, "The Suffolk County Court, 1671–1680," in Flaherty, ed., pp. 94–95.

15. Surrency, pp. 256–57.

16. Botein, p. 134.

17. Ibid. See also Friedman, pp. 85–86.

18. Julius Goebel, Jr., "The Courts and Law in Colonial New York," in Flaherty, ed., pp. 270–71.

19. Alan F. Day, "Lawyers in Colonial Maryland, 1660–1715," *American Journal of Legal History* 17 (1973): 145–65; Alfred Z. Reed, *Training for the Public Profession of the Law* (New York: Carnegie Foundation, 1921), p. 36.

20. Gawalt, p. 16; Robert Stevens, "Two Cheers for 1870: The American Law School," in Donald Fleming and Bernard Bailyn, eds., *Perspectives in American History* (Cambridge, Mass.: Harvard University Press, 1971), 5:409; Warren, pp. 16–18; Jackson T. Main, *The Social Structure of Revolutionary America* (Princeton, N.J.: Princeton University Press, 1965), pp. 101–2, 146–47.

21. Murrin, p. 430.

22. Stevens, pp. 412–13; Gerard W. Gawalt, "Massachusetts Legal Education in Transition," *American Journal of Legal History* 17 (1973): 27–50; Gary B. Nash, "The Philadelphia Bench and Bar, 1800–61," *Comparative Studies in Society and History* 7 (1964–65): pp. 204–8.

23. Botein, pp. 134–35.

24. Grinnell, pp. 173–83.

25. Murrin, pp. 435–37.

26. Botein, p. 135.

27. Murrin, p. 437.

28. A. G. Roeber, *Faithful Magistrates and Republican Lawyers* (Chapel Hill: University of North Carolina Press, 1981), pp. 133–34.

29. Friedman, p. 51. He also develops this argument on pp. 49–50 and 109–10.

30. Morris, pp. 207–8. See also Botein, p. 142.

31. On rural urban differences among lawyers, see Main, pp. 146–47; and Murrin, pp. 429–30.

32. These are the words of Henry Clay (1777–1852) quoted in Charles M. Haar, ed., *The Golden Age of American Law* (New York: Braziller, 1965), p. 42.

33. Hector St. John de Crevecoeur, *Letters from an American Farmer*, quoted in Richard E. Ellis, *The Jeffersonian Crisis: Courts and Politics in the Young Republic* (New York: Oxford University Press, 1971), p. 113. See also Gerard W. Gawalt, "Sources of Anti-Lawyer Sentiment in Massachusetts, 1740–1840," *American Journal of Legal History* 14 (1970): 283–307; and James P. Whittenburg, "Planters, Merchants, and Lawyers: Social Change and the Origins of the North Carolina Regulation," *William and Mary Quarterly* 34 (1977): 215–38; and Pound, on clerical opposition to lawyers.

34. Grinnell, pp. 81–82; Morris, pp. 426–28; Chroust, 2:5–11.

35. Main, p. 204.

36. Gawalt, *The Promise*, p. 36. See also Gerard W. Gawalt, "Sources of Anti-Lawyer Sentiment in Massachusetts, 1740–1840," *American Journal of Legal History* 14 (1970):283–307.

37. Morris; Gawalt, "Sources"; and Richard E. Ellis, *The Jefferson-*

ian Crisis: Courts and Politics in the Young Republic (New York: Oxford University Press, 1971), p. 112. See also Maxwell Bloomfield, *American Lawyers in a Changing Society, 1776–1836* (Cambridge, Mass.: Harvard University Press, 1976), chap. 2.

38. Warren, p. 221; Klein, p. 89.

39. Boorstin, p. 205.

40. Murrin, pp. 442–43.

41. Klein, pp. 94–95.

42. Roeber, pp. 147–49; and Gawalt, "Potent Politicians" (Washington, D.C., Mimeographed, earlier draft of *The Promise*), pp. 275–76.

43. Richard B. Morris, "The Legal Profession in America on the Eve of the Revolution," in Harry W. Jones, ed., *Political Separation and Legal Continuity* (Chicago: American Bar Association, 1976), p. 23.

44. Gawalt, "Potent Politicians," p. 279.

45. Gawalt, *The Promise*, p. 412.

46. Ibid., table 3, p. 40.

47. Gawalt, "Potent Politicians," p. 281. See also pp. 301–2; and Elizabeth Gasper Brown, "The Bar on the Frontier: Wayne County, 1796–1836," *American Journal of Legal History* 14 (1970): 137–56.

48. Roeber, p. 202.

49. Chroust, 2:42–43.

50. Warren, pp. 134–43; Friedman, pp. 109–10; Roeber, pp. 258–59; Aumann, pp. 34–40; and Kermit L. Hall, *The Politics of Justice: Lower Federal Court Selection and the Second Party System, 1829–61* (Lincoln: University of Nebraska Press, 1979), p. 158.

51. Chroust, 1:26–28.

52. Gary B. Nash, "The Philadelphia Bench and Bar, 1800–61," *Comparative Studies in Society and History* 7 (1964–65): 210–11; and Roeber, pp. 231–35.

53. On the tendency for lawyers to exploit antilawyer sentiment see Albert P. Melone, "Lawyer-Dominance Proposition: The Need for Additional Research," *Western Political Quarterly* 33 (1980): pp. 225–32.

54. Gawalt, *The Promise*, p. 105; and Ellis, pp. 199–203. On the background of this idea see Bloomfield, chap. 2.

55. Gawalt, *The Promise*, p. 105; and Ellis, pp. 111–22.

56. Ellis, p. 121.

57. Gawalt, "Potent Politicians"; and Roeber.

58. Ellis, p. 255. See also Roscoe Pound, "The Law Tradition as to the Lawyer," *Michigan Law Review* 12 (1914): 627–38, on the traditional conflict between clergy and bar in America.

59. Ellis, pp. 155–56.

60. Ibid., p. 164.

61. Nash, p. 211.

62. E.g., Roeber, pp. 256–61.

63. Gawalt, *The Promise*, pp. 168–97; and on the analogous attitude of legal and commercial interests toward juries see Morton Horwitz, *The Transformation of American Law* (Cambridge, Mass.: Harvard Univer-

sity Press, 1977), pp. 84–85, 141–43, 154–55.

64. Maxwell Bloomfield, "Law versus Politics: The Self-Image of the American Bar (1830–1860)," *American Journal of Legal History* 12 (1968): 306–23; Chroust, 2:69–72; and Ellis, p. 249.

65. Burton J. Bledstein, *The Culture of Professionalism* (New York: Norton, 1976), pp. 185–86. See also W. Raymond Blackard, "The Democratization of the Legal Profession in Nineteenth-Century America," *Tennessee Law Review* 16 (1940): 314–23; and Friedman, pp. 276–78. See also Gilb, p. 13; and James Willard Hurst, *The Growth of American Law* (Boston: Little, Brown, 1950), pp. 250–55, on the social class structure of the bar.

66. Terence Johnson, *Professions and Power* (London: Macmillan, 1972), p. 43. See also Daniel H. Calhoun, *Professional Lives in America* (Cambridge, Mass.: Harvard University Press, 1965), pp. 179–82; and more generally, Joan Jacobs Brumberg and Nancy Tomes, "Women in the Professions: A Research Agenda for American Historians," *Reviews in American History* (June 1982): 288; and Magali Sarfatti Larson, *The Rise of Professionalism: A Sociological Analysis* (Berkeley: University of California Press, 1977), pp. 124, 133; and Gawalt, *The Promise,* pp. 185–88.

67. Friedman, p. 278.

68. On the demise of strict educational requirements in this period see Gawalt, "Massachusetts Legal Education in Transition," *American Journal of Legal History* 17 (1973): 27–50; Stevens; and Reed.

69. Bloomfield, "Law versus Politics," p. 306.

70. Nelson; and see Friedman, p. 110, on the dangers of taking lawyer historians too seriously about the incompetence of lay judges.

71. Frank H. Miller, "Legal Qualifications for Office," *Annual Report of the American History Association* 1 (1899): 133–35.

72. Many have discussed the connection between lawyers and politics. Joseph A. Schlesinger reviews some of this literature in "Lawyers and American Politics: A Clarified View," *Midwest Journal of Political Science* 1 (1957): 26–39. More recently see Melone; and Mogens N. Pedersen, "Lawyers in Politics: The Danish Falketing and U.S. Legislatures," in Samuel C. Patterson and John C. Wahlke, eds., *Comparative Legislative Behavior: Frontiers of Research* (New York: Wiley, 1972), pp. 25–63. See also Heinz Eulau and John D. Sprague, *Lawyers in Politics: A Study in Professional Convergence* (Indianapolis: Bobbs-Merrill, 1964); and, for a historian's perspective, William Francis English, "The Pioneer Lawyer and Jurist in Missouri," *University of Missouri Studies* 21, no. 2 (1947); and Hurst, p. 352.

73. Alexis de Tocqueville, *Democracy in America* (New York: Vintage, 1945), 1:290.

74. Goebel, p. 270.

75. Gordon S. Wood, *The Creation of the American Republic, 1776–1787* (New York: Norton, 1969), pp. 12–13, 299–300; Goebel, p. 273; and Morton Horwitz, "The Emergence of an Instrumental Conception of

American Law, 1780–1820," in Fleming and Bailyn, eds., pp. 291–98.

76. Chroust, 2:56–79.

77. Perry Miller, *The Life of the Mind in America* (New York: Harcourt, Brace & World, 1965), p. 119.

78. Horwitz, "The Emergence," p. 326.

79. Wood, pp. 160–61.

80. Ibid., pp. 152–60.

81. Ibid., pp. 302–5.

82. Peter G. Fish, *The Politics of Judicial Administration* (Princeton, N.J.: Princeton University Press, 1973), p. 428.

83. Roeber, p. 259.

84. Keith H. Cox, "Lawyers, Population, and Society in New York," Bulletin no. 86 of the Cornell Rural Sociology Series, August 1977. On the survival of the colonial pattern discussed earlier through the nineteenth century see Gerard Gawalt, "Professional Diversity: The Impact of Industrialization on the Legal Profession in the Nineteenth Century" (paper delivered at the annual meeting of the American Studies Association, Memphis, Tenn., 1981).

85. Max Weber, *Law in Economy and Society* (Cambridge, Mass.: Harvard University Press, 1954), p. 321.

Chapter 2

1. See Linda Silberman et. al., *Non-Attorney Justice in the United States: An Empirical Study* (New York: Institute of Judicial Administration, 1979), appendix B, pp. 261–83.

2. The most obvious exception to this generalization is Vermont, where nonlawyers serve on "mixed benches" composed of two (lay) assistant judges and one (lawyer) presiding judge. These lay-lawyer courts have considerable civil jurisdiction, hear even the most serious criminal cases, and decide some appeals. The all-lawyer Vermont Supreme Court, however, has construed the authority of the assistant judges quite narrowly (see Chapter 3, p. 78).

3. John P. Dawson, *A History of Lay Judges* (Cambridge, Mass.: Harvard University Press, 1960), pp. 142–44 and 296. See also R. M. Jackson, *The Machinery of Justice in England* (Cambridge: Cambridge University Press, 1966), chap. 3, pt. 6.

4. Dawson, p. 297.

5. For a detailed account of the work of modern justices of the peace in England see Elizabeth Burney, *Magistrate, Court, and Community* (London: Hutchinson, 1979).

6. Chester Smith, "Justice of the Peace," *Encyclopedia of the Social Sciences* (1932), 8:524; and Isham G. Newton, "The Justice of the Peace—an American Dilemma," *Social Sciences* 34 (1959): 98.

7. Edwin C. Surrency, "The Courts in the American Colonies," *American Journal of Legal History* 11 (1967): 349–50.

8. Julius Goebel, Jr., and Raymond Naughton, *Law Enforcement in Colonial New York* (New York: Commonwealth Fund, 1944). See also Elizabeth Gasper Brown, "Frontier Justice: Wayne County," *American Journal of Legal History* 16 (1972): 126–53; Russell K. Osgood. "John Clark, Esq., Justice of the Peace," (Ithaca, N.Y., 1981, Mimeographed). More generally, see William E. Nelson, *The Americanization of the Common Law* (Cambridge, Mass.: Harvard University Press, 1975); Lawrence M. Friedman, *A History of American Law* (New York: Simon & Schuster, 1973) p. 110.

9. Goebel and Naughton, p. 136.

10. William Francis English, "The Pioneer Lawyer and Jurist in Missouri," *University of Missouri Studies* 21, no. 2 (1947); Charles A. Shinn, *Mining Camps: A Study in American Frontier Government* (New York: Knopf, 1948), chap. 16; John R. Wunder, *Inferior Courts, Superior Justice: A History of the Justice of the Peace on the Northwest Frontier* (Westport, Conn.: Greenwood, 1979); Ruth Y. Wetmore, "The Justice of the Peace in Kansas," University of Kansas Publications, no. 21 (Lawrence, Kans.: Governmental Research Center, 1960); Paul F. Douglass, *The Justice of the Peace Courts of Hamilton County, Ohio* (Baltimore: Johns Hopkins Press, 1932), chap. 2.

11. James Willard Hurst, *The Growth of American Law* (Boston: Little, Brown, 1950), pp. 147–48; Robert S. Keebler, "Our Justice of the Peace Courts—a Problem in Justice," *Tennessee Law Review* 9 (1930): 1–21; George Warren, *Traffic Courts* (Boston: Little, Brown, 1942), p. 188; and Bruce Smith, *Rural Crime Control* (New York: Institute of Public Administration, 1933), pp. 229–31.

12. Wunder, p. 117; Friedman, p. 146, on the impact of judicial election generally see p. 323; see also Brown, "Frontier Justice." It should be noted too that lawyers were not particularly well-educated in this period, often beginning practice after the briefest of clerkships. Friedman, pp. 278–82.

13. Alexis de Tocqueville, *Democracy in America* (New York: Knopf, 1945), 1:77.

14. Robert M. Ireland, "The Place of the Justice of the Peace in the Legislature and Party System of Kentucky," *American Journal of Legal History* 13 (1969): 202–22.

15. Shinn.

16. Hurst, pp. 93–96; Wickersham Commission, "Petty Offenses and Inferior Courts" (1931 Report on Criminal Procedure), reprinted in John A. Robertson, ed., *Rough Justice: Perspectives on Lower Criminal Courts* (Boston: Little, Brown, 1974), p. 6.

17. See Hurst, pp. 150–51; and Christine B. Harrington, "Delegalization Reform Movements: A Historical Analysis," in Richard L. Abel, ed., *The Politics of Informal Justice* (New York: Academic Press, 1982), 1:49. On the gradual undoing of these early reforms see Hurst, p. 93.

18. Burton J. Bledstein, *The Culture of Professionalism* (New York: Norton, 1978), chap. 3; see also Gawalt, "Professional Diversity: The

Impact of Industrialization on the Legal Professions in the Nineteenth Century"; and Magali Sarfatti Larson, *The Rise of Professionalism* (Berkeley: University of California Press, 1977), pp. 170–71.

19. Roscoe Pound, "The Causes of Popular Dissatisfaction With the Administration of Justice" (paper delivered at the annual convention of the American Bar Association, 1906). On Pound's attitude toward court reform see David Wigdor, *Roscoe Pound: Philosopher of Law* (Westport, Conn.: Greenwood, 1974). More generally see Larry Berkson, "A Brief History of Court Reform," in Berkson et al., *Managing the State Courts* (St. Paul: West, 1977).

20. See Herbert Harley, "Concerning the American Judicature Society," *Journal of the American Judicature Society* (now *Judicature*) 20 (1936): 9–12.

21. See Russell R. Wheeler and Howard R. Whitcomb, *Judicial Administration* (Englewood Cliffs, N.J.: Prentice-Hall, 1977), pp. 28–30 and 49–55; Peter G. Fish, *The Politics of Judicial Administration* (Princeton, N.J.: Princeton University Press, 1973); Larson, p. 138; Harrington, pp. 44 ff.

22. Chester Smith, "The Justice of the Peace System in the United States," *California Law Review* 15 (1927): 124.

23. *Index to Occupations, Alphabetical and Classified* (Washington, D.C.: Department of Commerce, Bureau of the Census, 1915), p. 15.

24. J. M. Levine quoted in W. F. Willoughby, *Principles of Judicial Administration* (Washington, D.C.: Brookings Institute, 1929), p. 302. See also Wickersham Commission; Austin W. Scott, "Small Claims and Poor Litigants," *American Bar Association Journal* 9 (1923): 457–59; Reginald Heber Smith, "Denial of Justice," *Judicature* 3 (1919): 12–26; Milton Strasburger, "A Plea for the Reform of the Inferior Court," *Case and Comment* 22 (1915–16): 20–24; and Simeon Baldwin and Clarence N. Callender quoted in Silberman, pp. 339–40.

25. Willoughby, pp. 302, 304.

26. Charles Evans Hughes quoted in Robertson, p. vii. See also Wickersham Commission, pp. 3–4; Warren, pp. 9–10; Douglass, p. v; and, more recently, Harry W. Jones, ed., *The Courts, The Public and the Law Explosion* (Englewood Cliffs, N.J.: Prentice-Hall, 1968), p. 125; and Byron W. Daynes, *An Assessment of Courts of Limited Jurisdiction*, Report no. 23 (Chicago: American Judicature Society, September 1968).

27. Reginald Heber Smith, p. 115. See also Harrington, p. 55; and Keebler, p. 5.

28. Keebler, p. 4.

29. Hurst, chap. 8.

30. Tumey v. Ohio, 273 U.S. 510 (1927).

31. See Institute of Judicial Administration, *The Justice of the Peace Today* (New York: Institute of Judicial Administration, 1965), p. 4.

32. E.g., Dugan v. Ohio, 277 U.S. 61 (1928), and at the state level Tari v. State, 117 O.S. 481, 159 N.E. 594, State v. Schelton, 205 Ind. 416 (1933), and Ex Parte Lewis, 47 Okla. Crim. 72 (1930). For one state's experience

see James A. Gazell, "A National Perspective on Justices of the Peace and Their Future: Time for an Epitaph?" *Mississippi Law Journal* 46 (1975): pp. 806–7.

33. Wm. J. Blackburn, *The Administration of Criminal Justice in Franklin County Ohio* (Baltimore: Johns Hopkins University Press, 1935), p. 145.

34. See Bruce Smith, pp. 243–44, where he argues that *Tumey* might encourage an all-salaried or all-volunteer lower-court bench, changes Smith regarded as highly desirable.

35. Tumey v. Ohio, p. 532.

36. See, e.g., Edson R. Sunderland, "A Study of Justices of the Peace and Other Minor Courts," *Connecticut Bar Journal* 20–21 (1946–47): 300–344.

37. Bellamy Partidge, *Country Lawyer* (Albany: Charles Evans Hughes Press, 1939), pp. 24–27, 29–31, 113–23, 273–75.

38. See Roscoe Pound's "The Administration of Justice in the Modern City," *Harvard Law Review* 26 (1912–13). See also Keebler, p. 11.

39. Pound, p. 312. On the persistence of this difference in enthusiasm for reform see Henry R. Glick and Kenneth N. Vines, *State Court Systems* (Englewood Cliffs, N.J.: Prentice-Hall, 1973), p. 17.

40. Silberman et. al., p. 340.

41. Institute of Judicial Administration, p. 13. See also Louis A. Kohn, "Modern Courts for Illinois," *Journal of the American Judicature Society* (now *Judicature*) 42 (1953); Warren, pp. 228–31; Hurst, pp. 89–92.

42. Chester Smith; Reginald Heber Smith; Hurst, p. 164.

43. T. L. Howard, "The Justice of the Peace System in Tennessee," *Tennessee Law Review* 13 (1934): 19.

44. Chester Smith, p. 134; see also Edwin R. Sunderland, "The Efficiency of Justices' Courts in Michigan," 4th Report, Judicial Council of Michigan, 1934, p. 208.

45. Chester Smith, p. 134. See also Keebler.

46. Keebler, pp. 11–12. On tolerance and even favor toward informality see Harrington, pp. 36, 45–46, and 50–57.

47. Howard, p. 19.

48. Ibid.

49. Ibid.

50. Douglass; Blackburn; H. K. Allen, "Administration of Minor Justice in Selected Illinois Counties," *Illinois Law Review* (now *Northwestern Law Review*) 31 (1937): 1047–55. On rural justice courts as a whole see Bruce Smith, chap. 7; and on traffic courts generally see Warren. Writing later but in much the same tradition see Wetmore; and Isham G. Newton.

51. Douglass, p. 57; see also Blackburn, p. 154.

52. Warren, pp. 203–4.

53. See, e.g., Douglass, pp. 24–25; Blackburn, p. 149.

54. Allen. See also Warren, pp. 208–9; Hurst, pp. 164–65; Blackburn, pp. 242–43.

55. See Bruce Smith, pp. 253–56; and Douglass, chap. 4.

56. Bruce Smith, p. 256; Douglass, p. 38.

57. Keebler, p. 11, and more recently see W.R.F. II, "The Justice of the Peace in Virginia: A Neglected Aspect of the Judiciary," *Virginia Law Review* 52 (1966): 158; Karan Knab, ed., *Courts of Limited Jurisdiction: A National Survey* (Washington, D.C.: National Institute of Law Enforcement and Criminal Justice, 1977), p. v; Lee Silverstein, "Small Claims Courts versus Justices of the Peace," *West Virginia Law Review* 58 (1955–56): p. 243.

58. Allen. See also Warren, pp. 210–11; and Howard.

59. Bruce Smith, p. 243.

60. Douglass, p. 51.

61. Bruce Smith, p. 246; and see Allen on the occupations of Illinois judges.

62. Blackburn, p. 148.

63. Keebler, p. 12. For remarks to the same effect but somewhat later, see, e.g., Arthur T. Vanderbilt, *The Challenge of Law Reform* (Princeton, N.J.: Princeton University Press, 1955), chap. 1.

64. Warren, p. 89. See also pp. 93–94.

65. Keebler; Newton; Silverstein; Bruce Smith, pp. 257–59; and Warren, pp. 192–97.

66. See also Warren, p. 237.

67. Wickersham Commission, p. 7.

68. Bruce Smith, pp. 260–61.

69. "Foreword, Reports of the Section of Judicial Administration," reprinted as Appendix A in American Bar Association, p. 143.

70. Keebler, p. 21. See also Kohn.

71. Wheeler and Whitcomb, pp. 80–82; Harrington, p. 48; Mary Volcansek, "Conventional Wisdom of Court Reform," in Berkson et al., pp. 18–23. Disagreement has emerged, however, on the degree to which courts should be centralized or "unified." See e.g. G. Alan Tarr, "Court Unification and Court Performance," *Judicature* 64 (1981): 356–68; Josef M. Broder et al., "The Hidden Consequences of Court Unification," *Judicature* 65 (1981): 10–17; and Larry Berkson and Susan Carbon, *Court Unification: History Politics and Implementation* (Washington, D.C.: National Institute of Law Enforcement and Criminal Justice, 1978).

72. On the continuing problems of limited jurisdiction courts generally see Wheeler and Whitcomb, pp. 80–82. For frequently cited condemnations of the justice of the peace in particular, see Kenneth E. VanLandingham, "The Decline of the Justice of the Peace," *Kansas Law Review* 12 (1964): 389–403; and Institute of Judicial Administration, p. 2.

73. Such proposals are described in Carl McGowan, "The Shape of Reform: Drafting the Court Organization Standards," in Wheeler and Whitcomb, pp. 65–69; Berkson et al., pp. 8–16; Knab, pp. vii–ix; Gazell, pp. 800–801; and see American Bar Association, *The Improvement of the Administration of Justice* (Chicago: ABA, 1971); and National Advisory Commission on Criminal Justice Standards and Goals, *Courts* (Wash-

ington, D.C.: NACCJSG, 1973), p. 162; Advisory Commission on Intergovernmental Relations, "For a More Perfect Union ... Court Reform" (1971).

74. See, e.g., Roman Tomasic and Malcolm M. Feeley, *Neighborhood Justice: Assessment of an Emerging Idea* (New York: Longman, 1982); and Benedict S. Alper and Lawrence T. Nichols, *Beyond the Courtroom* (Lexington, Mass.: Lexington, 1981); and Abel, vols. 1 and 2.

75. President's Commission on Law Enforcement and the Administration of Justice, *The Courts*, Task Force Report (Washington, D.C.: Government Printing Office, 1967).

76. Ibid., p. 36.

77. All of these quotations appear on p. 35 of the commission report. The inadequacy of these remarks as support for major policy recommendations is noted by Jack M. Kress and Sandra L. Stanley in *Justice Courts in the State of New York* (Albany: Association of Magistrates, 1976), p. 47.

78. See, e.g., VanLandingham; Allan Ashman and Pat Chapin, "Is the Bell Tolling for Nonlawyer Judges?" *Judicature* 59 (1976): 417–21; Zitah Wein-Shienk, "Limited and Special Jurisdiction," and Thomas M. Pomeroy, "Lingering Problem: Part-Time Courts," both in *Justice in the States* (Washington, D.C.: Department of Justice, 1971), pp. 125–30 and 130–39.

79. Kress and Stanley, p. 6.

80. Jon P. McConnell, "Some Trials of the Magistrate," *American Bar Association Journal* 54 (1968): 37.

81. Harry O. Lawson, "Commentary on the Process of Change," *Arizona State Law Journal* (1974): 629–30.

82. Sunderland, p. 326. See also Wetmore, pp. 9–10; and VanLandingham.

83. Paul E. Dow, *Discretionary Justice: A Critical Inquiry* (Cambridge, Mass.: Ballinger, 1981), p. 196. For the earlier epithets cited see p. 271.

84. Wesley Uhlmann, "Justifying Justice Courts," *Judicature* 52 (1968): pp. 22–26; Herbert S. MacDonald, "An Obituary Note on the Connecticut Justice of the Peace," *Connecticut Bar Journal* 35 (1961): 429; Allen Levinthal, "Minor Courts—Major Problems," *Journal of the American Judicature Society* 48 (1965): 188–92; Mildred J. Giese, "Why Illinois Proposes to Abolish Justice of the Peace," *Illinois Bar Journal* 46 (1958): pp. 754–813.

85. Ronald C. LaFace and Thomas G. Schultz, "The Justice of the Peace Court in Florida," *University of Florida Law Review* 18 (1965): 118. For other examples of such reasoning see Ronald J. Dolan and William B. Fenton, "The Justice of the Peace of Nebraska," *Nebraska Law Review* 48 (1969): 457–87; Knab, ed.; Anne C. Reppert, "Criminal Procedure ... Justice of the Peace Court—Increased Penalty upon Trial de Novo," *West Virginia Law Review* 75 (1972–73): 372–81; Gary L. Rosenthal, "The Right to a Legally-Trained Judge," *Harvard Civil*

Rights—Civil Liberties Law Review 10 (1975): 739–71; Lynda D. Nelson, "Gordon v. Justice Court," *Hastings Constitutional Law Quarterly* 2 (1975): 1177–1206; and James M. Coughlin, "The Constitutionality of Non-Attorney Judge Statutes," *Boston University Law Review* 55 (1975): 827–46.

86. F. S. Le Clercq, "The Constitutional Policy That Judges Be Learned in the Law," *Tennessee Law Review* 47 (1980): 737.

87. Jones, ed., pp. 143–44.

88. C.B.S., "Limiting Judicial Incompetence: The Due Process Right to a Legally-Learned Judge in State Minor Criminal Court Proceedings," *Virginia Law Review* 61 (1975): 1469.

89. This argument has its roots in the early campaign against justices of the peace. Chester Smith, e.g., claimed that when a decision comes up that may affect the justice's own social position, he "immediately begins balancing . . . his own interests with those to be affected" (p. 122).

90. James J. Cavenaugh, *The Lawyer in Society* (New York: Philosophical Society, 1963), pp. 55–57. See also John J. McCloy, "The Extracurricular Lawyer," *Washington and Lee Law Review* 15 (1958): pp. 182–83.

91. Theodore J. Fetter, ed., *State Courts: A Blueprint for the Future* (Williamsburg, Va.: National Center for State Courts, 1978), p. 119.

92. Silberman et al., pp. 102–22, 208–34, provide the most comprehensive recent discussion of possible roles lfor nonlawyer adjudicators. See also sources cited in the following footnotes.

93. Silberman et al., pp. 213–16; Milton M. Carrow and John H. Reese, "State Problems of Mass Adjudicative Justice," *Administrative Law Review* 28 (1976): 223–55; and Mary T. Hennessy, "Qualifications of California Justice Court Judges," *Pacific Law Journal* 3 (1972): 439–74.

94. E.g., Barbara Yngnesson and Patricia Hennessey, "Small Claims, Complex Disputes," *Law and Society Review* 9 (1975): 265.

95. National Center for State Courts, *Parajudges: Their Role in Today's Court Systems* (Denver, Colo.: National Center for State Courts, 1976).

96. Hennessy, p. 473 and see p. 472.

97. Student Note, "Justice Courts in Oregon," *Oregon Law Review* 53 (1974): 411–56; Lon T. Holden, "Justice Court Reform in Montana," *Montana Law Review* 34 (1973): 122–49; and E. Gardner Brownlee, "The Revival of the Justice of the Peace in Montana," *Judicature* 58 (1974): 373–79. On the subject of lay judge training in particular see Larry Berkson and Lenore Haggard, "The Education and Training of Judges in the United States," in Berkson and Carbon, pp. 142–49; and National Center for State Courts, *State Judicial Training Profile* (Denver, Colo.: National Center for State Courts, 1976).

98. Student Note, *Oregon Law Review*, p. 443.

99. Temporary Commission on the New York State Court System (Dominick Commission), *And Justice for All* (Albany, 1973), p. 22.

100. Ibid., p. 27.

101. Linda Silberman, "Non-Attorney Justice: A Survey and Proposed Model," *Harvard Journal of Legislation* 17 (1980): 540. To the same effect see Silberman et al., pp. 103–5.

102. Silberman, p. 540.

103. See Silberman et al., Chaps. 3 and 4.

104. On the more general concern for flexible, more accessible dispute resolution institutions, see Earl Johnson, "A Preliminary Analysis of Alternative Strategies for Processing Civil Disputes (Washington, D.C.: LEAA, 1977); and Fetter, ed. On the roots of these concerns see Harrington, pp. 35–37; and Abel, pp. 1–3, in the same volume. On various projects now in operation see Daniel McGillis, "Minor Dispute Processing: A Review of Recent Developments," pp. 60–76, in Tomasic and Feeley; and Robert C. Davis, "Mediation: The Brooklyn Experiment," pp. 154–70, in the same colume.

105. Alper and Nichols, pp. xi–xii. See also p. 247.

106. See Harrington, esp. p. 36. For a contemporary's perspective see Aumann, pp. 226–35.

107. Abel, Introduction; Sally Engle Merry, "The Social Organization of Mediation in Nonindustrial Societies," vol. 2; Abel, pp. 17–45; Eric A. Fisher, "Comment: Community Courts," *American University Law Review* 24 (1975): 1275–85.

108. Lewis R. Katz, "The Formation of Community Councils," in Robertson, p. 454. See also Frederick E. Snyder, "Crime and Community Mediation—the Boston Experience," *Wisconsin Law Review* (1978): 737–91.

109. "Foreword: Dispute Resolution," *Yale Law Journal* 88 (1979): 905–6.

110. "Dispute Resolution Act," P.L. 96–190, February 12, 1980. On its history and meaning see Paul Nejelski, "The 1980 Dispute Resolution Act," *Judges' Journal* 19 (1980): 33–45.

111. Royer F. Cook, Janice A. Roehl, and David I. Sheppard, *Neighborhood Justice Centers Field Test* (Washington, D.C.: Department of Justice, 1980), p. 10. For other statistics on referrals see William L. Felstiner and Lynne A. Williams, "Community Mediation in Dorchester, Massachusetts," in Tomasic and Feely, p. 149. See also Roman Tomasic, "Mediation as an Alternative Justice Movement," in the same volume, pp. 225–28.

112. Lawrence H. Cooke, "Community Dispute Resolution Centers Program Inaugurated," *New York State Bar Journal* (April 1982): 151.

113. Abel, p. 304. See also Tomasic. On the problem of equal adversaries in particular see Lon Fuller, "Mediation—Its Forms and Functions," *Southern California Law Review* 44 (1971): 305–39, esp. pp. 308, 330; and Davis, p. 119.

114. Sally Engle Merry, "Defining 'Success' in the Neighborhood Justice Movement," pp. 172–92. Tomasic and Feeley; Felstiner and Williams; Abel, pp. 297–98; and Robert M. Cover, "Dispute Relsolution:

A Foreword," *Yale Law Journal* 88 (1979): 910–15.

115.   E.g., Jerald S. Auerbach, "Burger's Golden Calf," *New Republic*
March 3, 1982: 9–10. For reasons why this could be expected to occur see
William Felstiner, "Influences of Social Organization on Dispsute Proc-
essing," pp. 44–59. Tomasic and Feeley.

116.   Daniel McGillis and Joan Mullen, *Neighborhood Justice Centers:
An Analysis of Potential Models* (Washington, D.C: Government Printing
Office, 1977), p. 75. See also David C. Shepard, Janice A. Roehl, and Roger
F. Cook, *Neighborhood Centers Field Test: An Interim Report* (Washing-
ton, D.C.: Government Printing Office, 1979). For a contrary opinion see
Robert Beresford and Jill Cooper, "A Neighborhood Court for Neigh-
borhood Suits," *Judicature* 61 (1977): 185–90, esp. pp. 186–87.

117.   See Abel, p. 304; and Chris McCormick and Geoff Mungham,
"Lawmen and Laymen and the Administration of the Lower Courts"
(paper presented at the annual meeting of the Law and Society Association, Madison, Wis., 1980).

118.   The issue is at least acknowledged in E. Keith Stott, Theodore J.
Fetter, and Laura L. Crites, *Rural Courts* (Denver, Colo.: National
Center for State Courts, 1977), p. 72.

119.   Katz, p. 454.

120.   Tomasic and Feeley, p. xliii.

121.   Harrington, pp. 45–46, explores this possibility.

122.   McCormick and Mungham, p. 12. For the same argument see
Yngvesson and Hennessey, pp. 221–28, esp. p. 227; Abel, p. 302.

123.   Institute of Judicial Administration, p. 1. See also Paul Dolan,
"Delaware Initiates Reform in Justice Courts," *National Civic Review*
(l1971): 321–25; VanLandingham. See also the statistics prepared by the
Council of State Governments in 1971 and reprinted in Silberman et al.,
p. 342.

124.   Gazell, pp. 806–7. See also Allan Ashman and David Lee,
"Non-Lawyer Judges: The Long Road North," *Chicago-Kent Law Review*
53 (1977): 567–69. See also Dolan and Fenton.

125.   Federal Magistrates Act of 1968, Pub. L. No. 90-578, Sec. 101, 82
Stat. 1113 (1969) codified and amended at 28 U.S.C. Sec. 638 (1976). There
have been other minor amendments since then. See Peter McCabe, "The
Federal Magistrates Act of 1979," *Harvard Journal of Legislation* 16
(1979): 343–401. See also Steven Puro et al., "The Developing Role of U.S.
Magistrates in the District Courts," *Judicature* 64 (1981): 436–49. See also
Charles A. Lindquist, "The Origin and Development of the U.S. Com-
missioner System," *American Journal of Legal History* 14 (1970): 1–16.

126.   Silberman et al., pp. 284–317.

127.   Wheeler and Whitcomb, pp. 47, 80; Carl Baer and Ellen Baer,
"Introduction: Judges and Court Reform, *Justice System Journal* 3
(1977): 99–104; Michael Powell, "Bar Associations in Professional and
Social Context" (paper delivered before the Law and Society Associa-
tion, Madison, Wis., 1980; and Jerome Carlin, *Lawyer's Ethics* (Beverly
Hills, Calif.: Sage, 1966), pp. 181–82.

128. Glick and Vines, p. 16.

129. Hurst, p. 361.

130. Fish, p. 427. See also Glick and Vines, pp. 15–16.

131. Beverly Blair Cook, *The Paradox of Judicial Reform*, Report no. 29 (Chicago: American Judicature Society, 1970), p. 15. See also Glick and Vines, p. 17; Gilb, p. 220; Berkson and Carbon, chap. 5.

132. See Silberman et al., pp. 92–93.

133. Kress and Stanley.

134. Kohn, p. 4.

135. See e.g., Institute of Judicial Administration; Lee Powell, ed., *Court Reform in Seven States* (Chicago: American Bar Association, 1980). For the effort in Florida see Talbot D'Alemberte, "Florida's Great Leap Forward," *Judicature* 56 (1973): 380–83. In California, Hennessey; in Tennessee, Leventhal.

136. For Illinois see Kohn; Griese; John A. Nordberg, "Farewell to Illinois J.P.s," *Chicago-Kent Law Review* 40 (1963): 23–34. For Connecticut see MacDonald, pp. 411–31; and Davis Mars "Court Reorganization in Connecticut," *Journal of the American Judicature Society* (now *Judicature*) 41 (1957); pp. 6–14.

137. Silberman et al., p. 24.

138. Mirjan Damaska, "A Foreign Perspective on the American Judicial System," in Fetter, ed., pp. 238–391.

Chapter 3

1. Brief for the American Judicature Society in North v. Russell (427 U.S. 328 [1976]) prepared by Allen Ashman, p. 12. Compare his argument with this one typical of the court-reform literature:

> No matter how well-meaning or intelligent, a lay person is lost in a judgeship unless trained in the capacity to identify legal issues, locate pertinent authority, and resolve controversies according to law. . . . The lay person is generally incapable of serving effectively as a judge because lay persons lack the training to render reasoned decisions according to law. (Frederic S. Le Clercq, "The Constitutional Policy That Judges Be Learned in the Law," *Tennessee Law Review* 47 [1980]: 740)

2. Consider, e.g., the records of the National Association for the Advancement of Colored People or the Women's Rights Project of the American Civil Liberties Union or the American Jewish Congress as coordinated, strategy-conscious litigating organizations (Clement E. Vose, *Caucasions Only* [Berkeley: University of California Press, 1959]; Karen O'Connor, *Women's Organizations' Use of the Courts* [Lexington, Mass.: Lexington, 1980]; Frank J. Sorauf, *The Wall of Separation* [Princeton, N.J.: Princeton University Press, 1976]. But see Stephen L. Wasby, "Is 'Planned Litigation' Planned?" (paper presented at the annual meeting of the American Political Science Association, Chicago, 1983).

3. Unanticipated conflicts, of course, can precipitate Supreme Court review. The conflicts between California and other state courts on the due process implications of adjudication by nonlawyer judges, for example, encouraged the Supreme Court to take up the matter in North v. Russell (427 U.S. 328 [1976]). On the significance of conflicts below to Supreme Court review generally see Doris Marie Provine, *Case Selection in the U.S. Supreme Court* (Chicago: University of Chicago Press, 1980).

4. See, e.g., Heard v. Moore, 290 S.W. 15 (Tenn. 1926).

5. This common law principle and citations supporting it appear in 48A C.J.S., section 15.

6. See the description of cases Thomas R. Trenkner provides in the annotation on eligibility for judicial office in 71 A.L.R. 3d 498.

7. The Institute of Judicial Administration provides a good synopsis of the cases in *Non-Attorney Justice in the United States* (New York: I.J.A., 1979), at pp. 180–84.

8. E.g., Ex parte Craig, 150 Tex. Crim. 598, 193 S.W.2d 178 (1946) and Ray v. Weaver, 586 S.W.2d 828 (Tenn. 1979).

9. Crouch v. Justice of the Peace Court, 6th Precinct, 440 P.2d 1000 (Ariz. App. 1968).

10. Decatur v. Kushner (253 N.E.2d 425 Ill. 1969).

11. State v. Lynch, 489 P.2d 697 (Ariz. 1971) and State v. Dziggel, 492 P.2d 1227 (Ariz. 1972).

12. State ex rel Moats v. Janco, 180 S.E.2d 174 (W.Va. 1971).

13. Melikian v. Avent, 300 F. Supp. 516 (Miss. 1969), p. 519.

14. Colton v. Kentucky, 407 U.S. 104 (1972). Appellant in that case raised a variety of objections to his conviction for disorderly conduct. The Court rejected them all, including defendant's argument that Kentucky's trial de novo procedure violated his right to due process. Colton's objection to this procedure was that he received a stiffer fine on retrial in the circuit court; he found no fault with the qualifications of the judge who originally tried him. The issue of judicial qualifications came up only in the Supreme Court's opinion, which justified de novo review in terms of safeguards missing in the courts of first instance, one of these being that "the judges may not be trained for their positions either by experience or schooling" (p. 114).

15. Argersinger v. Hamlin, 407 U.S. 25 (1972).

16. Ibid., p. 25.

17. Ibid., pp. 31, 33–34.

18. Ibid., p. 31, quoting Powell v. Alabama, 287 U.S. 45 (1932), pp. 68–69.

19. This argument proved successful in Gordon v. Justice Ct., 115 Cal. Rptr. 632, 12 Cal.3d 323, 525 P.2d 72 (1974). The case is discussed in detail infra.

20. See e.g., Ditty v. Hampton, 490 S.W.2d 772 (Ky. 1972).

21. Ibid.

22. Ibid., pp. 774–75.

23. Ibid., p. 777.

24. Gordon v. Justice Ct., 115 Cal. Rptr. 632, 12 Cal.3d 323, 525 P.2d (1974). Citations that follow are to Cal. Rptr.

25. The *Gordon* court cites this report and its conclusions favorably in fn. 8, pp. 636–37.

26. The lower court's opinion is reported in 108 Cal. Rptr. 912 (1973).

27. 115 Cal. Rptr., pp. 636–37.

28. Ibid., pp. 637–38.

29. Ibid., p. 636.

30. Ibid., p. 635. The emphasis noted in this quotation is in the original.

31. The Court of Appeals describes petitioners' evidence at 108 Cal. Rptr. 918.

32. 115 Cal. Rptr., p. 638. The decision requires California to make a lawyer judge available on demand. The state established circuit-riding lawyer judges for that purpose, each of whom covers one or more counties. E. Keith Stott et al. in *Rural Courts* (Denver, Colo: National Center for State Courts, 1977) discusses how this system works.

33. James M. Coughlin, "The Constitutionality of Non-Attorney Judge Statutes," *Boston University Law Review* 55 (1975): 827–46.

34. Gary L. Rosenthal, "The Right to a Legally-Trained Judge," *Harvard Civil Rights—Civil Liberties Law Review* 10 (1975): 739–71. See also C. Christopher Scruggs, "Due Process—Non-Attorney Judges," *American Journal of Criminal Law* 3 (1975): 341–54; Dorothy Robinson, "Right to an Attorney Judge in Justice Courts," *California Law Review* 63 (1975): 227–35; Lynda D. Nelson, "Gordon v. Justice Court: Defendant's Right to a Competent Tribunal," *Hastings Constitutional Law Quarterly* 2 (1975): 1777–1206; Elaine G. Rollins, "Is Trial before a Non-Attorney Judge Constitutional?" *Nebraska Law Review* 57 (1978): 233–43; Robert J. Hensley, Jr., "Due Process and Lay Judges," *North Carolina Central Law Journal* 6 (1975): 339–49; C.B.S. (Student Note), "Limiting Judicial Incompetence," *Virginia Law Review* 61 (1975): 1454–99; and Gerard A. Nebel, "Constitutional Law—Due Process—Permitting Non-Attorney Judges to Preside over Criminal Trials," *Vanderbilt Law Review* 28 (1975): 421–30.

35. Scruggs, p. 348.

36. E.g., Robert A. Kimsey, "The Justice of the Peace System under Constitutional Attack," *Utah Law Review* (1974): 861–70.

37. Coughlin. See also Robinson.

38. Rosenthal.

39. C.B.S., p. 1485.

40. See Nebel. See also Allan Ashman and Pat Chapin, "Is the Bell Tolling for Non-Lawyer Judges?" *Judicature* 59 (1976): 417–21.

41. Shelmadine v. Jones, Utah District Ct., 3d Dist. (Salt Lake City), 6/3/75, reported in 17 *Cr. L.* 2282.

42. Shelmadine v. Jones, 550 P.2d 207 (1976).

43. In Tennessee, Perry v. Banks, 581 S.W.2d 549, Henry and Fones dissenting, pp. 550–56. In Wyoming, Thomas v. Justice Court, 538 P.2d 42

(1975), Rose dissenting, pp. 54–56.

44. Thomas v. Justice Ct., p. 54.

45. In re Judicial Interpretation of 1975 Senate Enrolled Act No. 441, 332 N.E.2d 97 (1975).

46. See Tsiosdia v. Rianaldi, 547 P.2d 553 (N.M. 1976); In re Hewitt, 8 Misc.2d 202 (N.Y., 1975); and People v. Jones, N.Y. Law Jour., July 15, 1977, 14–15; Ex parte Ross, 522 S.W.2d 214 (Tex. Ct. Crim. App.), State v. Pfeiffer, 25 Or. App. 45, 548 P.2d 174 (1976); State v. Boone, 543 P.2d 945 (Kan. 1975).

47. Gordon v. Justice Ct., cert. den., 420 U.S. 938. Ditty v. Hampton, app. dismd., 414 U.S. 885.

48. North v. Russell, 427 U.S. 328 (1976).

49. Some of the details in this and the following paragraph come from an October 15, 1981, letter Eugene Goss wrote in response to my queries about the case.

50. For the progress of the case through the Kentucky courts, see North v. Russell, 427 U.S. 328 (1976), pp. 331–32.

51. North v. Russell, 516 S.W.2d 103 (1974).

52. North v. Russell 419 U.S. 1085 (1974).

53. Justice Palmore's March 121, 1975, opinion, appendix to 74-1409 (North v. Russell).

54. North v. Russell, 422 U.S. 1040 (1975).

55. Appellant's Brief on the Merits, p. 29.

56. Ibid., esp. pp. 24–27.

57. Official Reporter's Transcript of Evidence (examination by Mr. Eugene Goss, July 23, 1974), from appendix, no. 74-1409, p. 18.

58. Appellant's Brief, p. 29, quoting from Wolf v. Colorado, 338 U.S. 25 (1949).

59. Ibid.

60. Ibid., p. 30.

61. Appellee's Brief on the Merits, p. 16. See also p. 37: "The laws providing for police courts and the non-lawyer judges who preside in them should not be struck down solely on the basis of speculation. . . . The appellant has shown nothing to cause this Court to elevate the lawyer police court judge to a constitutional right."

62. Ibid., esp. pp. 3–4, 17, 20. The Court had applied this test in earlier cases involving fee-supported judges. It also used this approach to uphold a Tampa ordinance permitting lay clerks to issue arrest warrants (407 U.S. 345 [1972], esp. pp. 352–53).

63. Amicus Curiae Brief for the New York State Association of Magistrates (prepared by Eugene W. Salisbury and Duncan MacAffer), p. 14.

64. Justice Stevens appointed December 19, 1975, after oral argument in the case, took no part in the decision.

65. North v. Russell, 427 U.S. 328 (1976), p. 339.

66. Ibid., esp. pp. 334–35.

67. Ibid., p. 334.

68. Ibid., p. 337.

69. Ibid., p. 340.

70. See particularly fnn. 1, 3, and 4 and accompanying text.

71. Ibid., pp. 342–43.

72. Ibid., pp. 342–43.

73. Ibid., p. 345.

74. Allan Ashman and David Lee, "Non-Lawyer Judges: The Long Road North," *Chicago-Kent Law Review* 53 (1977): pp. 565–95. Ashman, it may be recalled, wrote the brief for the American Judicature Society in North v. Russell advocating abolition of nonlawyer judges.

75. Laughlin McDonald, "Speaking of Incompetence, Chief, What about Judges?" *Young Lawyer* (November 12, 1980): 41.

76. Vermont v. Dunkerley, 134 Vt. 523, 365 A.2d 131 (1976).

77. The controversy is discussed in a September 26, 1983, *Time* article (p. 62) and in an article by Tom Watkin for the *National Law Journal* (September 19, 1983), p. 8. I have also consulted with Thomas Lehner, Vermont State Court Administrator (telephone conversation of January 21, 1985).

78. State ex rel. Anglin v. Mitchell, 596 S.W.2d 779 (1980). The quotation is from Cooper and Hurbison dissenting, p. 792. Another divided case that was decided adversely to lay judges is Lecates v. Justice of the Peace Court, 637 F.2d 888 (3d Cir. 1980). Here lay judge jurisdiction was unaffected, but the Court of Appeals did require waiver of the state's surety bond requirement for paupers seeking lawyer-judge review of civil claims brought first before justices of the peace.

79. Young v. Konz, 88 Wash.2d 276, 558 P.2d 791 (1977); Jenkins v. Canaan Mun. Ct., 116 N.H. 616, 336 A.2d 208 (1976). Generally see Ashman and Lee; Larry D. Henin, "Side Judges in Vermont," *Vermont Law Review* 3 (1978): 147–64.

80. People v. Skrynski, 42 N.Y.2d 218, 336 N.E.2d 797 (1977).

81. Palmer v. Superior Court of Ariz., 114 Ariz. 279, 560 P.2d 797 (1977).

82. See Barbara Schulert, "Idaho Moves to Certify Nonlawyer Magistrates," *Judicature* 60 (1977): 455–56; Treiman v. State, ex rel. Miner, 343 So.2d 819 (Fla. 1977).

83. Ashman and Lee, p. 579. The States that interpreted *North* loosely to permit nonlawyer judges even without de novo lawyer review found some support for their position in fn. 6 of the majority's opinion in *North*. That footnote, quoting language from another case, stated: "States are entitled to some flexibility in responding to constitutional command" (North v. Russell, 427 U.S. 328 [1976], p. 338).

84. 42 N.Y.2d 218, 336 N.E.2d 797 (1977).

85. The statute provides for removal of misdemeanors from the town and village courts for prosecution by indictment upon motion when the superior court judge finds "good cause to believe that the interests of justice so require." The section has been interpreted to require some showing of prejudice for removal. People v. Rosenberg, 59 Misc. 342 (Court of General Sessions, New York County 1908) is a leading case.

See, e.g., People v. Prisco, 68 Misc.2d 493 (County Court, Suffolk County 1970); People v. Lovejoy, 66 Misc.2d 1003 (County Court, Tompkins County 1971); and People v. Banaszak, 76 Misc.2d 397 (County Court, Monroe County 1973).

86. Cases holding removal to a lawyer judge required upon defendant's request: People v. Dean, 96 Misc.2d 781 (1978); and by the same judge an unpublished opinion in People v. Breeds, Tompkins Co. Ct., May 5, 1980. See also Simpson v. Swartwood, 69 A.D.2d 954 (1979). Cases holding to the contrary, that removal is *not* automatic: People v. Jones, N.Y. Law Journal, July 15, 1977, 14–15; unpublished decision by Hon. Lee Towne Adams, Ct. in People v. Witherell, Chatauqua Co. Ct., Oct. 16, 1978; Legal Aid v. Scheinman, 73 A.D.2d 411 (1980), aff. 53 N.Y.2d 12 (1981); People v. Schultz, 114 Misc.2d 939 (Sup. Ct., Onondaga Co., 1982); unpublished decisions by Hon. J. Robert Houston in People v. Frankenberger et al., Livingston Co. Ct., Jan. 15, 1982 (upon motion) and Feb. 16, 1983 (upon appeal); and the unpublished decision of Norman A. Mordue in People v. Mossow, Oswego Co. Ct., March 24, 1983.

87. People v. Charles F., 470 N.Y.2d 342, 458 N.E.2d 801 (1983).

88. *New York Times* (December 28, 1983), p. A-22.

89. North v. Russell, 516 S.W.2d 103 (1974).

90. Theodore J. Fetter, "A History of the Lay Judge," *State Court Journal* (Fall 1978): 9. On the general problems appellate courts face in litigation raising broad social policy issues see Donald L. Horowitz, *The Courts and Public Policy* (Washington, D.C.: Brookings Institute, 1977).

91. Peter W. Sperlich discusses the jury competence issue in "The Case for Preserving Trial by Jury in Complex Civil Litigation," *Judicature* 65 (1982): 394–419. On the problem of self-representation in criminal cases see Faretta v. California, 422 U.S. 806 (1974).

Chapter 4

1. John Paul Ryan and James H. Guterman, "Lawyer versus Non-Lawyer Town Justices," *Judicature* 60 (1977): 274.

2. See "Understanding Misdemeanor Courts: A Review of the Literature and Recent Case Law," in James J. Alfini, ed., *Misdemeanor Courts: Policy Concerns and Research Perspectives* (Washington, D.C.: Department of Justice, 1981), p. 1. See also James J. Alfini and Rachel N. Doan, "A New Perspective on Misdemeanor Justice" *Judicature* 60 (1977): 425–34; and U.S. Department of Justice and Bureau of the Census, *National Survey of Court Organization* (Washington, D.C.: Department of Justice, 1973), p. 4.

3. James Willard Hurst, "The Functions of Courts in the United States: 1950–1980," *Law and Society Review* 15 (1980–81): 407. See also E. Keith Stott, Theodore J. Fetter, and Laura L. Crites, *Rural Courts: The Effect of Space and Distance on the Administration of Justice* (Denver, Colo.: National Center for State Courts, 1977). These authors

also suggest that rural courts "have remained a neglected area of concern" (p. xv).

4. Department of Justice (*National Survey*), p. 5. Russell R. Wheeler and Howard R. Whitcomb make the same point in *Judicial Administration* (Englewood Cliffs, N.J.: Prentice-Hall, 1977), p. 75. Nor are these differences between states a function simply of differences in caseloads, population, or other obvious factors. Rodney H. Maybry found per capita variations in court costs of nearly 100 percent in two states similar in income, population, crime rate, and education. He also found much variation in the extent to which court systems are locally or centrally financed. *An Economic Investigation of State and Local Judicial Services* (Washington, D.C.: LEAA, 1977), pp. 2–11.

5. Alfini and Doan. See more generally John Paul Ryan, Allan Ashman, Bruce D. Sales, and Sandra Shane-DuBow, *American Trial Judges* (New York: Free Press, 1980).

6. For a state-by-state census see Linda Silberman et al., *Non-Attorney Justice in the United States* (New York: Institute of Judicial Administration, 1979), pp. 253–60.

7. The total number of civil and criminal cases handled by the town and village courts in 1983, according to the state Department of Audit and Control, was 2,749,192.

8. See Uniform Justice Court Act, sections 2001, 2005, and 2300. See also Criminal Procedure Law, sections 510.20 and 510.30.

9. Uniform Justice Court Act, sections 201–208, 2300(d)(2), and 1801–12.

10. See New York Constitution, article 6, section 20, and Uniform Justice Court Act, section 105.

11. Administrative Order of the Chief Justice, December 15, 1983, amending section 17.2 of pt. 17 of the Rules of the Chief Judge of the State of New York (22 NYCRR 17.2). These changes took effect on January 1, 1984. Before that time, lawyer justices were under no obligation to attend any classes.

12. The number of justices responding in proportion to the estimated total population of justices as of December 1980 was:

	Population	No. Responding	% Response
Total respondents:	2,222	1,539	59
Nonlawyers	1,647	1,223	74
Lawyers (all)	575	316	55
Lawyers, city judges	137	64	47
Lawyers, town and village justices	438	252	58

13. Irwin Edman, ed., *The Philosophy of Plato*, trans. Benjamin Jowett (New York: Modern Library, 1956), pp. 522–23.

14. Carl Sandburg, "The Lawyers Know Too Much."

15. William Shakespeare, *Henry VI*, vol. 2, act 5, sc. 2, line 84. See *Standard Quotations*, comp. Burton Stgevenson (New York): Funk & Wagnall, 1953).

16. Roscoe Pound, "The Lay Tradition as to the Lawyer," *Michigan Law Review* 12 (1914): 628. For a more extended discussion, see Pound's famous "The Causes of Dissatisfaction with the Administrative of Justice," *Reports of the American Bar Association* 29 (1906): 395, 397.

17. Stuart Scheingold, *The Politics of Rights* (New Haven: Yale University Press, 1974), p. 151. See also Judith M. Shklar, *Legalism* (Cambridge, Mass.: Harvard University Press, 1964); Michael Barkun, *Law without Sanctions* (New Haven: Yale University Press, 1968), p. 77.

18. John J. Bonsignore, "Law School: Caught in the Paradigmatic Squeeze," in Bonsignore, ed., *Before the Law*, 2d ed. (Boston: Houghton Mifflin, 1979), p. 215. To the same effect see Duncan Kennedy, "Legal Education as Training for Hierarchy," in David Kairys, ed., *The Politics of Law* (New York: Pantheon, 1982), pp. 40–61. For a different perspective, see Wagner Thielens, Jr., *The Socialization of Law Students* (New York: Arno Press, 1980), esp. pp. 283–84, where the author discusses law student opinion about the "makings" of a lawyer. Many students apparently believe the most important characteristics of a lawyer are acquired *before* law school. See Fran Zemans and Victor Rosenbloom, *The Making of a Public Profession* (Chicago: American Bar Foundation, 1981). See also Robert Stevens, "Law Schools and Law Students," *Virginia Law Review* 59 (1973): pp. 551–708; and Howard Erlanger and Douglas A. Klegon, "Socialization Effects of Professional School: The Law School Experience and Student Orientations to Public Interest Concerns," *Law and Society Review* 13 (1978): 11–35, for empirical evidence that attitudinal changes during law school are moderate and not necessarily directly related to classroom experiences.

19. Bonsignore, p. 217. For a similar analysis see Joel Seligman, *The High Citadel: The Influence of the Harvard Law School* (Boston: Houghton Mifflin, 1978).

20. Ibid., p. 218.

21. Scheingold, p. 159.

22. Scott Turow, *One L: An Inside Account of Life in the First Year at Harvard Law School* (New York: Putnam's, 1977), p. 296.

23. Ibid., p. 297.

24. Scheingold, p. 158; Seligman. For evidence that an analogous socialization process occurs in elite business schools, see Peter Cohen, *The Gospel according to the Harvard Business School* (New York: Penguin, 1973).

25. Abraham S. Goldstein, "The Unfulfilled Promise of Legal Education," in Geoffrey G. Hazzard, ed., *Law in Changing America* (Englewood Cliffs, N.J.: Prentice-Hall, 1968), p. 159. See also Turow, p. 261, where he complains: "I am still a little discomfited by a place which is so cheerfully assumed to be the training ground for the power elite."

See also Thielens, pp. 427–29.

26. Chester H. Smith, "The Justice of the Peace in the United States," *California Law Review* 15 (1927): 127–28.

27. National Commission on Law Observance and Enforcement (Wickersham Commission), *Report on Criminal Procedure*, selection included in John A. Robertson, ed., *Rough Justice: Perspectives on the Lower Criminal Courts* (Boston: Little, Brown, 1977), p. 7. See also Kenneth Vanlandingham's complaint in the same volume that the lay judge "administers unequal justice without regard to law" (p. 42).

28. The law review literature praising the pro-lawyer-judge result in Gordon v. Justice Court and condemning the differing result in North v. Russell offers many good examples of such reasoning.

29. Senate Select Task Force on Court Reorganization, *The Price of Local Justice* (Williamsburg, Va.: National Center for State Courts, 1978), p. 24.

30. The medians in conservation cases are 2 percent for nonlawyers, 0 percent for lawyers. The two medians are identical for small claims and civil cases, 5 percent in each group. Motor-vehicle cases constituted 75 percent of the median nonlawyer justice's caseload and 70 percent of the lawyer's caseload.

31. See Senate Task Force, p. 24.

32. The difference in means exhibits the same gap, with 63 percent for lawyer judges and 46 percent for nonlawyers.

33. The median number of trials for all lawyer city, town, and village judges responding to this survey was four. For nonlawyers the median was one. Regression analysis indicated that caseload and population, not educational status, explain differences in the number of jury trials.

34. The median number of days nonlawyer judges estimated between the typical demand for a jury trial and its occurrence was thirty. For lawyers this figure was forty.

35. Answers broke down this way:

	Lawyers (%) (N=167)	Nonlawyers (%) (N=613)
Comments on plea bargaining:		
Inadequate staff, time, etc.	25	13
Justice to defendant	48	44
Combination of lines 1 and 2	17	7
Prosecutorial abuse	5	11
Unfair to public	4	24
Other	1	1
	100	100

$$\chi^2 = 64.582, \ p = .0001$$

36. James J. Alfini and Rachel N. Doan, "A New Perspective on Misdemeanor Justice," *Judicature* 60 (1977): 430–31. See also James J. Alfini, ed., *Misdemeanor Courts: Policy Concerns and Research Perspectives* (Washington, D.C.: Department of Justice, 1981), pp. 13–15; and Harold H. Bruff, "Arizona's Inferior Courts," *Law and the Social Order* (1973), p. 14.

37. See Alfini; and Alfini and Doan, p. 430. See also John Paul Ryan et al., *American Trial Judges: Their Work Styles and Performance* (New York: Free Press, 1980), pp. 63–64, which also notes the greater frequency of plea bargaining among urban judges.

38. The question was: "In the past twenty years courts have interpreted the Constitution to require increasing attention to procedural safeguards in criminal cases. Do you think this trend has gone:

	Lawyers (%) (N=297)	Nonlawyers (%) (N=1,174)
Much too far	15	26
Somewhat too far	30	35
About far enough	49	35
Not quite far enough	6	2
Not nearly far enough	0	1
	100	99

$$\chi^2 = 35.216, p = .0001$$

39. Correlations between the rights question and the propensity to dismiss at various stages in proceedings were all less than .09, accounting for less than 1 percent of the variance. Cross-tabular analysis comparing those critical of rights and those satisfied or enthusiastic produced no statistically significant patterns in responses to questions on whether judges took prior not guilty pleas into account in sentencing and whether judges were willing to accept a police officer's bail recommendation.

40. Thirty-nine percent of the lawyers reported they did not dismiss arraignments compared with 37 percent of the nonlawyers; 42 percent of the lawyers and 58 percent of the nonlawyers apparently never dismiss at preliminary hearings, and 25 percent of the lawyers and 56 percent of the nonlawyers never dismiss during trial.

41. With the frequency with which one party is represented in small claims and whether a justice is a lawyer or not as independent variables, regression on the propensity to dismiss at each stage in the proceedings produced: (a) at arraignment, $R^2 = .0017$; (b) at preliminary hearing, $R^2 = .033$; (c) at trial, $R^2 = .078$. The latter two R^2s were almost entirely attributable to the counsel variable.

42. Sixty percent of the lawyers and 61 percent of the nonlawyers answered "no" to this question. Of the minority that noted that police officers do sometimes recommend bail:

	Lawyers (%) (N=246)	Nonlawyers (%) (N=955)
Frequency judge follows officer's bail recommendation:		
Less often than not	44	55
As often as not	54	44
More often than not	1	0
	99	99

$$\chi^2 = 3.493, \, p = .3216$$

43. The question was: "When a defendant pleads not guilty and is later found guilty after a trial, do you take this into account in sentencing?" (no/yes). The judges who answered "yes" were asked how they took this factor into account. Sixty percent of those who responded "yes" answered this part of the question.

44. Twenty percent of the lawyers, however, gave mixed responses, as opposed to 6 percent of the nonlawyers.

45. The justices conducted this research because of a lawsuit they were considering which challenged the constitutionality of adjudication by nonlawyer judges: People v. Jones, *New York Law Journal* (July 5, 1977), pp. 14–15. The statistics on appeals appear at the end of the opinion.

46. Student Note, "Justice Courts in Oregon," *Oregon Law Review* 53 (1974): 427–28. See also Silberman et al., pp. 66–67, which reports that nonlawyer judges consider most of their cases "simple" and find legal questions rare in their courts. Most disputes, they reported, are over factual matters.

47. Milton M. Carrow and John H. Reese, "State Problems of Mass Adjudicative Justice: The Administrative Adjudication of Traffic Violations—a Case Study," *Administrative Law Review* 28 (1976): pp. 223–55, 253.

48. Silberman et al., pp. 94–95.

49. Ibid., pp. 95–97.

50. Ibid., p. 105.

51. Ibid., pp. 115, 105.

52. Ibid., p. 98.

53. Ryan and Guterman, p. 280n.1.

54. The questionnaire contained twenty-one items; the article does not say why three were omitted.

55. The information is graphically presented; the article does not include actual means. Of the seventeen items for which some differences were discernible, fifteen indicated greater lay favor toward police and prosecutors, and two were in the opposite direction; no difference was discernable on one item. Nor do the authors include any data on actual frequencies or on standard deviations or other information about

distribution around the means (ibid., pp. 276–77).

56. Questionnaire, item 48.

57. Lay judges were more likely to respond negatively to the proposal that free day-care should be made available to indigent mothers.

58. Five of thirty-three nonlawyers but only one of forty-five lawyers answered this way where motor-vehicle cases were concerned. In three other types of cases, the differences between the two groups were less.

59. Recall that all city courts are staffed by lawyer judges and that lawyers also tend to serve in the busiest town and village courts.

60. See especially Harry Kalven and Hans Zeisel, *The American Jury* (Chicago: University of Chicago Press, 1971); and John Baldwin and Michael McConville, *Jury Trials* (Oxford: Clarendon Press, 1979). Kalven and Zeisel found an overall agreement rate of 78 percent. Of the 22 percent disagreement, 19 percent was between a jury that acquitted and a judge who would have convicted, and only 3 percent was the reverse (p. 58). Baldwin and McConville's study of British jury verdicts over two decades later produced a strikingly similar pattern (pp. 37–51). The tendency for juries to be more lenient was apparently well-established and well-known at least a century earlier. As William Forsyth observed in 1878:

> With respect to the jury system as a means of protecting inno-
> cence, it may be safely averred that it is the rarest of accidents
> when an innocent man is convicted in this country. . . . But can it
> with equal truth be asserted that juries never acquit in ordinary
> cases when they ought to condemn? I fear not. This is no doubt the
> vulnerable point of the system, that feelings of compassion for the
> prisoner, or of repugnance to the punishment which the law
> awards, are sometimes allowed to overpower their sense of duty.
> They usurp in such cases the prerogative of mercy. (*History of
> Trial by Jury*, republished in 1971 by Burt Franklin)

61. Kalven and Zeisel, p. 495.

62. For a convenient sampling of various opinions see Charles W. Joiner, *Civil Justice and the Jury* (Englewood Cliff, N.J.: Prentice-Hall, 1962). For a decidedly negative view see Dale W. Broeder, "The Functions of the Jury: Facts or Fictions?" *University of Chicago Law Review* 21 (1954): 386, but esp. p. 412 where Broeder complains:

> Persons who look with favor upon the jury's legislative powers
> generally think only one way, of the murder case, for example,
> where the defendant shot his wife's paramour in a fit of blind rage,
> or where the community's most able and God-fearing doctor
> administered poison to put his best friend out of misery. Where the
> prejudices of the community are shrouded in the verdict's mys-
> tery to carve out an exception from a rule whose normal operation
> would permit the defendant to go free, law-dispensing becomes
> less palatable. The bonafide white male conviction of a Negro for
> leering at a white girl at a distance of over sixty feet is a Southern

exception to the ordinary assault rule. Other examples must be legion, the white-washing of lynchers is also law-dispensing.

63. See McKinney's Consolidated Laws of New York Annotated (1980), chap. 29A, pt. 2, sections 1801–14.

64. Responses to the question asking judges to characterize their small claims proceedings broke down this way:

	Lawyers (%) (N=243)	Nonlawyers (%) (N=1,164)
Very informal	27	39
Somewhat informal	57	42
Somewhat formal	14	15
Formal	2	4
	100	100

$$\chi^2 = 21.050, p = .001$$

65. Results to the question of how frequently judges "split the difference" in small claims were:

	Lawyers (%) (N=224)	Nonlawyers (%) (N=1,180)
Don't split	34	30
Less than 10 percent of the time	8	14
10–24 percent	24	22
25–50 percent	29	30
Over 50 percent of the time	4	4
	99	100

$$\chi^2 = 7.411, p = 1,157$$

66. The average in courts of nonlawyer judges is 9 percent. The difference in medians, a more reliable measure given the tremendous differences between judges, is even greater, 15 percent for lawyers and 2 percent for nonlawyers.

67. Probabilities that these patterns could occur by chance were all .05 or less.

68. The precise question was: "Do you ever sentence a defendant to an unusual punishment designed especially to the offender or the offense, such as ordering a litterer to clean up a roadside?" Judges responded this way:

	Lawyers (%) (N=304)	Nonlawyers (%) (N=1,206)
I never have	38	46
I have a few times	46	43
I do this fairly often	16	11
	100	100

$$\chi^2 = 8.552, p = .0139$$

69. Of course the question of proper disposition can easily be complicated further by a letter from defendant, representation by counsel, or a personal appearance in court. Usually then an explanation is offered, and the judge must determine its believability as well as its relevance.

70. The pattern is similar in drunk-driving cases. Here I asked for considerations relevant to reductions:

Considering It Relevant (%)

Considerations	Lawyers (%) (N=259)	Nonlawyers (%) (N=1,165)	χ^2	p
Record of alcohol-related offenses	96	97	.231	.6306
Marital status	42	41	.216	.6419
Age	50	36	17.848	.0001
Employment status	62	64	.417	.5186
Demeanor of defendant	62	53	6.996	.0032
Other	33	21	18.680	.0001

71. Both groups cite punishment as most important, 87 percent of the lawyers and 86 percent of the nonlawyers describing it as "very" or "quite" important. Reform was the next most important concern. Fifty-five percent of the lawyers and 53 percent of the nonlawyers cite "deterring others" as "very" or "quite" important, an importance only 26 percent of the lawyers and 27 percent of the nonlawyers assigned to "keeping defendant 'out of circulation.'"

72. These were the responses:

	Lawyers (%) (N=272)	Nonlawyers (%) (N=1,157)
Reforming defendant:		
Very important	40	51
Quite important	22	20
Of some importance	25	19
Of little importance	8	7
Not important	4	3
	99	100

$$\chi^2 = 11.193, p = .0245$$

73. Hans Zeisel and Gerhard Casper, "Lay Judges in the German Criminal Courts," *Journal of Legal Studies* 1 (1972): 135–39. These statistics are in table 40, p. 190.

74. Stanislaw Pomorski, "Comment: Lay Judges in the Polish Criminal Courts: A Legal and Empirical Description," *Case Western Reserve Journal of International Law* 7 (1975): 198–209.

75. Ibid., p. 206. Seventy-five percent of these differences involved

lay-judge arguments for leniency.

76. Casper and Zeisel, pp. 143–44.

77. This information is reprinted in appendix C (pp. 516–19) of Kalven and Zeisel.

78. Casper and Zeisel, e.g., state: "Our objective was to obtain data on the influence the lay judges have on the verdicts rendered by the tribunals on which they sit" (p. 143).

79. The mixed bench, in fact, grew out of the jury in Germany and Poland. See ibid., pp. 135–41; and Pomorski, p. 199.

80. This is true in all three court systems. Pomorski was the most explicit about the effects of this domination. He reported that, in 60 percent of the cases the apprentice judges observed, the lawyer presiding completely dominated discussion, discouraging any active participation from the lay judges (p. 204). See also John H. Langbein, "Mixed Court and Jury Court: Could the Continental Alternative Fill the American Need?" *American Bar Foundation Research Journal* (1981): 200. The lawyer judge's authority and liberal grounds for appeal, Langbein argues, provide protection against lay nullification of binding legal rules, a jury power Langbein considers undesirable. He suggests that America try mixed benches to enhance lay participation in adjudication.

81. Langbein, pp. 206–8.

82. Apparently selection systems in Germany at least are not entirely successful in getting a representative lay bench. The bias is toward males, the middle class, and civil servants. See Zeisel and Casper, pp. 130–35; and more generally see "Lay Judges and Assessors: A Comparative Perspective," in Silberman et al., pp. 346–93. This material was prepared by John P. Richert of Stockton State College who is working on a book on this subject. See also Richert's conference paper, "Lay Assessors in German Criminal Courts" (delivered at the annual meeting of the Law and Society Association, Amherst, Mass., June 1981).

83. Jerry Beatty, Justin Green, Russell M. Ross, and John R. Schmidhauser, *The Iowa Unified Court System* (1974, Mimeographed). This report appears in a much shortened form in *Judicature* 58 (1975): 380–89.

84. John Hogarth, *Sentencing as a Human Process* (Toronto: University of Toronto Press, 1971); and Daniel Decker et al., *Deer Hunting Violations and Law Enforcement in New York* (Ithaca, N.Y.: Department of Natural Resources, 1980).

85. Hogarth, p. 213.

86. See John Hogarth, *Technical Appendices to Sentencing as a Human Process* (University of Toronto, 1972, Mimeographed), technical appendix 6, "Relationship of Social Characteristics of Magistrates to Age and Behavior," pp. 131–34.

87. Ibid. The reference to this material in the text occurs at p. 213.

88. Decker et al. sent their questionnaire, which consisted primarily of hypothetical deer cases and extenuating circumstances, to 1,907 town

and village justices and 196 environmental conservation officers. Seventy-five percent of the justices responded, in part due to a four-wave mailing. The purpose of the research was to compare the attitudes of conservation officers and justices toward sentencing and to determine whether justices in the Adironacks area sentenced less severely than others in the state (p. 2). I asked the authors to design their survey to include legal education as an independent variable. Education was, it turned out, more important than geographical location in predicting sentencing views.

89. See printout prepared by Decker et al. for the author and available upon request. Lawyer and nonlawyer judges differed only slightly in what factors they take into account in sentencing, the lawyers paying slightly more attention to defendant's record. Whether the differences on questionnaire hypotheticals accurately reflect actual sentencing differences, however, is unclear. When the researchers checked a sample of five questionnaires against actual fines recorded at state offices, they found that actual penalties tended to be smaller. They did not, however, compare lawyer and nonlawyer judges in this respect.

90. Information on the construction of this index appears in the report, p. 10.

91. Silberman et al. The authors set out the questions that guided their investigation on pp. 17–18. Three of the ten questions they outlined concerned the possibility that lay judges might offer a special, more mediation-oriented perspective on adjudication. Their general finding of no significant differences between lawyer and nonlawyer judges (pp. 94–95) thus applies to discretionary matters as well as issues involving procedural guarantees defendants enjoy in criminal cases.

92. Jack Spence, *Search for Justice: Neighborhood Courts in Allende's Chile* (Boulder, Colo.: Westview, 1979). See also his article, "Institutionalizing Neighborhood Courts: Two Chilean Experiences," *Law and Society Review* 13 (1978): 138–82.

93. Spence, pp. 163–64.

94. Spence was particularly interested in the dynamics of dispute processing in Chilean squatter settlements, where the legitimacy of the locally elected judges was a crucial issue. The fact that the neighborhood judges were laypersons and the state-authorized judges were lawyers was incidental to the primary objectives of his study.

Chapter 5

1. See Joseph F. Zimmerman, *The Government and Politics of New York State* (New York: New York University Press, 1981), pp. 265–68.

2. New York State Constitution, article 6, section 17(d), Public Officers Law, section 3, Village Law, section 3-300.

3. The Uniform Justice Court Act, which became effective in 1967, changed these titles.

4. Frederick Miller, "Court Reform: The New York Experience," in Lee Powell, ed., *Court Reform in Seven States* (Chicago: American Bar Association, 1980), p. 109.

5. Russell Wheeler and James Whitcomb, *Judicial Administration* (Englewood Cliffs, N.J.: Prentice-Hall, 1977), pp. 81–82.

6. Judiciary Law, section 220. See also Zimmerman, p. 265.

7. See 26 Op. State Compt. 238 (1970). Kress and Stanley found that 97 percent of the town and village justices surveyed at the annual convention held court in public buildings. Most of these judges believed these facilities were good or excellent, and 91 percent believed their local citizenry supported better court facilities. This sample appears either better housed or more optimistic than the judicial population I surveyed, 30 percent of which rated financial support "not quite adequate" or "seriously deficient." Only 26 percent rated this support "very good."

8. Senate Task Force, p. 25.

9. The Senate Task Force noted a similar variety in facilities in its 1979 report on New York's justice courts, p. 26. Dolan and Fenton report the same pattern in their 1969 survey of justices of the peace in Nebraska. They note that judges held court in police stations, town halls, and their own homes and businesses, over half the judges surveyed believing that their surroundings reduced the dignity of their courts. Ronald J. Dolan and William B. Fenton, "The Justice of the Peace in Nebraska," *Nebraska Law Review* 48 (1969): 457–87.

10. Town law prevents judges in all but the smallest towns from actually hiring their wives or other dependants as clerks unless the town authorizes the position (see Op. State Compt. 64-1036). Sixty percent of the judges Kress and Stanley surveyed had no clerical assistance. Many of those who did have clerks received relatively little assistance even so: nearly 30 percent of the clerks received $1,000 or less per year (Kress and Stanley, p. 44). See also Senate Task Force, p. 8.

11. The Senate Task Force reported annual judicial salaries as low as $1 and as high as $12,500 in a single county (p. 14). See also Kress and Stanley, pp. 122–27, for figures on selected towns and for a county-by-county analysis of salary variation.

12. The Department of Audit and Control requires that all fines and other moneys be deposited within seventy-two hours of receipt and forwarded to the state monthly with a report of the sections of law involved and disposition dates. The Department of Motor Vehicles requires a separate filing of all motor vehicle cases. The Criminal Disposition Reporting Unit of the Office of Court Administration requires a series of reports, one at each stage of proceedings.

13. Max Weber, *Law in Economy and Society*, ed. Max Rheinstein (Cambridge, Mass.: Harvard University Press, 1954), p. 349.

14. Senate Task Force, p. 35.

15. See Beverly Blair Cook, *The Paradox of Judicial Reform*, Report no. 29 (Chicago: American Judicature Society, 1970).

16. *Justice Court Topics*. The editor of this monthly bulletin is

Herbert A. Kline, a Binghamton attorney.

17. New York Vehicle and Traffic Law, sections 225 and 235 (McKinney 1970). See also section 2251 (McKinney 1978 supp.).

18. See, e.g., the association's (undated) 1981 press release opposing the Department of Motor Vehicle's proposal for a $100,000 federal grant to fund a demonstration project in Syracuse, Rome, Utica, Troy, Yonkers, White Plains, and several smaller cities: "The State Magistrates Association emphatically opposes any attempt by the Department of Motor Vehicles to establish a statewide adjudication pilot project and urges the New York State Legislature to refrain from adopting implementing legislation which would remove traffic matters from the local courts to an administrative agency."

19. See Uniform District Court Act, sections 101–2300. See Kress and Stanley, p. 144, for a summary of instances where voters have rejected proposals for eliminating town and village courts.

20. The commission's authority derives from article 6, section 22 of the New York State Constitution and article 2-A of the state judiciary law. The commission publishes an annual report that includes, along with the year's activities, a brief history of judicial disciplinary bodies in New York and a table of total commission action to date (New York State Commission on Judicial Conduct, *Annual Report* [March 1984], p. 168).

21. Judges called before the commission have to provide their own counsel. Individuals also bear the expense of traveling to wherever the commission is sitting. Commission members and their staff, on the other hand, are paid for their efforts.

22. "State's Justice Courts Flourish," *Syracuse Herald Journal* (May 1982).

23. N.Y.S. Comm. (1980 Report), p. 51.

24. N.Y.S. Comm., *Ticket-fixing: The Assertion of Influence in Traffic Cases*, interim report (June 20, 1977), p. 3.

25. Kress and Stanley, p. 107.

26. See Silberman et al., p. 61. See case studies by Harold H. Bruff, "Arizona's Inferior Courts," *Law and the Social Order* (1973): 1; Bruff found that the appeal rate in traffic cases was 2.7 percent and 1.4 percent in misdemeanor cases; Student Note, "Justice Courts in Oregon," *Oregon Law Review* 53 (1974): 411. For a brief history and critique of trial de novo see Stephen R. Bing and S. Stephen Rosenfeld, *The Quality of Justice in the Lower Criminal Courts of Metropolitan Boston*, Lawyer's Comm. for Civil Rights (Williamsburg, Va.: National Center for State Courts, 1970), pp. 37–40 and 96–98.

27. See Town Law, section 27, and Village Law, section 4-410. See also Kress and Stanley, pp. 111–12.

28. The reimbursement formulas are complicated. They are set out, along with reporting procedures, in the Department of Audit and Control's *Handbook for Town Justices and Village Justices* (Mimeographed). See also Senate Task Force, p. 9; and Kress and Stanley, p. 112. For specifics, see Vehicle and Traffic Law, section 1803; Uniform Justice

Court Act, sections 1191 and 2020; and General Municipal Law, section 99-1. For recent changes in the civil fees see Uniform Justice Court Act, section 1911(a). The new fees provide $10 for most filings in civil cases other than small claims, where the repayment schedule remains unchanged.

29. Figures supplied by Department of Audit and Control, August 1984.

30. Charles G. Rose, "President's Message," *Magistrate* (May 1978): 3.

31. Uniform Justice Court Act, section 105(d), and Town Law, section 60-a.

32. Senate Task Force, p. 9.

33. Ibid., pp. 30–33; Vehicle and Traffic Law, section 1600, and Opinion of the State Comptroller, pp. 83–137.

34. Ibid., p. 9.

35. Senate Task Force, p. 7. I did not distinguish between town and village justices on my questionnaire.

36. Village Law, section 3-301. Many villages have avoided the problem of town-village competition for judicial business by leaving the village judgeships unfilled. Kress and Stanley, pp. 31, 148. It should be noted, however, that village justices are susceptible to competition from town justices whose jurisdictions encompass them. Some town boards attempt to solve the problem of forum shopping and competition for cases by making one judgeship honorary only, and enforcing this decision with a miniscule salary for the inactive judge. Towns can also eliminate judges by submitting the matter to a townwide vote.

37. Vehicle and Traffic Law, section 1803(5).

38. Stott et al., p. 5.

39. $R^2 = .08$, with population, caseload, and whether a justice is a lawyer or not as independent variables, and acquaintance with defendants as the dependent variable. Standardized estimates = .075 (caseload), .113 (population), and .152 (lawyer/nonlawyer). $R^2 = .11$ with the same independent variables and acquaintance with civil plaintiffs as the dependent variable. Standardized estimates = .290 (caseload), .273 (population), and .261 (lawyer/nonlawyer).

40. See Donald D. Jackson, *Judges* (New York: Atheneum, 1974).

41. The median population for justices with a high-school education or less is 2,500, compared to 3,000 for justices with some college. Caseloads are proportionately less too (300 v. 400 for college-educated justices). The median age for the high-school-or-less group was fifty-three compared to forty-seven for college-educated justices. The median high-school-educated judge had spent 80 percent of his or her life in the community, had five other relations living there, and had parents who had lived locally thirty years. The median college-educated judge had resided locally 50 percent of his or her lifetime, had one relative locally, and had parents who did not live within the jurisdiction.

42. Seventy-eight percent of the city judges serve in jurisdictions in

which their parents have resided, and 76 percent have other relatives in the community, usually more than one. For 60 percent, their parents had lived in the community for over fifty years. On local roots at this level, see Ryan and Guterman. These authors studied a somewhat different cross-section of lawyer and nonlawyer judges but reached many of the same conclusions about background characteristics.

43. Evidence from several sources suggests that some rural, part-time judges take office only reluctantly, often under pressure from friends and acquaintances. See, e.g., Senate Task Force, p. 8; and Wetmore, pp. 53–55. Most stay in office less than two terms, another indication of the limited attractiveness of the job for many. Senate Task Force, p. 7; Wetmore, p. 54; Goldenson et al.; Bruff.

44. Elvin Hatch, *Biography of a Small Town* (New York: Columbia University Press, 1979), pp. 270–71.

45. These lawyer judges are older and clearly better established than some lawyers in comparable positions elsewhere. Wheeler and Whitcomb describe the typical lawyer judge at this level as marginal; as such they are either young and inexperienced or older and unsuccessful. New York's lawyer town and village judges do not fit this stereotype. They are more like the small-town lawyers Joel Handler described in *The Lawyer and His Community: The Practicing Bar in a Middle-sized City* (Madison: University of Wisconsin Press, 1967), esp. pp. 22–31.

46. Kress and Stanley also report a wide occupational mix in their study (p. 38). These authors also reported a gap between lay and lawyer incomes in 1976. The lawyers they surveyed all earned over $30,000 annually, while over half the nonlawyers earned $20,000 or less.

47. See Silberman et al., pp. 74–75; Wetmore, pp. 65–72; Goldenson et al.; Hennessey; Bruff; Jerry Beatty et al., *The Iowa Unified Court System* (1974, Mimeographed); and Dennis L. Toombs, "The Part-Time Lay Justice of the Peace in Texas," *Public Affairs Comment* (May 1983).

48. Jonathan D. Casper reports that criminal defendants discover this fact, too, and that it runs counter to their expectations (*American Criminal Justice: The Defendant's Perspective* [Englewood Cliffs, N.J.: Prentice-Hall, 1972], pp. 135–44). Even the case law reveals limits on judicial authority. See, e.g., U.S. v. Ostendorff, 371 F. 2d 730 (1967), where the court finds it necessary to affirm the judge's power to be more than "a bump on a log" or "a referee in a prize fight" (p. 732). The number of cases on this question of judicial participation in the trial suggests that an active judicial role remains controversial.

49. Maureen Mileski, "Courtroom Encounters: An Observational Study of a Lower Criminal Court," *Law and Society Review* 6 (1971): 473; Raymond Nimmer, "Judicial Reform: Informal Processes and Competing Effects," in Herbert Jacob, ed., *The Potential for Reform of Criminal Justice* (Beverly Hills, Calif.: Sage, 1974), pp. 207–34; and Malcolm Feeley, *The Process Is the Punishment* (New York: Russell Sage, 1979), esp. pp. 3–34. Herbert Jacob and James Eisenstein discuss this approach and its implications in *Felony Justice: An Organizational Analysis of*

Criminal Courts (Boston: Little, Brown, 1977), pt. 1, pp. 3–64. See also Edward J. Clynch and David W. Neubauer, "Trial Courts as Organizations: A Critique and Synthesis," *Law and Policy Quarterly* 3 (1981): 69–94; Marcia J. Lipetz, "Routine and Deviations: The Strength of the Courtroom Workgroup in a Misdemeanor Court," *International Journal of the Sociology of Law* 8 (1980): 47–60; Suzann and Leonard Buckle, *Bargaining for Justice: Case Disposition and Reform in the Criminal Courts* (New York: Praeger, 1977).

50. See, e.g., Gribetz v. Edelstein, 66 A. D. 2d 788 (Dec. 5, 1978), where the court states: "A District Attorney may dictate the terms under which he will agree to consent to accept a guilty plea and where his terms are not met, he may withhold such consent; the withholding of such consent by statutory mandate renders the court without authority to accept a plea to anything less than the entire indictment."

51. This unpublished poem was supplied by its author, Woodruff A. Gaul, a town justice in New York.

52. Silberman et al., pp. 265–83. See also Wheeler and Whitcomb, pp. 78–79; these authors discuss the amount local governments spend on local courts.

53. See Silberman et al., pp. 265–83, for which states these are.

54. Stott et al., p. 4. In New York, according to one study, two-thirds of the 931 towns and 354 villages across the state with courts have no lawyer residents. Jack M. Kress and Sandra L. Stanley, *Justice Courts in the State of New York* (New York State Association of Magistrates, 1976), pp. 13, 25. On the pattern in New York, see *The Price of Local Justice*, a report prepared by the New York State Senate Select Task Force on Court Reorganization (Williamsburg, Va.: National Center for State Courts, 1978), p. 1; see also John Paul Ryan and James H. Guterman, "Lawyer versus Non-Lawyer Town Justices," *Judicature* 60 (1977): 272–80.

Chapter 6

1. See Henry R. Glick, "The Politics of State-Court Reform," in Philip L. DuBois, ed., *The Politics of Judicial Reform* (Lexington, Mass.: Lexington, 1982), pp. 17–33; and in the same volume, Frank Munger, "Movements for Court Reform: A Preliminary Interpretation," pp. 51–67; and Larry J. Cohen, "Assessing Judicial Competence; A Prolegomenon," pp. 165–75. For an argument that social scientists neglect reality in model building see Austin Sarat, "Doing the Dirty Business of Coping with Crime: The Contemporary 'Crisis' of American Criminal Courts," reprinted in Peter F. Nardulli, ed., *The Study of Criminal Courts: Political Perspectives* (Cambridge, Mass.: Ballinger, 1979), pp. 59–79.

2. See Richard A. Watson and Rondal G. Downing, *The Politics of the Bench and the Bar* (New York: Wiley, 1969), p. 6; Henry R. Glick, "The

Promise and Performance of the Missouri Plan: Judicial Selection in the 50 States," *University of Miami Law Review* 32 (1978): pp. 509–71, esp. 539–40; and Philip L. Dubois, *From Ballot to Bench: Judicial Elections and the Quest for Accountability* (Austin: University of Texas Press, 1980).

3. Glick, "The Politics," pp. 28–29.

4. Cohen, p. 170. See also Joel Grossman, *Lawyers and Judges: The ABA and the Politics of Judicial Selection* (New York: Wiley, 1965), esp. p. 52.

5. Reinhold Bendix and Gunther Roth, *Scholarship and Partisanship: Essays in Honor of Max Weber* (Berkeley: University of California Press, 1971), p. 148.

6. Magali Sarfatti Larson, *The Rise of Professionalism: A Sociological Analysis* (Berkeley: University of California Press, 1977).

7. Ibid.

8. See survey results reported by Yankelovich, Skelly, and White in Theodore J. Fetter, ed., *State Courts: A Blueprint for the Future* (Williamsburg, Va.: National Center for State Courts, 1978), pp. 5–69.

9. Report of the Senate Select Task Force on Court Reorganization, *The Price of Local Justice* (Williamsburg, Va.: National Center for State Courts, 1978).

10. Sarat, p. 61.

11. Charles A. Whittaker, "Lawyers, Laymen and Traffic Courts: Concerted Effort Needed for Improvement," *American Bar Association Journal* 49 (1963): 334–35.

12. Abraham S. Blumberg discusses this problem in the context of law practice in "The Practice of Law as Confidence Game: Organizational Cooption of a Profession," *Law and Society Review* 1 (1967): 16–39.

13. See Andrew Abbott,"Status and Status Strain in the Professions," *American Journal of Sociology* 86 (1981): 819–35; and, on the role women play as buffers between the public and more elite male-dominated professions, see Joan Jacobs Brumberg and Nancy Tomes, "Women in the Professions: A Research Agenda for American Historians," *Reviews in American History* (June 1982): 275–96, but esp. p. 288.

14. See e.g., Senate Select Task Force, pp. 22–23; see E. Keith Stott et al., *Rural Courts* (Denver, Colo.: National Center for State Courts, 1977), pp. 4–5, for the same opinion from a broader cross-section of rural judges. See also Linda J. Silberman et al., *Non-Attorney Justice in the United States: An Empirical Study* (New York: Institute of Judicial Administration, 1979), esp. pt. 3, "Final Report: A Vignette of the Lay Court," pp. 36–101; Jack M. Kress and Sandra L. Stanley, *Justice Courts in the State of New York*, (Albany: Association of Magistrates, 1976). The authors subtitled their book *"The Courts Closest to the People,"* and they refer to New York's nonlawyer justices as "citizen-justices"; and see Senate Select Task Force, p. 22.

15. See, e.g., Mildred J. Giese, "Why Illinois Proposes to Abolish

Justice of the Peace Courts," *Illinois Bar Journal* 46 (1958): 815:

> It can surely be expected that the circuit judges, who would be responsible after the transitional period for the appointment of magistrates and for the operation of the court system in their circuits, would be sufficiently interested in the quality of the magistrates they appoint and supervise to appoint lawyers to this position. It can also be expected that many lawyers would be interested in serving as magistrates because of the dignity of that new office and the opportunity it would afford for possible future selection as a circuit judge or associate circuit judge.

16. See Jerry Beatty et al., *The Iowa Unified Court System* (1974, Mimeographed).

17. Ibid., p. 73.

18. Ibid., pp. 56–58, 73–74.

19. James L. Gibson probed this issue systematically in "Knowing One's Constituency: Processes Linking Judges to their Districts" (paper presented at the annual meeting of the Law and Society Association, Toronto, Canada, June 1982). The paper contains a useful discussion of the relevant literature.

20. On the pattern in federal districting see Richard J. Richardson and Kenneth N. Vines, *The Politics of Federal Courts: Lower Courts in the U.S.* (Boston: Little, Brown, 1970).

21. Tumey v. Ohio, 273 U.S. 510 (1927).

22. Ibid., p. 532.

23. For a classic attack on the principle of judicial elections from a prime mover in the court-reform movement see Arthur T. Vanderbilt, *The Challenge of Law Reform* (Princeton, N.J.: Princeton University Press, 1955), chap. 1, pp. 3–35; for information on selection trends, see Larry C. Berkson, "Judicial Selection in the United States: A Special Report," *Judicature* 64 (1980): 176–93.

24. Watson and Downing provided the major analysis of influence in state merit selection; at the federal level the major work is Joel Grossman.

25. See the annual report of the New York State Commission on Judicial Conduct for Membership. Article 2-A of the State Judiciary Law, the commission's governing statute, requires that at least two members of the panel be lay persons.

26. E.g., Brian Wooley, "Lay Judges: The Illiterate Bench," *Nation* (October 4, 1975): 304–5; Howard James, *Crisis in the Courts* (New York: McKay, 1968); and Robertson, ed., esp. p. xix. For early indictments, see Raymond Moley, *Tribunes of the People* (New Haven: Yale University Press, 1932); Warren, chap. 9.

27. Dennis C. Colson discusses this case at length in "Would a Lay Justice Be Just?" *Idaho Law Review* 13 (1977): 351–71.

28. Murray Edelman, "The Political Language of the Helping Professions," *Politics and Society* 4 (1974): 304.

29. Burton J. Bledstein, *The Culture of Professionalism* (New York:

Norton, 1978), pp. x–xi.

30. Susan S. Silbey, "Making Sense of the Lower Courts," *Justice System Journal* 6 (1981): 13.

31. See, e.g., Alan D. Freeman, "Antidiscrimination Law: A Critical Review," in Kairys, pp. 96–116.

32. Alexis de Tocqueville, *Democracy in America* (New York: Random House, 1945), 1:291–97. Examples of modern-day de Tocqueville-like arguments applied to different lay institutions in different settings are: A. R. Rickard, "A Defense of the English Lay Magistracy," *Judicature* 59 (1975): 140–44; and Jesse Berman, "The Cuban Popular Tribunals," *Columbia Law Review* 69 (1969): 1317–54.

33. John Richert, "Lay Judges and Assessors: A Comparative Perspective," reprinted in Linda Silberman et al., *Non-Attorney Justice in the United States: An Empirical Study* (New York: Institute of Judicial Administration, 1979), appendix G, p. 350. This report is an excellent summary of much of the lay judge literature worldwide.

34. Ibid., pp. 350–53.

35. For a summary of this debate see A. Scheflin, "Jury Nullification—the Right to Say No," *Southern California Law Review* 45 (1972): 168; Mortimer R. and Sanford H. Kadish, *Discretion to Disobey: A Study of Lawful Departures from Legal Rules* (Stanford, Calif.: Stanford University Press, 1973); and Hans Zeisel, " . . . And Then There Were None: The Diminution of the Federal Jury," *University of Chicago Law Review* 38 (1971): 710.

36. For a good description of a system that does encourage audience participation, see Berman. Court sessions are held in the evenings in easily accessible areas, and judges are encouraged to facilitate audience participation in the Cuban popular tribunals, according to Berman.

37. In the Soviet Comrades' Courts, apparently, procedures and offenses are not clearly specified; government policy favors informality above all. In the Cuban popular tribunals, on the other hand, both substantive offenses and procedural guidelines are clear, the result of considerable rewriting of the preexisting legal code by lawyers following the revolution (see Bernard A. Ramundo, "The Comrades' Court: Molder and Keeper of Socialist Morality," *George Washington Law Review* 33 [1965]: 692–727; and Berman).

38. Contrast Berman, p. 338, with the system described by Nico Roos in "Political Aspects of the Functioning of Lay Judges in the Dutch Social Security Tribunals" (paper presented at the annual meeting of the Law and Society Association, Amherst, Mass., June 1981).

39. See S. D. Ross, "A Comparative Study of the Legal Profession in East Africa," *Journal of African Law* 17 (1973): 279–99; and J. Keaning, "Some Remarks on Law and Courts in Africa," *Integration of Customary and Modern Legal Systems in Africa* (Ilf-Ife, Nigeria: University of Ilf Press, 1971), pp. 66–71.

40. Richert, p. 360.

41. Canada until quite recently constituted a notable exception. See

John Hogarth, *Sentencing as a Human Process* (Toronto: University of Toronto Press, 1971), pp. 45–47.

42. Peter W. Sperlich, "The Theory and Practice of Lay Adjudication: East German Commissioners and United States Jurors" (paper presented at the Twelfth World Congress of the International Political Science Association, Rio de Janeiro, Brazil, August 1982", p. 50.

43. M. L. Friedland, "Magistrates Courts: Functioning and Facilities," *Criminal Law Quarterly* 11 (1968–69): 52; for comments to the same effect concerning the British magistrates' courts see Burney, p. 218.

44. Roderick Haig-Brown, "The Lay Mind in the Law," *University of British Columbia Law Review* 9 (1974): 6–7.

45. Michael Lipsky, "The Assault on Human Services: Street-Level Bureaucrats, Accountability, and the Fiscal Crisis," in Scott Greer et al., eds., *Accountability in Urban Society* (Beverly Hills, Calif.: Sage, 1978), pp. 15–38, esp. p. 17.

46. See, e.g., R. H. Maudsley and J. W. Davies, "The Justice of the Peace in England," *University of Miami Law Review* 18 (1964): 517–60, esp. p. 559; and Elizabeth Burney, *J.P.: Magistrate, Court, and Community* (London: Hutchinson, 1979), chap. 11, pp. 199–211; see also Ramaldo.

47. See Burney, chap. 9, pp. 146–64, for a good discussion; see also Richard (Richard is a justices' clerk in several jurisdictions); and see R. M. Jackson, *The Machinery of Justice in England*, (Cambridge: Cambridge University Press, 1966), p. 170.

48. Harold J. Laski, "Judiciary," in *Encyclopedia of the Social Sciences* (1932), 7:465.

49. Ibid.

50. For a summary of examples see Ben W. Palmer, "The Vestigial Justice of the Peace," *American Bar Association Journal* 47 (1961): 380–85.

51. The author chose to remain anonymous, with identification only as "A Chairman of Quarter Sessions." The article is "The Lay Justices: Some Criticisms and Suggestions," *Criminal Law Review* (1961): 658.

52. See the issue of *Judicature* devoted to the issue of the jury's role in complex litigation (vol. 65 [1982], nos. 8–9), esp. the article by Peter W. Sperlich, "The Case for Preserving Trial by Jury in Complex Litigation," pp. 394–419.

53. See Henry W. Ehrmann, *Comparative Legal Cultures* (Englewood Cliffs, N.J.: Prentice-Hall, 1976), pp. 102–3; and sources cited in the discussion of mixed-bench systems in Chapter 5, pp. 116–17.

54. Stanislaw Pomorski, "Lay Judges in the Polish Criminal Courts: A Legal and Empirical Description," *Case Western Reserve Journal of International Law* 7 (1975): 202.

55. Roos, p. 13.

56. Silberman et al., pp. 68–94.

57. Zenon Bankowski and Geoff Mungham explore this problem at length in "Law and Lay Participation," in M. B. Blegvad et al., eds., *European Yearbook in Law and Sociology* (The Hague: Martinus Nijhoff,

1979); these authors conclude that true lay participation is a contradiction in terms in a modern legal system.

58. Ibid., p. 21.

59. Burney, p. 216.

60. Richert, p. 350; on the decline of lay participation generally, see pp. 359–63; and Ehrmann, p. 103.

61. See Earl Johnson, Jr., and Elizabeth Schwartz, *A Preliminary Analysis of Alternative Strategies for Processing Civil Disputes* (1977, Mimeographed); but cf. John H. Langbein, "Mixed Court and Jury Court. Could the Continental Alternative Fill the American Need?" *American Bar Foundation Research Journal* (1981): 195–219.

62. Haig-Brown, p. 4.

INDEX